LEADERSHIP
—— BY ——
CYRUS THE GREAT

Unlocking Xenophon's Cyropaedia

DARIUS LAHOUTIFARD

IMPORTANT LEGAL NOTICES & DISCLAIMERS

DEDICATION

To the People of Iran,

Cyrus the Great's Children—

May your pursuit of freedom be realized and safeguarded

for generations to come.

TABLE OF CONTENTS

ACKNOWLEDGMENTS

The journey of bringing "Leadership by Cyrus the Great" to life has been one of discovery, inspiration, passion, love, and immense support from many individuals who contributed to the realization of this project.

First and foremost, I am deeply grateful to my family for their unwavering support and continuous feedback during my journey, especially Cyrus and Elisa.

I must also express my profound gratitude to Xenophon, the original author of Cyropaedia. His insightful portrayal of leadership and his ability to distill the qualities of a great leader have stood the test of time, making this work a cornerstone of leadership literature. Without Xenophon's foundational work, the wisdom and principles that have shaped this book would not have been possible.

A special thanks to the scholars, translators, authors, and historians who have contributed in various ways to the study of Cyropaedia over the centuries, beginning with Henry Graham Dakyns, who translated it from Greek to English. I would also like to express particular gratitude to Larry Hedrick for inspiring ideas that guided my approach and encouraged me to take it a step further in modernization and leadership education. The diversity of previous works opened my eyes to new possibilities, enabling me to create a more engaging and insightful experience for readers, while deepening the focus on the leadership lessons within Cyropaedia.

To the artists, designers, proofreaders, and assistants—with a special mention of Siavash Sarlak—as well as Chat GPT-4o, Google GEMINI, and DALL.E 3, who have made this book not just a read, but an experience.

I would also like to acknowledge the feedback from my social media followers, early readers, and my friends and colleagues, whose perspectives helped refine the ideas presented here. Your contributions, whether in the form of voting for the cover design, constructive criticism, or words of encouragement, have been deeply appreciated.

Lastly, I extend my heartfelt thanks to the readers who have engaged with this work. Your interest in the leadership principles of Cyrus the Great is what truly brings this book to life. I hope the lessons within these pages inspire and guide you on your own leadership journey, just as they have guided prominent leaders throughout history.

EDITORIAL REVIEWS & QUOTES

"When you start learning Greek, the first book you should read is Cyropaedia."

Thomas Jefferson, Founding Father

"Cyropaedia, the earliest book on leadership, is still the best."

Peter Drucker, The inventor of modern management

"Cyrus triumphed not just through conquest but also by showing singular tolerance and mercy to those he defeated. Discover the wise leadership principles of the Persian King Cyrus the Great in Darius Lahoutifard's great new book."

Navi Radjou, Author and TED Speaker

PREFACE

Nearly twenty years ago, I stumbled upon Xenophon's *Cyropaedia*, a work that immediately captivated me with its sweet and insightful portrayal of Cyrus the Great's childhood. However, despite my enthusiasm, I found myself unable to progress beyond the first twenty pages. The editions I owned, translated in the nineteenth century from Greek to English, presented numerous challenges: they lacked structure, featuring no titles, subtitles, images, introduction, or preface, and were written in an antiquated language that was difficult to read.

This frustration was particularly poignant given the book's historical significance. *Cyropaedia* was reportedly a profound influence on the framers of the U.S. Constitution, a favorite of Thomas Jefferson, who considered it essential reading for his children and grandchildren and was praised by Peter Drucker as the best book on leadership. Moreover, the concepts within *Cyropaedia*, along with the Cyrus Cylinder, are regarded as foundational to the first human rights charter. Here was a text of immense value, yet it remained largely inaccessible to modern readers.

Thus, the book remained an unpolished gem; its exceptional value was recognized primarily by scholars and academics who had the patience and dedication to delve into its depths. Unfortunately, this treasure trove of wisdom was out of reach for the average person and even the typical leader. Most corporate leaders, lacking the inclination to sift through ancient texts, miss out on these timeless lessons. However, if these lessons are presented in a manner that directly addresses their everyday challenges, they would undoubtedly find them invaluable.

Years later, I came across and read Larry Hedrick's edition of *Cyropaedia*. Larry did a commendable job of organizing the content with chapters and subtitles to underscore military and leadership lessons, hence the title of his book: *The Arts of Leadership and War*. While he addressed some issues, such as the archaic language and the lack of structure, his edition introduced new complications. The original eight books, each comprising four to eight chapters, were transformed into a single book with eighteen chapters. Additionally, the narrative was reimagined to be fictitiously voiced by Cyrus himself, which I found somewhat disconcerting. Xenophon's frequent praise for Cyrus made this narrative style seem narcissistic; it's quite different to hear someone say you are the greatest versus proclaiming it yourself. I was left wondering if it was still *Cyropaedia* or a new book inspired by *Cyropaedia*. Nonetheless, Larry's approach of highlighting key lessons, even briefly in subtitles, was a concept I greatly appreciated.

Inspired by Larry's idea but aiming to avoid the issues I identified, I sought to make Xenophon's masterpiece accessible in a way that retains the book's original chapters, sections, characters, descriptions, and dialogues, while adding titles and subtitles and editing the text into an easier-to-read language. To make it attractive to leaders, I extracted the leadership lessons, not just as subtitles as Larry did, but into full paragraphs explaining the lesson and using the event or action from the book, right when it happened, as an example to illustrate the leadership lesson. I added summaries to each chapter, allowing busy leaders to skip the detailed dialogues that are beautiful novel-style stories for those who enjoy reading novels but are not necessarily needed for the lessons. To make the whole experience even more pleasant, I included pictures of real or fictitious paintings illustrating the events.

When I refer to leaders in this book, I am not limiting the term to corporate CEOs or army generals. Leadership, as I define it, is the ability to motivate people to act toward achieving a common goal. This concept applies to small business owners, managers, directors, vice presidents, Chief-X-Officers, mayors, governors, political party leaders, teachers, coaches, social media influencers, and even heads of households. In the smallest form of leadership, even in couples, one partner often takes the lead while the other enjoys following. Leadership skills are essential across various roles and aspects of society.

Although the focus on leadership is clear, this book is also a pleasant experience for those who enjoy history, novels, biographies, world cultures, and the rich heritage of the Persians, Middle-Easterners, and the people of the Mediterranean regions.

This project has been a labor of love, driven by my belief in the enduring relevance of Cyrus the Great's leadership principles. I hope this book will serve not only as a historical account but also as a practical guide for leaders seeking to learn from one of history's greatest figures.

I am deeply grateful to the many scholars and historians who have previously brought Xenophon's work to light, as well as to my friends and family for their unwavering support throughout this journey.

May the timeless wisdom of Cyrus the Great inspire and guide you as it has done for countless others throughout history.

Artwork derived from a hand sketch by the artist Siavash Sarlak.

INTRODUCTION

Purpose and Relevance of Xenophon's Cyropaedia

Cyropaedia, or the Education of Cyrus, is an invaluable text that chronicles the life, education, and leadership of Cyrus the Great. Written by Xenophon, it details Cyrus's journey from his childhood, through his conquests and governance, to his death. The book serves not only as a historical account but also as a guide for personal and leadership development, offering timeless lessons on how we can educate ourselves based on Cyrus's exemplary life.

Cyrus the Great: A Legacy of Leadership and Justice

Cyrus the Great, founder of the Achaemenid Empire, is celebrated for his extraordinary leadership and vision. His legacy has been praised by numerous historical figures. Herodotus, the ancient Greek historian, described Cyrus as a ruler who combined military prowess with wisdom and benevolence. The Roman statesman Cicero referred to him as a model of kingly virtue. Even modern scholars like Peter Drucker have acknowledged his impact, with Drucker calling *Cyropaedia* the best book on leadership ever written.

Cyrus's influence extends into religious texts as well. In the Bible, he is revered as a liberator who fulfilled God's will by freeing the Jews from Babylonian captivity. The Book of Isaiah refers to him as the "Anointed of the Lord," and he is praised for his decree allowing the Jews to return to Jerusalem and rebuild their temple.

One of Cyrus's most notable achievements was his progressive approach to human rights. He is credited with abolishing slavery in his empire, setting a precedent for future generations. His respect for the cultures and religions of the lands he conquered was unprecedented at the time. This respect is encapsulated in the Cyrus Cylinder, often considered the world's first charter of human rights. The Cylinder proclaims Cyrus's policies of religious tolerance and freedom, highlighting his enlightened rule.

Cyrus is also known as the Father of Persians, Liberator of the Babylonians, and Law-giver for the Greeks. His leadership style was marked by a unique blend of compassion and strength, earning him the admiration of not only his contemporaries but also of future generations. His ability to unite diverse peoples under a single administration, respect local customs, and promote justice and equity set a high standard for leadership that remains relevant today.

Historical Context

Xenophon of Athens (c. 430 – probably 355 or 354 BC) was a Greek military leader, philosopher, and historian. At the age of 30, Xenophon was elected as one of the leaders of the retreating Greek mercenaries, the Ten Thousand, who had been part of Cyrus the Younger's attempt to seize control of the Achaemenid Empire. His leadership during this retreat demonstrated his military genius and established precedents for logistical operations and combat maneuvers that have influenced military strategies for centuries.

Xenophon's *Anabasis* recounts his adventures with the Ten Thousand, providing a unique first-hand account of a military leader's experience in antiquity. This work, along with *Cyropaedia*, inspired future leaders, including Alexander the Great, who admired and sought to emulate Cyrus's leadership style. The influence of Xenophon's writings extended widely, impacting various interpretations of leadership and governance.

Xenophon's Multifaceted Life

A student and friend of Socrates, Xenophon documented several Socratic dialogues, including *Symposium*, *Oeconomicus*, *Hiero*, and *Memorabilia*. His works offer a unique perspective on Socratic thought, complementing Plato's more famous accounts. *Memorabilia*, in particular, was influential, inspiring Zeno of Citium to found the Stoic school of philosophy. Through his writings, Xenophon significantly contributed to the preservation and dissemination of Socratic philosophy.

For millennia, scholars have debated whether Xenophon should be categorized primarily as a general, historian, or philosopher. Quintilian, in his *Orator's Education*, ultimately placed Xenophon alongside Plato as a philosopher, recognizing the eloquence and depth of his philosophical works. Despite this, today Xenophon is best known for his historical writings, such as *Hellenica*, which continues directly from Thucydides' *History of the Peloponnesian War* and covers subsequent significant events in Greek history.

Xenophon's Legacy and Style

Xenophon's life and works were deeply intertwined with the major historical and philosophical currents of his time. Although born an Athenian citizen, Xenophon became closely associated with Sparta, Athens' traditional rival. His experiences as a mercenary and leader, service under Spartan commanders, and friendship with King Agesilaus II provided a unique perspective on Spartan society. His accounts, particularly the *Constitution of the Lacedaemonians* and the royal biography of Agesilaus, remain primary sources for understanding Spartan culture.

Xenophon's contributions to literature and philosophy earned him the title of "Attic Muse" for the sweetness of his diction, as noted by Diogenes Laërtius. Cicero and Quintilian also praised his mastery of Greek composition, highlighting the elegance and persuasive power of his writing. His works, spanning multiple genres and written in plain Attic Greek, continue to be used in educational settings for translation exercises, underscoring their lasting significance and clarity.

Alexander the Great's Influence by *Cyropaedia* and Cyrus

Alexander the Great was deeply influenced by *Cyropaedia* and the figure of Cyrus the Great. He admired Cyrus as an ideal ruler, which is reflected in his efforts to emulate Cyrus's leadership style and strategies. Alexander's education included studying Xenophon's works, which shaped his views on governance and military tactics. This influence is evident in several actions taken by Alexander, such as his respectful treatment of Cyrus's tomb and his efforts to incorporate Persian customs and administrative practices into his own empire. The *Cyropaedia* provided Alexander with a model of leadership that emphasized justice, wisdom, and effective governance, principles that Alexander sought to implement during his reign. This influence highlights the lasting impact of Xenophon's work on subsequent generations of leaders.

Machiavelli and a Machiavellian View of Cyropaedia

The *Cyropaedia* has been considered the bible of leadership for centuries, with various interpretations by different authors. Niccolò Machiavelli, the Renaissance political philosopher, also drew inspiration from the *Cyropaedia*. In *The Prince*, Machiavelli presents a pragmatic and often ruthless approach to leadership, epitomized by the phrase "the end justifies the means." He saw in Cyrus's driven character a justification for this principle, although this view is a significant exaggeration and misinterpretation of Xenophon's portrayal. While *Cyropaedia* emphasizes the importance of justice, wisdom, and ethical leadership, Machiavelli focused on Cyrus's ambition and effectiveness, offering a more cynical view of power.

Jefferson and Cyropaedia

Thomas Jefferson, one of America's Founding Fathers, was profoundly inspired by Xenophon's *Cyropaedia*. Jefferson, known for his deep intellectual curiosity and extensive reading, saw in Cyrus's character an embodiment of leadership qualities that resonated with his own values and aspirations for the new American republic. The *Cyropaedia*'s depiction of Cyrus as a leader who valued justice, wisdom, and effective governance influenced Jefferson's thoughts on leadership and governance, contributing to his vision for America [Richard Frye and Afshin Zand].

Jefferson owned two editions of the *Cyropaedia* and made detailed notes in his Commonplace Book, reflecting his keen interest in the work. He admired Cyrus's secular approach to governance, which included the separation of church and state, a principle that became a cornerstone of American democracy. Jefferson's engagement with the *Cyropaedia* is evident in his drafting of the Virginia Statute for Religious Freedom, which later influenced the First Amendment of the U.S. Constitution [Richard Frye and Afshin Zand]. His regard for the text underscores its significant impact on his thinking and the foundational principles of the United States.

Audience

This book is designed for a broad audience, including those seeking insights into leadership, history enthusiasts, and readers who enjoy biographies and novels. Whether you are a corporate CEO, a small business owner, a political leader, or someone fascinated by ancient cultures, this book offers a rich tapestry of lessons and narratives. Teachers and coaches can find inspiration in Cyrus's strategies, while history enthusiasts will appreciate the detailed recounting of his life and times. The narratives also appeal to readers who enjoy immersive storytelling, offering a blend of historical facts and engaging tales from ancient Persia and the Mediterranean regions.

Structure of the Book

This edition of *Cyropaedia* is structured to provide maximum clarity and utility. Each chapter begins with a summary, followed by the original text, modernized for readability. Key leadership lessons are extracted and elaborated upon within the context of the narrative, providing practical insights alongside the historical account. Additionally, visual elements such as illustrations and paintings are included to enhance the reading experience and bring the events to life.

Conclusion

The *Cyropaedia* is more than just a historical text; it is a treasure trove of wisdom and insight that has stood the test of time. This edition, subtitled *Xenophon's Cyropaedia Unlocked*, seeks to honor Xenophon's work by making it accessible and relevant for contemporary readers. As you journey through the pages, may the timeless lessons of Cyrus the Great inspire and guide you, whether you are a leader, a history enthusiast, or simply someone who enjoys compelling narratives. This edition aims to reveal the insights and principles embedded in Xenophon's narrative, offering a clearer path to understanding and applying these lessons in today's world.

BOOK I

Cyrus's Childhood
And Education

I.1

Obedience and Leadership
Cyrus's Unique Approach to Governance

Why Cyropaedia?

The Challenge of Leadership: Human Disobedience

We've often thought about how democracies are frequently replaced by the desire for a different kind of government. Monarchies and oligarchies are often overthrown by popular movements. Aspiring dictators often fall, some right away with a single action. Those who manage to hold power even briefly are seen as remarkably wise and successful.

We noticed a similar pattern in families: whether big or small, even the head of a small household can't always count on everyone's obedience.

One thought led to another, and we started thinking: drovers can definitely be called rulers of their cattle, and horse breeders, rulers of their horses. Essentially, all herdsmen can be seen as governors of the animals they care for. If we trust our senses, it's clear that flocks and herds obey their keepers more readily than people obey their leaders. Watch how cattle follow their herdsmen wherever they're guided, graze where they're told, and stay away from forbidden areas. They give their produce to their master to use as he wishes. We've never seen a flock band together against their keeper, either to disobey him or to refuse him control of their produce. Instead, they're more likely to show hostility to other animals than to the owner who benefits from them. But with humans, it's different; people quickly unite against those trying to rule over them.

The Leadership of Cyrus, a First of its kind

But when we came to understand the character of Cyrus the Persian, our perspective changed. We saw a man who had gained the obedience of thousands of his fellow humans, from countless cities and tribes. We had to ask ourselves if governing people is truly an impossible or even a difficult task, as long as it's done the right way. Cyrus, as we know, received the most willing obedience from his subjects, even though some lived so far away that it would take days and months to reach them. Among these subjects were people who had never seen him and knew they never would, yet they still chose to obey him.

Cultivate Respect through Exemplary Leadership

The power of earning respect rather than demanding it cannot be overstated. Effective leaders don't rely on fear or coercion; instead, they lead by example, displaying unwavering integrity, wisdom, and dedication to the welfare of their team. Focus on building authentic relationships, demonstrating ethical behavior, and making decisions that consistently reflect your commitment to your team's success. True loyalty and willing obedience come from respect that is earned through actions.

Authority and Loyalty by Remote People

Cyrus outshone all other monarchs, both those who inherited their power and those who built their empires through their own efforts. No Scythian, despite their large numbers, has ever dominated a foreign nation. In fact, the Scythian would be happy just to keep control over his own tribe and people. The same goes for the Thracians and the Illyrians, and all other nations we know of. In Europe, their condition is still one of independence and separation, which seems permanent. This was the state of Asia when Cyrus, with a small Persian force, began his journey. The Medes and Hyrcanians accepted his leadership willingly, but he conquered Syria, Assyria, Arabia, Cappadocia, both Phrygias, Lydia, Caria, Phoenicia, and Babylonia. He established his rule over the Bactrians, Indians, Cilicians, Sakians, Paphlagonians, Magadidians, and many other tribes whose names challenge the memory of the historian. Finally, he brought the Greeks in Asia under his control, and by moving along the coast, he also conquered Cyprus and Egypt.

It's clear that among these many nations, few, if any, spoke the same language as Cyrus or understood each other. Yet, Cyrus managed to control this vast territory through sheer force of personality, making everyone bow before him. No one dared to challenge him.

At the same time, he inspired a deep desire in everyone to please him and win his favor. They all wanted to follow his judgment alone. He united a complex mix of nationalities so vast that it would have exhausted a person just to travel across his empire in any direction from the central palace.

Given his remarkable achievements, we wanted to know more about his background, his natural talents, and how he was trained to become such an excellent leader. We gathered information from various sources and made our own inferences, which we will now share.

Leveraging Personality and Leadership to Unify Diverse Groups

The ability to unite people from different backgrounds, languages, and customs is a hallmark of great leadership. Develop your personal charisma and communication skills to craft and articulate a vision that resonates with a diverse group of stakeholders. By inspiring collective action and building cohesive, high-performing teams, you can achieve remarkable success. This ability to unite and motivate diverse groups is essential in today's globalized world as well as local diverse communities.

I.2

The Persian Path to Leadership;
A Structured Journey from Youth to Eldership

The Heritage and Qualities of Cyrus

The story goes that Cyrus's [Kūrosh in Persian] father was Cambyses, [Kambūjiyeh in Persian] a king of the Persians and one of the Perseidae, who trace their lineage back to Perseus. *[Editor's note: Perseus, A half-God in Greek mythology, was believed by the Greeks to be the ancestor of the Persians. Fact-based history tells us that Persians were simply the habitants of Persia, a region in the South of the Iranian Plateau, with their capital called Parseh, which developed later into Persepolis, the capital of the Persian Empire. This can also be read in the Cyrus Cylinder, where Cyrus states that he is from Anshan (near Parseh and Pasargad in Persia, just like his father and ancestors.]* **His mother was Mandana** *[a popular given name among Persians, Mandane according to Xenophon]*, **the daughter of Astyages,** *[Āstiyāg or Ishtovigo in Persian] king of the Medes [Maad in Persian].*

According to songs and stories from the East, Cyrus was naturally very handsome and had a deep love for humanity, knowledge, and honor. He was willing to endure any hardship and face any danger for the sake of glory. Blessed with such qualities, his memory remains alive in the hearts of people to this day. He was raised according to Persian laws and customs, which aimed at the common good but followed different principles than those of most nations.

Establishing a Foundation of Integrity and Preventive Governance

Most states allow their citizens to raise their children as they see fit and let adults live their lives as they wish, then impose penalties for wrongdoings like theft, assault, adultery, and disobedience. However, Persian laws aimed to prevent any desire for wickedness or shameful conduct from the start.

In their cities, they have an open space called Free Square, where the palace and public buildings are located. No goods are sold there, and hawkers and peddlers are banned to maintain grace and order.

This square is divided into four parts: one for boys, another for youths, a third for grown men, and the last for those past military age. The law requires citizens to gather there at specific times. Boys and grown men must be there at daybreak. Elders have more flexible schedules but must also attend on certain days.

Young men must sleep near the public buildings with their weapons, except for married men who are exempt unless notified otherwise. Frequent absences are frowned upon.

Each group has twelve governors, corresponding to the twelve Persian tribes. Elders govern the boys, chosen for their ability to guide them well. Grown men govern the youths, selected on the same principle. The best candidates lead the grown men to ensure they perform their duties. Elders also have their leaders to ensure they fulfill their roles completely.

Building a Strong Nation Starts with its People

The Persian system emphasizes the importance of early education and preventive governance to cultivate righteousness and justice from a young age. Unlike other societies that impose penalties after wrongdoings occur, the Persians focus on instilling ethical values and self-discipline to prevent the desire for misconduct. This proactive approach not only reduces the incidence of crime but also fosters a society where individuals are naturally inclined to act with integrity. Modern leaders can adopt this by emphasizing ethical education and character development, ensuring that individuals are guided by strong moral principles from the outset.

We'll now review the specific obligations required of various classes, showcasing the Persian dedication to enhancing the caliber of their citizens. Persian children are enrolled in schools with a primary focus on mastering the concepts of justice and righteousness, stating outright their attendance is for this very learning, a sentiment as naturally expressed by them as it is for us to talk about children learning the alphabet. Teachers dedicate most of their day to adjudicate disputes among the students, reflecting the reality that, in the microcosm of their school world as in the larger adult world, opportunities for legal grievances are ever-present. It's anticipated that accusations, such as theft, violence, fraud, and slander, will arise. When accusations are made, they are thoroughly investigated, and the guilty parties are punished accordingly.

Not only is punishment meted out to those found guilty, but also to those who falsely accuse their peers. Among the various accusations, one particularly serious charge is handled without hesitation: the charge of ingratitude, a complaint often avoided in adult courts yet one that breeds much animosity. If a student is found guilty of not returning a favor when fully capable, they are severely punished. The logic is straightforward: someone ungrateful is more likely to neglect their duties towards the gods, their parents, their country, and their friends. Dishonor, they believe, follows closely behind ingratitude, making it the prime mover of all sorts of vile actions.

Leadership through Discipline: The Power of Example

> Leaders should set clear goals and objectives. They should show and emphasize a clear path to advancement based on merit and fulfilling one's duties.

Furthermore, the youths are educated in moderation and self-control, immensely aided by the dignified conduct of their seniors, showcased daily. They are also taught to follow their leaders, a virtue significantly reinforced by the elders' visible compliance with authority. The instruction on moderation in eating and drinking benefits greatly from two practices: firstly, the elders' habit of not satisfying their personal desires until dismissed by their superiors, and secondly, the rule requiring students to eat their meals not with their mothers but with their instructor, and only when permission is granted. The basic meal they bring from home consists of dry bread with nasturtium as a relish, and for drinking; they carry a cup to fill from the nearest stream. Moreover, they are trained in the arts of archery and javelin throwing.

Transitioning to Young Adulthood: Building Community and Self-Restraint

The students pursue their studies until they reach the ages of sixteen or seventeen, at which point they graduate to the status of young men. Upon reaching this stage, their new responsibilities involve, for a decade, nightly guarding of the public buildings, a duty serving dual purposes: protecting the community and fostering self-restraint, especially vital during these formative years. By day, they make themselves available for state service, gathering around the public buildings when needed. Furthermore, during the king's frequent hunting expeditions, they accompany him, fully equipped with bows and arrows, a sheathed dagger or "sagaris" beside their quiver, a lightweight shield, and two javelins for varied use—one for throwing and another for close combat, if necessary.

Embracing the Hunt: Preparing for War

The rationale behind the public endorsement of hunting is clear: it mirrors the conditions of warfare, with the king leading the hunt just as he leads in battle, to ensure that his men are well-prepared for the demands of war. This form of exercise is unparalleled in preparing for military engagement, acclimating individuals to early mornings, and conditioning them to withstand both heat and cold. It trains them to march and sprint, to launch arrows and javelins swiftly upon spotting their target, and, crucially, to sharpen their instincts against formidable animals. In facing such challenges, they learn the importance of timing their strikes and defending against attacks, skills directly transferable to the battlefield.

Sustaining Through Simplicity: Lessons in Endurance

As young men, their hunting expeditions are characterized by slightly improved but fundamentally similar provisions to their younger days, emphasizing the lesson that simplicity does not hinder, but rather enhances, resilience. They refrain from eating during the hunt unless a break is necessitated, at which point they consume what is essentially a modest meal. This practice ensures their readiness for similar conditions in warfare. The satisfaction derived from simple food and water, when faced with hunger and thirst, underscores the value of basic sustenance.

Maintaining Skills and Civic Engagement: A Foundation for Leadership

Those remaining in the city engage in continuous improvement of their skills and apply the lessons learned in their youth in various civic duties. Through competitions and public service, they not only hone their abilities but also contribute to the safety and order of their community. This period of engagement lays the groundwork for their eventual transition into roles of greater responsibility and leadership.

Advancing to Adulthood: Leadership and Civic Duty

After completing this ten-year phase, these individuals officially take their place as adults within the society. As adults, their daily routine encompasses presenting themselves for state service, demonstrating a readiness to contribute to the collective needs and well-being of their community. Whenever a military expedition is organized, these seasoned men are deployed, not with the lighter arms of their youth but equipped for close combat, symbolizing their transition into more formidable roles. This period is marked by a shift from learning and guarding to active participation and leadership, embodying the full spectrum of their training and education.

Eldership: The Pinnacle of Service and Wisdom

After twenty-five years of dedicated service, these individuals ascend to the esteemed status of elders, a role that signifies not only age but a profound depth of experience and wisdom. No longer required to engage in the physical demands of military service, their focus shifts towards governance, judicial responsibilities, and the nurturing of societal values. Their accumulated knowledge and insight make them the pillars of the community, tasked with resolving disputes, both minor and major, and selecting those among them fit for various leadership roles.

This transition into eldership represents the culmination of a lifelong journey of personal development, service, and leadership, embodying the societal ideals of wisdom, justice, and the collective good. Through this structured progression from youth to elder status, the Persian system illustrates a comprehensive approach to leadership development, emphasizing the importance of each phase in preparing individuals for the responsibilities and challenges of the next.

Progressive Responsibility and Civic Engagement

The structured progression from youth to eldership in Persian society underscores the significance of gradually increasing responsibilities and active civic engagement in leadership development. Each stage of life builds on the previous one, preparing individuals for more complex roles and greater responsibilities. This approach ensures that by the time individuals reach elder status, they are well-rounded and experienced leaders. Modern leaders can apply this by creating clear pathways for career progression, providing opportunities for professional growth, and encouraging community involvement. This holistic approach to leadership development ensures that future leaders are not only skilled but also deeply connected to the values and needs of their communities.

Civic Engagement and Leadership: A Continuum of Growth

The Persian model of citizen development emphasizes a continuum, where each stage of life builds upon the lessons and experiences of the previous, creating a seamless transition from learner to leader, from individual contributor to guardian of tradition and values. This holistic approach ensures that by the time one reaches elder status, they are not only well-versed in the practical aspects of leadership and governance but are also imbued with the philosophical and ethical principles necessary for wise decision-making.

In essence, the Persian approach to leadership and citizenship education offers timeless lessons on the value of discipline, the importance of service, and the pursuit of excellence. By meticulously crafting a society where each member is guided through a structured developmental journey, they fostered a community capable of sustaining its values, defending its principles, and advancing its collective interests.

Discipline Shapes Excellence

> Self-control and a commitment to healthy habits are essential for building strong individuals, a strong company or a strong society.

The Persian Path to Governance and Education: A Foundation for Leadership

To fully understand Persia's approach to governing, let's take a step back. Building on what we've already discussed, we can keep this brief. Estimates suggest Persia has around 120,000 citizens, and interestingly, no one is excluded from holding positions of honor or office based solely on birth.

In fact, every Persian has the opportunity to send their children to state-run schools focused on fostering righteousness and justice. Those who can afford to raise their children without needing them to work send them to these schools. For those who can't, this privilege isn't available.

Once a young person completes these schools, they're eligible to join the ranks of the youths. But those who haven't gone through this initial training can't participate. Similarly, the youths who've fulfilled their expected duties can eventually progress to the level of men and share in positions of honor and leadership. However, there's a requirement: they must dedicate their full time to being part of the youth group. If they don't meet this requirement, they can't advance further.

Finally, those who have lived virtuous lives as grown men can ultimately take their place among the elders. This council of elders is essentially a group where every member has completed the entire cycle of esteemed learning. This, in the Persians' view, is the system and the training that will bring them the very pinnacle of excellence.

Even today, there's evidence of their ancient self-control and the strict rules that maintained it. To this day, it's still considered improper for a Persian to spit in public, blow their nose, show signs of flatulence, or be seen going to the bathroom. And let's face it, they wouldn't be able to uphold these standards unless they were accustomed to moderation in their diet and trained to exercise and work hard, ensuring these bodily urges are addressed in other ways.

Fostering Leadership through Education

Investing in the education and well-being of your team and your people is the foundation of a successful society, community, corporation or nation.

So far, we've been discussing Persia as a whole. Now, let's rewind and explore Cyrus's life story, starting from his childhood.

I.3

A Meeting of Generations
Cyrus's Visit to Media

Summary

This chapter recounts young Cyrus's visit to his maternal grandfather, Astyages, the king of Media. Through a series of anecdotes, the narrative illustrates Cyrus's intelligence, charm, and quick-wittedness as he navigates the opulent and sophisticated world of the Median court. The interactions between Cyrus, his grandfather, and the court attendants highlight cultural contrasts and the boy's ability to adapt and excel in different environments.

Early Promise: Cyrus's Exceptional Upbringing and Natural Abilities.

Up until around the age of twelve, Cyrus was raised in the way we've described. He consistently stood out among his peers for his exceptional ability to learn and his noble and manly approach to every responsibility.

Around this time, Astyages requested his daughter and her son, Cyrus, to visit him. He was very eager to see Cyrus because of all he'd heard about the boy's nobility and good looks. So, Mandana traveled to Astyages's court, bringing her son Cyrus with her.

As soon as they met, the young boy, upon learning that Astyages was his maternal grandfather, embraced him and kissed him affectionately, just like the naturally warm and friendly boy he was. It was as if he'd been raised by his grandfather all along and they were old playmates. Then he took a closer look and noticed that the king had his eyes lined with kohl and his cheeks painted, and that he wore a wig, which was the Median fashion at that time. It's important to note that these decorative elements, along with the purple robes, tunics, necklaces, and bracelets, all originated with the Medes, not the Persians. Even today (at the time Xenophon wrote it), Persians back home tend to stick with their simpler clothing and way of life.

Cyrus, struck by his grandfather's grandeur, couldn't take his eyes off him and exclaimed, "Oh, Mother, how magnificent Grandfather looks!" His mother then asked him who he thought was more handsome, his father or his grandfather. Without hesitation, he replied, "Father is the best-looking man in all of Persia, while Grandfather is by far the most handsome Mede I've ever seen, whether at home or abroad."

Hearing this, Astyages showered the boy with affection and presented him with a beautiful robe, bracelets, and necklaces as tokens of honor. Whenever Astyages rode out, the boy would ride beside him on a horse with a golden bridle, just like King Astyages himself. Cyrus, with his heart that valued beauty as much as respect, was delighted with the exquisite robe and overjoyed to learn how to ride. After all, horses were a rare sight in Persia, a mountainous country not exactly known for horse breeding.

Feast and Wit

Now Cyrus and his mother were having a meal with the king. Astyages, wanting Cyrus to enjoy the feast and not miss his home, offered him all sorts of delicacies. According to the story, Cyrus exclaimed, "Oh, grandfather, you must be working so hard to reach for all these dishes and taste all this amazing food!"

Astyages replied, "Isn't this meal much better than what you had in Persia?" The story goes that Cyrus responded, "Our way is much simpler and faster, grandfather. We get hungry and want to eat, so bread and meat get us satisfied right away. But you Medes take so many turns and wind about so much, it's a wonder if you ever get to the goal that we reach quickly."

"Well, my boy," said his grandfather, "we don't mind the long way. Try the dishes yourself and see how good they are."

Cyrus observed, "One thing I do notice, grandfather, is that you don't seem to like them much yourself." When Astyages asked how he knew that, Cyrus answered, "Because when you touch plain bread, you don't wipe your hands. But when you take these fancy dishes, you use your napkin right away, like you're annoyed your fingers got dirty."

"Well, well, my boy," said the king, "just enjoy the feast and eat well. We'll send you back to Persia strong and healthy." With that, he had dishes of meat and game placed in front of Cyrus. The boy was surprised by the abundance and exclaimed, "Grandfather, do you give me all this to do what I want with it?"

"Of course I do," said the king.

Generosity and Playfulness

Without hesitation, Cyrus took one dish after another and gave them to the attendants around his grandfather. With each gift, he said something like, "This is for you, for teaching me to ride;" "And this is for you, because you gave me a javelin, I still have it;" "This one is for you, because you serve my grandfather so nicely;" "And this is for you, sir, because you honor my mother." He kept going until he had given away all the meat he had been given.

"But you haven't given a single piece to Sacas, my butler," said his grandfather, "and I honor him more than all the rest."

Now, this Sacas was a good-looking man. He had the job of bringing people to see the king or stopping them if the timing wasn't right. But when his grandfather asked why he didn't give Sacas a piece of meat, Cyrus eagerly replied, like a boy who didn't know fear, "Why do you honor him so much, grandfather?"

Astyages laughed and said, "Can't you see how nicely he mixes the drinks and serves the wine?" Indeed, these royal cup-bearers are very skilled. They mix the wine with great elegance and pour it into cups without spilling a drop. When they hand the goblet, they hold it just right for the guest to take.

"Grandfather," said Cyrus, "tell Sacas to give me the bowl. Let me pour the wine as nicely as he does and win your favor." So, the king told the butler to hand him the bowl. Cyrus took it and mixed the wine just like he had seen Sacas do. Then, with great seriousness and skill, he brought the goblet to his grandfather and offered it with such style that his mother and Astyages both laughed out loud. Cyrus then laughed too and hugged his grandfather, saying, "Sacas, your time is up! I'll take your job for sure. I can be just as good a cup-bearer as you— and I won't drink the wine myself!"

The king's butler, when he offers the wine, has to dip a ladle in the cup first, pour a little into his hand, and sip it. This is to make sure that if there's poison in the cup, it affects him first.

So, to keep the joke going, Astyages asked why Cyrus didn't taste the wine, even though he did everything else like Sacas. The boy answered, "I was afraid there might be poison in the bowl. When you had your birthday feast, I could see clearly that Sacas had put in poison for you all."

"And how did you figure that out, my boy?" asked the king.

"Because I saw how you all got dizzy and staggered. You started talking loudly, and no one understood what the others were saying. Then you began singing in a funny way that made us laugh. Even though you wouldn't listen to the singer, you all said it was a great performance. Then you boasted about your strength, but when you got up to dance, you couldn't even keep your balance. You all seemed to forget you were king and subjects. I figured out that you must be celebrating that 'free speech' we hear about because you never stopped talking."

"Well, boy," said Astyages, "does your father never lose his head when he drinks?"

"Certainly not," said the boy.

"What happens then?" asked the king.

"He quenches his thirst," answered Cyrus, "and that's it. No harm comes from it. You see, he doesn't have a Sacas to mix his wine for him."

"But, Cyrus," his mother interjected, "why are you so unkind to Sacas?"

"Because I hate him," the boy answered. "Many times, when I wanted to see my grandfather, this old villain stopped me. Please, grandfather, let me manage him for three days."

"And how would you do that?" Astyages asked.

"I'll stand in the doorway just like he does. When he wants to go in for breakfast, I'll say, 'You can't have breakfast yet: HE is busy with some people.' When he comes for dinner, I'll say, 'No dinner yet: HE is in his bath.' And as he gets hungrier, I'll say, 'Wait a little: HE is with the ladies of the court.' I'll torment him just like he torments me by keeping me away from you, grandfather."

The boy delighted his elders with these words. During the day, if he saw that his grandfather or uncle needed anything, no one could get it for them faster than Cyrus. Nothing seemed to make him happier than to please them.

Persuasion and Perseverance

When Mandana started thinking about going back to her husband, Astyages begged her to leave Cyrus behind. She said that while she wanted to please her father in everything, it would be hard to leave the boy if he didn't want to stay.

Then the old man turned to Cyrus, saying, "My boy, if you stay with us, Sacas will never stop you from coming to me. You can come whenever you want, and the more you come, the happier I will be. You will have horses to ride, mine and as many others as you like. When you leave, you can take them with you. At dinner, you can do things your way and eat how you like. I will give you all the game in my parks and paradises and get more for you. Once you learn to ride, you can hunt, shoot, and throw the javelin like a man. You will have boys to play with and anything else you wish for. Just ask me, and it will be yours."

Then his mother asked him if he would rather stay with his grandfather in Media or go back home with her. He immediately said he would rather stay. When she asked him why, he answered, "Because at home, I'm considered the best at shooting and throwing the javelin. But here, I know I'm the worst at riding, and that really bothers me, mother. If you leave me here and I learn to ride, when I go back to Persia, you'll see that I will outdo all our brave men on foot. When I return to Media, I'll show my grandfather that, despite his splendid cavalry, he won't have a better horseman than his grandson to fight for him."

His mother then said, "But what about justice and righteousness, my son? How can you learn them here when your teachers are at home?"

"Oh," said Cyrus, "I already know all about them."

"How do you know that?" asked Mandana.

"Because," the boy replied, "before I left home, my teacher thought I had learned enough to judge cases and set me to try them. I remember once, I got a whipping for a bad judgment."

"I will tell you about that case. There were two boys, a big boy and a little boy. The big boy's coat was small, and the small boy's coat was huge. So the big boy took the little boy's coat and gave him his own small coat while he wore the big one himself. In my judgment, I decided it was better for both to have the coat that fit them best. But I never got to finish my sentence because my teacher thrashed me and said the verdict would have been excellent if I were deciding what fit and what did not. But my job was to decide to whom the coat belonged. The point was, who had the right to it: the one who took it by force or the one who had it made and bought it? My teacher taught me that what is lawful is just, and what goes against the law is based on violence. Therefore, he said, the judge must always ensure his verdict aligns with the law. So, you see, mother, I have justice all figured out already. And if there's anything more I need to know, I have my grandfather here to teach me."

"But," replied his mother, "what people consider just and righteous at your grandfather's court isn't seen the same way in Persia. For instance, your grandfather has made himself master over everyone among the Medes. But in Persia, equality is considered essential to justice. Your father must perform his duties to the state and receive his due. The measure of these is not his own desire but the law. Be careful, or you might be punished when you return to Persia if you learn to love not kingship but tyranny and believe you alone should have more than everyone else."

"Ah, but mother," said the boy, "my grandfather is better at teaching people to have less than their share, not more. Can't you see," he cried, "how he has taught all the Medes to have less than himself? So don't worry, mother. My grandfather will never teach me or anyone else how to get too much."

I.4

Cyrus's Early Years in Media

Summary

Young Cyrus stayed with his grandfather, Astyages, the king of Media, where he quickly made friends and endeared himself to both his companions and their parents. Astyages, deeply fond of Cyrus, indulged his every wish. Cyrus's intelligence and eagerness to help made him a beloved figure in the Median court. As he grew, his talkativeness and wit evolved into a more reserved yet still charming demeanor. His bravery and enthusiasm for hunting were evident, often leading him to take risks. Despite occasional recklessness, his dedication and determination impressed those around him. Eventually, Cyrus returned to Persia, leaving a lasting impression on Media, where he had won the hearts of everyone, including his grandfather, who gifted him generously. His departure was marked by heartfelt farewells and demonstrations of affection and generosity, reflecting the deep bonds he had formed.

A Talkative and Witty Boy

So, the boy kept talking. Eventually, his mother went home, and Cyrus stayed behind and was raised in Media. He quickly made friends with his companions and won their hearts. He also won over their parents with his charm and genuine affection for their sons. In fact, when the parents wanted a favor from the king, they would ask their children to get Cyrus to arrange it for them. Whatever the request was, Cyrus's kind heart and ambitious nature made him do his best to get it done.

On his part, Astyages couldn't refuse his grandson's slightest wish. Once, when Astyages was sick, Cyrus refused to leave his side. He couldn't hold back his tears, and everyone could see how terrified he was at the thought of his grandfather dying. If the old man needed anything during the night, Cyrus was the first to notice. He would jump up to wait on him and bring him whatever he thought would please him. Thus, he won the old king's heart.

In those early days, the boy was quite talkative, possibly due to his upbringing. His teacher had trained him to give reasons for his actions whenever he made a judgment and to expect the same from others. Moreover, his curiosity and thirst for knowledge made him ask everyone he met about various things. His quick wit meant he was always ready with an answer to any question asked of him, so talkativeness became second nature to him. But, just like a boy whose body has outgrown his age shows signs of youthfulness, Cyrus's talkativeness left an impression of simplicity and warm-heartedness, not arrogance. People would rather listen to him chatter endlessly than sit beside him in silence.

However, as he grew older and transitioned from childhood to youth, Cyrus became more careful with his words and quieter in his tone. At times, he was so shy that he would blush in the presence of his elders. The old boldness and impulsiveness, like a puppy jumping on everyone, master and stranger alike, were almost gone.

He became more reserved, but his company was still very charming. It's no surprise, really. Whenever there was a competition between him and his friends, he never challenged them in things he excelled at. Instead, he chose activities where he felt he was not as good, claiming he would outdo them all. He would jump on a horse to shoot or throw a javelin before he had even settled properly. When he lost, he was the first to laugh at his own failure.

Continuously Embracing New Challenges for Self Development

He didn't try to avoid defeat by giving up. Instead, he took pride in his determination to do better next time. Soon, he became as good a horseman as his peers. Eventually, due to his hard work, he surpassed them all. The thinning game in the king's preserves began to show his skill. With all the chasing, shooting, and spearing, the animal population decreased so much that Astyages struggled to gather enough for him.

One day, Cyrus saw that his grandfather couldn't keep up with his need for game, despite his goodwill. He said, "Grandfather, why should you go through so much trouble to find game for me? If you let me hunt with my uncle, I could pretend every animal we encounter was raised just for my enjoyment!"

Despite his eagerness to go hunting, Cyrus had lost the old childish way of getting what he wanted by coaxing. He hesitated for a long time before approaching the king again. In the past, he had quarreled with Sacas for not letting him in. Now, he played the part of Sacas against himself and couldn't find the courage to intrude until he felt it was the right moment. He even begged the real Sacas to tell him when it was okay to approach.

The old butler's heart was won, and he, like everyone else, completely adored the young prince.

At last, when Astyages saw that Cyrus was really set on hunting in the open country, he allowed him to go with his uncle. However, he made sure to send a group of experienced mounted guards to watch over him and protect him from any dangerous situations or wild animals.

Boldness while Learning the Hunt

Cyrus asked his escorts many questions about the animals they encountered. He wanted to know which animals he should avoid and which ones he could hunt. They told him to be careful of bears, wild boars, lions, and leopards, as many people had been attacked and killed by these dangerous creatures. But antelopes, deer, mountain sheep, and wild asses were safe enough to hunt. They also warned him to be cautious of dangerous places, as many riders had fallen off cliffs to their deaths.

Cyrus seemed to listen to all their advice. But then he saw a stag and forgot all the warnings. He immediately gave chase, focusing only on the animal ahead. His horse slipped and almost threw him over its head, but Cyrus managed to stay on and the horse regained its footing. When they reached a flat area, Cyrus threw his javelin and killed the stag, a beautiful big creature.

Still thrilled with his success, the guards rode up and scolded him severely. They asked if he couldn't see the danger he had put himself in and warned that they would certainly tell his grandfather. Cyrus, who had dismounted, stood quietly and listened with his head down while they reprimanded him. But then he heard the call of another hunt. He quickly jumped on his horse again as a wild boar charged at them. He met the boar head-on, drew his bow, and shot the animal in the forehead, killing it.

Now his uncle felt it was time to scold him personally. He thought Cyrus's boldness was too much. But the more he scolded, the more Cyrus begged to take the spoil as a present for his grandfather. His uncle finally replied, "But if your grandfather finds out you chased these animals yourself, he will scold both you and me for letting you go."

Cyrus responded, "Let him whip me if he wants, after I give him my animals. You too, uncle, can punish me however you choose, but please don't refuse me this."

So Cyaxares [*Huvakhshtr in Persian*] had to give in, saying, "Have it your way then. You are almost like our king already."

Thus, Cyrus was allowed to bring his trophies home and presented them to his grandfather. "See, grandfather, here are some animals I have shot for you." He did not show his weapons in triumph. He just laid them down with the blood still on them where he hoped his grandfather would see them.

Astyages replied, "I must accept with pleasure every gift you bring me, but I don't want any of them at the risk of your life."

Cyrus said, "If you really don't want them, grandfather, will you give them to me? I will share them with the other boys."

"With all my heart," said the old man. "Take them or anything else you like and give them to whoever you wish."

So Cyrus took the spoil and divided it with his friends, saying, "What foolishness it was when we hunted in the park! It was no better than hunting animals tied by a string. First, it was such a small place. And then, what poor creatures the animals were, some limping, others injured! But the real animals on the mountains and plains are magnificent, so big, sleek, and glossy! The stags leap as if they have wings, and the wild boars charge like warriors in battle! Their size and strength make them easy targets. Even when they're dead, they look better than those poor park creatures did when alive! But you," he added to his friends, "can't your fathers let you go out to hunt too?"

"They would gladly let us," they answered, "if only the king gave the order."

"Well," said Cyrus, "who will ask Astyages for us?"

"You should do it," they said. "You are the best one to persuade him."

"No, not me!" cried Cyrus. "I don't know what's come over me. I can't speak to my grandfather anymore. I can't look him in the face. If this keeps up, I'm afraid I'll become no better than an idiot. And yet, when I was a little boy, they tell me I was good at talking."

His friends retorted, "Well, that's a problem. If you can't help us, we'll have to find someone else."

Cyrus felt hurt by this. He went away in silence, determined to be brave, and went to his grandfather, but not without planning how to bring up the topic.

He began, "Tell me, grandfather, if one of your slaves ran away and you caught him, what would you do?"

"What else should I do," the old man answered, "but put him in chains and make him work?"

"But if he came back on his own, how would you treat him then?"

"I would whip him as a warning not to do it again, then treat him as if nothing had happened."

"Then it's time to get a birch ready for your grandson," said the boy, "because I plan to take my friends and run away on a hunting trip."

"Very kind of you to tell me beforehand," said Astyages. "But listen, I forbid you to leave the palace grounds. It would be foolish to lose my daughter's precious child for a day's hunting."

So Cyrus obeyed and stayed home, but he was silent and sad. Astyages saw how upset the boy was and decided to make him happy by organizing a hunting party himself. He gathered a large group of horsemen and foot soldiers, including Cyrus's friends. They drove the animals down to the flat country where the horses could easily chase them, and then the hunt began in grand style.

Following royal custom, Astyages ordered that no one was to shoot until Cyrus had his fill of hunting. But Cyrus insisted, "Grandfather, if you want me to enjoy myself, let my friends hunt with me, and we'll all try our best."

So Astyages let everyone go while he watched. He saw how they raced to catch the animals and how their ambition drove them to chase and throw their javelins. He was especially pleased to see how Cyrus couldn't keep quiet from excitement, calling out to his friends by name whenever he spotted the prey. It delighted the old man to hear how happily the boy laughed and praised his friends without any jealousy.

Finally, it was time to head home. They returned, carrying their impressive trophies. After that, the king was so pleased with the day's hunting that he often went out with his grandson, bringing along all the boys to make Cyrus happy.

Thus, Cyrus spent his early life, sharing in and contributing to everyone's happiness, and bringing no sorrow to anyone.

Cyrus's First Battle at Age Fifteen Was a Victory

But when Cyrus was about fifteen years old, the young Prince of Assyria planned a hunting party to celebrate his upcoming marriage. He had heard that there was a lot of game on the borders of Assyria and Media, untouched because of the war, so he chose this area for his hunt. For safety, he took a large escort of cavalry and infantry to drive the beasts from their lairs into the open fields where it was easier to hunt.

The prince went to the Assyrian outposts where a garrison was stationed and there he and his men prepared to have supper, intending to start the hunt at dawn.

As evening fell, a night-watch consisting of a considerable number of horse and foot soldiers arrived from the city to relieve the garrison on guard. The prince realized he had a large force at his disposal: the two garrisons and the troop for the hunt. He then thought it might be a good idea to raid the Medes' land. This would add more excitement to the hunt and provide many animals for sacrifices.

So, he got up early and led his army out. He gathered the foot soldiers at the frontier while he and his cavalry rode up to the border fortresses of the Medes. He stopped there with the majority of his company to prevent the garrisons from coming out. Meanwhile, he sent select men forward in groups with orders to raid the country, capture everything they found, and bring the loot back to him.

While this was happening, news reached Astyages that the enemy had crossed the border. He quickly set out to help, leading his own bodyguard and his son with whatever troopers were ready, leaving instructions for others to follow quickly. When they saw the Assyrians, lined up in order and motionless, they stopped as well.

Now, seeing that everyone else was rushing to help, Cyrus also wanted to join in. He put on his armor for the first time, hardly believing it was true, since he had longed for this moment so often. The armor, made by his grandfather, fit him perfectly and looked beautiful. He mounted his horse and rode to the front. Astyages, surprised to see him, told him to stay by his side now that he was there.

Cyrus, looking at the enemy horsemen, asked, "Grandfather, are those men our enemies, standing so quietly by their horses?"

"Yes, they are our enemies," said the king.

"And are those riding over there enemies too?" asked the boy.

"Yes, to be sure," replied his grandfather.

"Well, grandfather, they look like a sorry bunch with poor horses! It would be good for some of us to charge them!" Cyrus suggested.

"Not yet, my boy," answered his grandfather. "Look at the mass of horsemen there. If we charge now, their friends will attack us before we are fully ready."

"Yes, but if you stay here ready to receive our supporters, those men will be afraid to move. The raiders will drop their loot as soon as they are attacked," suggested Cyrus.

Astyages saw the wisdom in what the boy said and, impressed by his sense and awareness, ordered his son to take a squadron of horsemen and charge the raiders. "If the main body moves to attack," he added, "I will charge them myself and keep them busy here."

Cyaxares took a detachment of horsemen and galloped forward. Cyrus, seeing the charge, darted ahead, leading the way with Cyaxares close behind and the rest following. As soon as the raiders saw them, they abandoned their loot and fled.

Cyrus and his troopers cut some of them down immediately, while others slipped past. They pursued these as well, catching and cutting them down too. Cyrus was always at the front, like an eager young hound, focused only on the hunt and the capture.

When the Assyrian army saw their friends in trouble, they pushed forward, thinking the pursuit would stop once their movement was noticed. But Cyrus didn't slow down. In his excitement, he called on his uncle by name, chasing the fugitives relentlessly. Cyaxares followed closely, perhaps thinking of what his father Astyages would say if he hung back. The others followed too, with even the faint-hearted turning into heroes for the moment.

Seeing their furious attack and the enemy moving forward in tight formation to meet them, Astyages decided to advance without delay. He feared his son and Cyrus might get hurt if they crashed into the enemy in disorder.

The Assyrians saw the king's movement and halted, leveling their spears and bending their bows. They expected that, as usual, their attackers would stop when within range and exchange shots until evening. But now, they saw their own men being chased by Cyrus and his comrades, while Astyages and his cavalry were already within bowshot. This was too much for them, and they turned and fled.

The Medes pursued them, cutting down both horses and men they caught, and killing those who fell. They didn't stop until they reached the Assyrian foot soldiers.

Daring Borders Madness

Here, they finally drew rein, fearing a hidden ambush, and Astyages led his army away. He was very pleased with his cavalry's success, but he didn't know what to say to Cyrus. The battle and victory were due to him, but the boy's daring bordered on madness. Even on the way home, Cyrus behaved strangely; he rode around alone, looking into the faces of the dead. Those in charge had a hard time dragging him to Astyages. Cyrus was glad to have them as a shield between himself and the king, as he saw his grandfather's stern expression.

So things went in Media, and the name of Cyrus was on everyone's lips, in songs and stories. Astyages, who always loved him, was amazed by the boy. Meanwhile, his father, Cambyses, was happy to hear such news about his son. But hearing that Cyrus was already acting like a grown man, he decided it was time to call him home to complete his training.

The story tells how Cyrus responded to the summons, saying he would return home at once so his father wouldn't be upset, and his country wouldn't blame him. Astyages also felt it was his duty to send the boy back but gave him horses and other gifts, as many as he wanted, not only out of love but because he had high hopes for the boy's future.

Farewell to Media and Departure for Persia

When the time came for Cyrus to leave, everyone came out to see him off—children, lads his age, grown men, and old men on their horses, including King Astyages. According to the chronicle, no one had dry eyes as they turned back home.

Cyrus himself, they say, rode away in tears. He gave gifts to all his friends, sharing what Astyages had given him. Finally, he took off his splendid Median cloak and gave it to one friend to show how much he cared. His friends took the gifts but brought them back to Astyages, who sent them to Cyrus again. Once more, Cyrus sent them back to Media with this message for his grandfather: "If you want me to hold my head up when I come back, let my friends keep the gifts I gave them." Astyages did as the boy asked. *(Note from the editor: This is a perfect example of Persians "taarof", which is still a typical behavior among Persians, showing an extreme level of generosity, hospitality and kindness, even though sometimes it may be costly and consequently annoying or not deeply desired).*

And here, if a tale of boyish love is not out of place, we might tell how, when Cyrus was just about to leave and the last good-byes were being said, each of his kinsmen, in the Persian fashion—and to this day the custom holds in Persia—kissed him on the lips as they wished him Godspeed. *(Note from the editor: by "this day", the author, Xenophone, is referring to his era. Modern Persian heterosexual males never kiss each other on the lips but very often on the cheeks).*

Now, there was a certain Mede, as beautiful and brave a man as ever lived, who had been in love with Cyrus for a long time. When he saw the kiss, he stayed behind. After the others had left, he went up to Cyrus and said, "Am I the only one of your kindred you refuse to recognize, Cyrus?"

Cyrus answered, "What, are you my kinsman too?"

"Yes, assuredly," the other replied.

The lad rejoined, "Ah, then that is why you looked at me so earnestly. I think I've seen you look at me like that more than once before."

"Yes," answered the Mede, "I have often wanted to approach you, but as often, heaven knows, my heart failed me."

"But why should that be," said Cyrus, "seeing you are my kinsman?" And with that, he leaned forward and kissed him on the lips.

Then the Mede, emboldened by the kiss, took heart and said, "So in Persia it is really the custom for relatives to kiss?"

"Truly yes," answered Cyrus, "when we see each other after a long absence or when we part for a journey."

"Then the time has come," said the other, "to give me a second kiss, for I must leave you now." With that, Cyrus kissed him again and so they parted.

But the travelers had not gone far when suddenly the Mede came galloping after them, his horse covered with foam. Cyrus caught sight of him and asked, "Did you forget something? Is there something else you wanted to say?"

"No," said the Mede, "it is just that it feels like a long, long time since we met."

"Such a little, little while you mean, my kinsman," answered Cyrus.

"A little while!" repeated the other. "How can you say that? Don't you understand that the time it takes to wink is an eternity if it separates me from the beauty of your face?"

Then Cyrus burst out laughing despite his tears and told the unfortunate man to take heart and leave. "I will soon be back with you again, and then you can stare at me to your heart's content without ever blinking."

I.5

Cyrus's Return to Persia and Rise

Summary

Cyrus returned to Persia from Media and spent a year adjusting back to Persian life, initially facing ridicule but eventually winning admiration for his modesty and generosity. After this period, Astyages died, and Cyaxares, Cyrus's uncle, took the throne of Media. The Assyrian king, having conquered neighboring tribes and seeing the Medes as a significant threat, planned to attack Media. In response, Cyaxares requested help from the Persians. The Persian council appointed Cyrus to lead the forces, comprising 10,000 archers, 10,000 slingers, 10,000 targeteers, and 1,000 Peers. Cyrus motivated his troops with a powerful speech, emphasizing dedication, hard work, and the pursuit of honor. He prepared meticulously, ensuring provisions and health for his soldiers. Cyrus set out with his father's blessings, ready to face the challenges ahead and uphold the principles of wise and just leadership.

Media Needs Cyrus

So, Cyrus left his grandfather's court and returned to Persia. He spent another year as a boy among boys. At first, the other boys laughed at him, thinking he must have learned luxurious ways in Media. But when they saw he could enjoy simple Persian food just as much as they did and noticed how, during festivals, he would give away his share of the treats instead of asking for more, they realized his inherent nobility and superiority. Eventually, they admired him once more.

When this part of his training was over, and it was time for him to join the young men, the same thing happened again. He excelled in his duties, endured hardships, respected his elders, and obeyed authority better than anyone else.

In time, Astyages died in Media, and Cyaxares, the brother of Cyrus's mother, took the throne. By then, the king of Assyria had subdued all the tribes of Syria, conquered the king of Arabia, brought the Hyrcanians under his rule, and was besieging the Bactrians. He thought that if he could weaken the power of the Medes, it would be easy to extend his empire over all the surrounding nations, as the Medes were the strongest of them all.

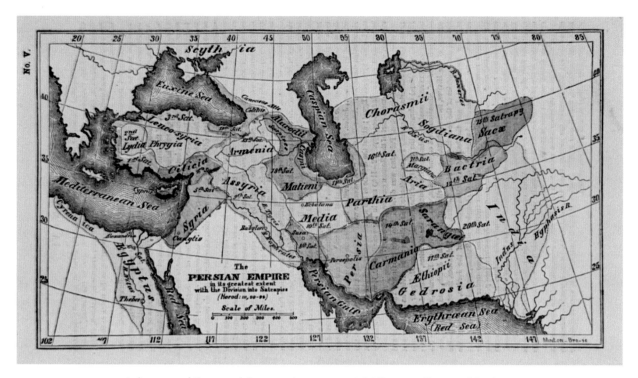

Achaemenid Imperial Satraps (source: a 1855 Persian Empire Map)

So, he sent messengers to every part of his domain: to Croesus, king of Lydia, to the king of Cappadocia, to both the Phrygias, to the Paphlagonians and the Indians, to the Carians and the Cilicians. He told them to spread lies about the Persians and the Medes, saying these were great and powerful kingdoms united by marriage and would soon attack their neighbors unless they were stopped first. The nations listened to the messengers and allied with the king of Assyria. Some were convinced by his words, and others were won over with gifts and gold, for the Assyrian king was very wealthy.

Cyaxares, the son of Astyages, was aware of these plots and prepared on his side. He sent word to the Persian state and to Cambyses, the king, who was married to his sister. He also sent for Cyrus, begging him to come quickly with any force the Persian Council might provide. By this time, Cyrus had completed his ten years among the youths and was now enrolled with the grown men.

Cyrus Appointed to Assemble the Army and Lead It for Media

Cyrus was eager to go, and the Council of Elders appointed him to lead the force for Media. They instructed him to choose two hundred men from the Peers, and each of them was to choose four others from their fellows. This formed a body of a thousand Peers. Each of the thousand had orders to raise thirty men from the commoners—ten targeteers, ten slingers, and ten archers—thus forming three regiments: 10,000 archers, 10,000 slingers, and 10,000 targeteers, in addition to the thousand Peers. The entire force was placed under Cyrus's command.

As soon as he was appointed, Cyrus offered a sacrifice. When the omens were favorable, he chose his two hundred Peers, and each of them chose their four comrades. Then he called the whole body together and addressed them for the first time:

Cyrus's First Motivational Speech to Prepare for The Battle

"My friends, I have chosen you for this task, but this isn't the first time I've judged your worth. Since my boyhood, I've observed your dedication to what our country honors and your disdain for what it despises. I want to explain why I accepted this position and why I ask for your help.

I believe our forefathers were as good as we are. They lived their lives striving for the same deeds of valor we honor now. Yet, despite their worth, I don't see what good they achieved for the state or themselves.

I can't believe that virtue is practiced just so the brave and good fare no better than the base. People don't give up momentary pleasures to say goodbye to all joy forever. No, self-control is training to reap greater joy in the future. A man will work hard to become an orator, not because oratory is his ultimate goal, but to influence others and achieve something noble.

Similarly, we who are trained in the arts of war don't labor to fight endlessly. We hope to one day win and secure wealth, happiness, and honor for ourselves and our city. If some have worked hard all their lives but find old age has taken their strength before they reap the benefits, they seem like farmers who sow and plant well but let the harvest rot. Or like an athlete who trains hard but never competes, deserving to be called a fool.

Let that not be our fate, my friends. From boyhood, we've been trained in the ways of honor and nobility. Now, let's face our enemies. They may be skilled with javelins and bows and ride well, but they aren't true warriors if they fail when endurance is needed.

You, however, are not like them. To you, night is like day. Your training has taught you that hard work leads to happiness. Hunger is a daily companion, and water quenches your thirst like a lion at a stream. You have something rare and valuable: the love of honor and glory. You seek honor and gladly face hard work and danger to earn it."

"Now if I said all this about you, and my heart were not in my words, I would only be deceiving myself. For if you didn't fulfill my hopes, the shame would fall on me. But I have faith in you, based on experience. I trust in your goodwill towards me and our enemy's lack of wisdom. You will not disappoint my expectations. Let's go forth with a light heart; we have no bad reputation to fear. No one can say we unlawfully covet another man's goods. Our enemy strikes the first blow for an unjust cause, and our friends call us to protect them. What is more lawful than self-defense? What is nobler than helping those we love?

And you have another reason to be confident. In starting this campaign, I have not forgotten the gods. You have been with me and seen how I strive to win their blessing in all things, big and small.

And now," he added, "there is no need for more words. I will leave you to choose your own men. When all is ready, you will march into Media at their head. Meanwhile, I will return to my father and start ahead of you, so that I can learn what I can about the enemy as soon as possible and make all necessary preparations. With God's help, we will achieve glory on the field."

Cyrus's Journey and Wisdom from Cambyses

Such were his orders, and they set about them at once. But Cyrus himself went home and prayed to the gods of his father's house, to Hestia and Zeus, and to all who had watched over his family. [Editor's note: Unlike the Greek, Cyrus had supposedly faith in Ahura Mazda, as a follower of the monotheistic religion, Zoroastrianism, and not in the Greeks Gods as Xenophone seems to believe.] After his prayers, he set out for the war, and his father accompanied him on the road. As they exited the city, a dramatic display of thunder and lightning split the sky, interpreted by them as a blessing. After that, they continued without further divination, confident in the signs from the Ruler of the gods.

As they went on their way, Cyrus' father said, "My son, the gods are kind to us and favor your journey. They have shown this in the sacrifices and the signs from heaven. You don't need another person to tell you this, because I made sure you learned this art. You can understand the counsels of the gods yourself, without needing an interpreter. You can see with your own eyes and hear with your own ears, understanding the divine signs for yourself. This way, you won't be at the mercy of any soothsayers who might deceive you, or be lost without guidance if you're without a seer. Your own learning allows you to understand and follow the warnings of the gods."

The Role of Effort and Divine Favor

Effort and preparation are essential to achieving success and earning favor, both human and divine. One cannot simply rely on prayers or wishes without putting in the necessary work and training.

"Yes, father," answered Cyrus, "I remember your teachings and pray to the gods continually for their favor and guidance. I recall you saying that, as with men, so with the gods, it's natural for the prayers of those who remember them in good times to be heard more favorably than those who only turn to them in times of need. You said this is how we should treat our earthly friends as well."

"True, my son," said his father. "Because of all my teachings, you can now pray to the gods with a lighter heart and more confidence, knowing you have always remembered them."

"Even so," said Cyrus, "I feel towards them as though they were my friends."

"And do you remember," asked his father, "certain other conclusions we reached? We agreed that there are certain things the gods allow us to achieve through learning, study, and training. Success in these areas is the reward of effort, not idleness. Only when we have done all that is our duty can we rightly ask for blessings from the gods."

"I remember very well," said Cyrus. "You used to say that a man has no right to pray to win a cavalry charge if he has never learned to ride, or to triumph over master bowmen if he cannot draw a bow. He shouldn't expect to bring a ship safely to harbor if he doesn't know how to steer, or reap a bountiful harvest if he hasn't sown any grain. Nor should he pray to come home safely from battle if he takes no precautions. All such prayers are against the very laws of heaven. Those who ask for things they haven't worked for shouldn't be surprised if they fail to receive them from the gods, just as a petition against the law on earth would have no success with men."

The Leaders' Noble Goal and What Sets Them Apart

True leadership is about guiding and governing others to meet their needs and helping them become their best selves. A noble leader should not seek distinction through luxury and ease but through foresight, wisdom, and a strong work ethic. Cyrus knew that ruling well and nobly is the greatest of all works, and he strived to be a leader who provided for his people and stood out for his dedication and wisdom rather than for his comfort and wealth.

"And do you remember," said his father, "how we thought it would be a noble achievement if a man could truly train himself to be beautiful and brave, earning all he needed for his household and himself? We said that was something to be proud of. But if he went further and had the skill to guide and govern other men, providing for all their needs and making them the best they could be, that would be truly marvelous."

"Yes, father," answered Cyrus, "I remember it well. I agreed with you that ruling well and nobly was the greatest of all works, and I still think that way. But when I look at the world and see the poor quality of the men who manage to hold power and the kind of opponents we are likely to face, I feel it would be disgraceful to bow before them instead of confronting them on the battlefield. All of them, starting with our own friends here, believe that a ruler should be different from his subjects by the splendor of his banquets, the wealth in his coffers, the amount of sleep he gets, and his freedom from trouble and pain. But I believe a ruler should stand out not by living easily but by his forethought, wisdom, and eagerness for work."

Collaborate with Partners, but don't rely on them for critical resources.

Effective leaders understand the importance of collaboration with partners but ensure they have their own critical resources secured. Relying solely on external support can be risky, as unforeseen circumstances may arise. Cyrus learned from his father that while Cyaxares promised supplies for their campaign, it was essential to have independent provisions and preparations to guarantee the welfare of his troops and maintain their respect and confidence.

"True, my son," the father answered, "but you know the struggle is not just against people but also against circumstances, which may not be easily overcome. You know that if supplies were not available, you would lose your government."

"Yes," Cyrus answered, "and that is why Cyaxares is undertaking to provide for all of us who join him, no matter our numbers."

"So," said the father, "you really mean that you are relying only on these supplies from Cyaxares for your campaign?"

"Yes," answered Cyrus.

"And do you know what they amount to?"

"No," he said, "I cannot say that I do."

"And yet," his father went on, "you are prepared to rely on what you do not know? Do you forget that tomorrow's needs will be high, not to mention today's expenses?"

"Oh, no," said Cyrus, "I am well aware of that."

"Well," said the father, "suppose the cost is more than Cyaxares can handle, or suppose he actually meant to deceive you, how would your soldiers fare?"

"Ill enough, no doubt," answered Cyrus. "And now tell me, father, while we are still in friendly country, do you know of any resources that I could secure for myself?"

"You want to know where you could find resources of your own?" repeated his father. "And who is to find that out if not the one who holds the keys of power? We have given you an infantry force that you wouldn't trade for one twice its size; and you will have the cavalry of Media to support you, the finest in the world. I believe none of the nearby nations will refuse to serve you, whether to win your favor or out of fear of disaster. These are matters you must carefully examine with Cyaxares, so that nothing you need is ever lacking. Also, for habit's sake, you should devise some means for securing your revenue.

Remember this above all—never delay collecting supplies until you need them. Use your time of abundance to prepare for times of scarcity. You will gain better terms from those you depend on if you are not seen as desperate. Moreover, you will avoid blame in the eyes of your soldiers. That in itself will earn you more respect. Wherever you want to help or harm, your troops will follow you more eagerly if they have all they need. And your words will carry more weight when your power to help or hurt is evident."

"Yes, father," Cyrus said, "I believe everything you say is true, especially because, as it stands, none of my soldiers will thank me for the pay they are promised. They know the terms Cyaxares has offered for their help, but whatever they get above that amount, they will see as a gift and will likely feel more gratitude to the giver."

"True," said his father, "and really, for a man to have a force with which he could serve his friends and take vengeance on his foes, and yet neglect the supplies for it, would be as disgraceful, wouldn't it, as for a farmer to have lands and workers but let the fields lie barren for lack of tillage?"

"No such neglect," answered Cyrus, "will ever be blamed on me. Whether through friendly lands or hostile, trust me, in this business of supplying my troops with what they need, I will always do my part."

"Well, my son," his father continued, "do you remember certain other points we agreed must never be overlooked?"

"How could I forget them?" answered Cyrus. "I remember coming to you for money to pay the teacher who claimed to have taught me generalship, and you gave it to me, but you asked many questions. 'Now, my boy,' you said, 'did this teacher you want to pay ever mention economy among the things a general ought to understand? Soldiers, like servants in a house, depend on supplies.' I had to admit that not a word had been said about that. Then you asked if he had taught anything about health and strength, since a true general must think about these matters as well as tactics and strategy. Again, I had to say no. You asked if he had taught me any of the arts that are most useful in war. Once again, I had to say no. Then you asked if he had taught me how to inspire enthusiasm in my men, because in every undertaking, there is a huge difference between energy and lack of spirit. I shook my head, and your questions continued: 'Had this teacher stressed the importance of obedience in an army or the best ways to maintain discipline?' And finally, when it was clear that even this had been ignored, you exclaimed, 'What, then, does your professor claim to have taught you under the name of generalship?' To that, I could only answer that he taught me tactics. And then you laughed a little and reviewed your points: 'What use are tactics to an army without supplies, health, discipline, or knowledge of useful arts in war?' You made it clear that tactics and maneuvers are only a small part of generalship. When I asked if you could teach me the rest, you advised me to learn from those reputed to be great generals. So, I sought out those authorities.

As for our present supplies, I was persuaded that Cyaxares intended to provide enough. Regarding the health of the troops, I knew that cities that valued health appointed medical officers, and generals who cared for their soldiers took out a medical staff. When I found myself in this position, I immediately focused on the matter. I flatter myself, father," he added, "that I will have an excellent staff of surgeons and physicians with me."

Watch on Your People's Health; and Prevention is better than Cure

A leader must prioritize the health and well-being of their team, focusing on prevention rather than relying solely on remedies. Cyrus's father, Cambyses, advised him that while doctors can treat illnesses, it is crucial to prevent them by choosing healthy locations for camps and maintaining a disciplined lifestyle. By ensuring the team members are always engaged and never idle, a leader can maintain a healthy and effective team, ready to face any challenge.

His father replied, "Well, my son, but these excellent men are like tailors who patch torn garments. When people are ill, doctors can fix them up, but your care for their health should go deeper. Your main goal should be to prevent your men from getting ill in the first place."

"And how can I succeed in that?" asked Cyrus.

"I presume that if you are to stay in one place for a while, you will find a healthy spot for your camp. If you focus on this, you can hardly fail. People constantly discuss which places are healthy and which are not, and their own health is the clearest evidence. But you won't just choose a site; you'll remember the care you take for your own health."

"My first rule," said Cyrus, "is to avoid overeating, which is most oppressive to the system. My second rule is to work off everything that enters the body. This seems the best way to maintain health and gain strength."

"My son," Cambyses answered, "these are the principles you must apply to others."

"What!" said Cyrus. "Do you think it will be possible for the soldiers to diet and train themselves?"

"Not only possible," said his father, "but essential. An army, to fulfill its function, must always be engaged in either hurting the enemy or helping itself. Supporting even one idle person is difficult, a household harder, and an army hardest of all. There are more mouths to feed, less initial wealth, and greater waste. Therefore, an army should never be idle."

"If I understand you," said Cyrus, "you think an idle general is as useless as an idle farmer. Here and now, I promise that with God's help, the working general will show you that his troops have all they need and are in excellent health. I think," he added, "I know a way to train the men in various branches of war. Let the officer propose competitions and offer prizes. The skill level will rise, and he will soon have a body of troops ready for any service required."

"Nothing could be better," his father replied. "Do this, and you will watch your regiments at their maneuvers with as much delight as if they were a chorus in a dance."

Inspire Your People and Develop Hope and Wisdom

> To inspire enthusiasm in your team, kindle hope, but be cautious not to raise false expectations. Cyrus's father advises that false promises can lead to loss of credibility. Save your assurances for moments of critical importance and let your agents handle uncertain situations. Moreover, to secure obedience, a leader must be seen as wiser than those they lead. Genuine wisdom, not mere pretense, earns true respect and voluntary obedience.

"And then," continued Cyrus, "to rouse enthusiasm in the men, there is nothing, I think, like the power of kindling hope?"

"True," answered his father, "but that alone would be like a huntsman always rousing his pack with the view-halloo. At first, the hounds will respond eagerly, but after being misled a few times, they will refuse the call even when the prey is really there. And so it is with hope. Let a man raise false expectations often enough, and in the end, even when hope is real, he may cry the good news in vain. He should refrain from speaking positively when he cannot be certain; his agents can do it instead. He should save his own appeal for the critical moments of supreme danger and not waste his credibility."

"By heaven, a most admirable suggestion!" cried Cyrus, "and one much more to my liking!

"As for enforcing obedience, I hope I have had some training in that already. You began my education by teaching me to obey you when I was a child. Then you handed me over to masters who did the same. Later, when we were lads, my fellows and I, our governors stressed obedience above all. Our laws themselves enforce this dual lesson: 'Rule thou and be thou ruled.' When I study the secret of it, I see that the real incentive to obedience lies in the praise and honor it brings versus the discredit and punishment for disobedience."

"That, my son," said his father, "is the road to compulsory obedience. But there is a shorter way to a nobler goal: voluntary obedience. When the interests of people are at stake, they will gladly obey the man they believe is wiser than themselves. You can see this everywhere: how the sick man begs the doctor for advice, how a whole ship's crew listens to the pilot, how travelers cling to the one who knows the way better. But if people think that obedience will lead to disaster, then nothing—neither penalties, persuasion, nor gifts—will rouse them. No one accepts a bribe to their own destruction."

"You mean," said Cyrus, "that the best way to secure obedience is to be thought wiser than those we rule?"

"Yes," said Cambyses, "that is my belief."

"And what is the quickest way," asked Cyrus, "to win that reputation?"

"None quicker, my lad, than this: wherever you wish to seem wise, be wise. Examine any case, and you will find this true. If you wanted to be thought a good farmer, horseman, physician, or flute-player without really being one, imagine the tricks you would need to keep up the pretense! Suppose you got a following to praise you and burdened yourself with all kinds of paraphernalia. What would come of it? You might succeed in deceiving people at first, but eventually, the truth would come out, and the impostor would be revealed."

"But," said Cyrus, "how can a man truly attain the wisdom that will serve his turn?"

Leading by Example, Wisdom and Empathy

A leader must lead by example, demonstrating wisdom through careful actions and decisions. Showing genuine care and empathy for those you lead is essential. Cyrus's father emphasizes that a commander must endure the same hardships as their followers, sharing in their joys and sorrows. This shared experience fosters loyalty and respect. The leader's challenges are mitigated by the honor of their role and the public nature of their actions.

"Well, my son, it is clear that where learning leads to wisdom, learn you must, just as you learned your battalion drill. But for matters beyond mortal learning or foresight, you can only become wiser than others by communicating with the gods through divination. Always, wherever you know that something ought to be done, ensure it is done and done with care. Care, not carelessness, is the mark of a wise man."

"And now," said Cyrus, "to win the affection of those we rule—and there is nothing, I think, more important—surely the path to follow is clear for anyone who wants their friends' love. We must show that we do them good."

"Yes, my child, but to always do good for those we want to help isn't always possible. Only one way is ever open, and that is the way of sympathy. We must rejoice with them when they are happy, share their sorrow when things go wrong, help them in their difficulties, fear disaster for them, and guard against it by foresight. These, rather than actual benefits, are the true signs of friendship."

"And in war, if the campaign is in summer, the general must share in the sun and heat, and in winter, in the cold and frost, and in all labors, the toil and fatigue. This will help make him beloved by his followers."

"You mean, father," said Cyrus, "that a commander should always be braver and stronger in everything than those he commands."

"Yes, my son, that is my meaning," said he. "But remember this: the princely leader and the private soldier may have similar bodies, but their sufferings are not the same. The leader's pains are always lightened by the glory that comes with his role and by knowing all his acts are done in the public eye."

"But now, father, suppose the time has come, and you are sure your troops are well supplied, healthy, able to endure fatigue, skilled in the arts of war, eager for honor, and ready to show their mettle. Wouldn't you think it wise to try the chance of battle without delay?"

"By all means," said his father, "if you are likely to gain by the move. But if not, the more I felt confident in our superiority and the power of our troops, the more I would be inclined to stay on guard, just as we put our greatest treasures in the safest place."

"But how can a man be sure he will gain?"

Don't Be Tender with Your Enemy

A successful leader must employ strategy, craft, and deception against opponents. Training for war involves learning to outsmart and outmaneuver the enemy, using tactics that ensure victory. Cyrus's father emphasizes the need to be just and upright with friends and citizens but ruthless and strategic with enemies. He advises using various cunning methods, such as attacking when the enemy is vulnerable and setting traps. This approach ensures that leaders can effectively safeguard their people and achieve success in their campaigns.

"Ah, there you come," said his father, "to a most important matter. This is no easy task. If your general is to succeed, he must be an arch-plotter, a master of craft, full of deceits and stratagems, a cheat, a thief, and a robber, always outsmarting his opponent."

"Heavens!" said Cyrus, laughing, "is this the kind of man you want your son to be!"

"I want him to be," said his father, "as just and upright and law-abiding as any man who ever lived."

"But how come," said his son, "that the lessons you taught us in boyhood and youth were exactly the opposite of what you teach me now?"

"Ah," said his father, "those lessons were for friends and fellow-citizens, and for them they still hold true. But for your enemies—don't you remember you were also taught to do much harm?"

"No, father," he answered, "I would say certainly not."

"Then why were you taught to shoot? Or to hurl the javelin? Or to trap wild boars? Or to snare stags with cords and caltrops? And why did you never meet the lion, bear, or leopard in a fair fight but always tried to gain some advantage over them? Can you deny that all that was craft and deceit and fraud and greed?"

"Of course," answered the young man, "in dealing with animals, but with humans, it was different. If I was ever suspected of trying to cheat another, I was punished, I know, with many stripes."

"True," said his father, "and for that matter, we did not permit you to draw a bow or hurl a javelin against humans. We taught you to aim at a mark. But why did we teach you that? Not to injure your friends, either then or now, but so that in war, you would have the skill to make the bodies of living men your targets. So also, we taught you the arts of deceit and craft and greed and covetousness, not among men, but among beasts. We did not mean for you to turn these skills against your friends. In war, we wanted you to be better than raw recruits."

"But, father," Cyrus answered, "if doing good and doing harm are both things we ought to learn, wouldn't it have been better to teach them in actual practice?"

Then his father said, "My son, we are told that in the days of our forefathers, there was once such a teacher. This man taught his boys righteousness in the way you suggest: to lie and not to lie, to cheat and not to cheat, to slander and not to slander, to be greedy and not greedy. He explained the difference between our duty to friends and our duty to enemies. He even went further and taught that it was just and right to deceive even a friend for his own good, or to steal his property.

And with this, he had to teach his pupils to practice on one another what he taught them, just as people in Hellas teach lads in the wrestling school to fence and feint, and train them by practicing with one another. Some of his students showed such excellent skills in deception and overreaching, and perhaps no lack of interest in making money, that they did not even spare their friends but used their tricks on them.

So, an unwritten law was framed by which we still abide, telling us to teach our children, as we teach our servants, simply and solely not to lie, not to cheat, and not to covet, and if they did otherwise, to punish them, hoping to make them humane and law-abiding citizens.

But when they reached manhood, as you have, it seemed the risk was over, and it was time to teach them what is lawful against our enemies. At your age, we do not believe you will act savagely against your fellows, with whom you have formed ties of friendship and respect since childhood. Similarly, we do not talk to the young about the mysteries of love, for if lightness were added to desire, their passion might sweep them beyond all bounds."

"Then, in heaven's name, father," said Cyrus, "remember that your son is but a backward scholar and a late learner in this lore of selfishness, and teach me all you can that may help me to outsmart the foe."

"Well," said his father, "you must plot and plan, regardless of the size of his force and your own, to catch his men in disorder when yours are all arranged, unarmed when yours are armed, asleep when yours are awake, or wait until he is visible to you and you are invisible to him, or until he is struggling over difficult terrain and you are in your fortress and can give him a warm welcome there."

"But how," asked Cyrus, "can I catch him in all these mistakes?"

"Simply because both you and he will often be in some such situations; both of you must eat sometime; both of you must sleep; your men must scatter in the morning to satisfy the needs of nature, and, for better or worse, whatever the roads are like, you will be forced to use them. You must consider all these necessities, and wherever you are weaker, be most on guard, and wherever your foe is most vulnerable, press the attack."

Then Cyrus asked, "And are these the only cases where one can apply the great principle of greed, or are there others?"

"Oh, yes, there are many more; indeed, in these simple cases, any general will be sure to keep a good watch, knowing how necessary it is. But your true cheat and prince of swindlers is the one who can lure the enemy on and throw him off his guard, allow himself to be pursued, and get the pursuers into disorder, lead the foe into difficult ground and then attack him there.

Indeed, as an eager student, you must not limit yourself to the lessons you have learned; you must show yourself as a creator and discoverer. You must invent strategies against the foe, just as a real musician is not content with the mere basics of his art but sets himself to compose new themes. And if, in music, it is the novel melody that wins popularity, in military matters, it is the newest contrivance that stands the highest because it gives you the best chance of outwitting your opponent.

And yet, my son, I must say that if you did no more than apply against human beings the devices you learned to use against the smallest game, you would have made considerable progress in this art of outsmarting. Do you not think so yourself? To snare birds, you would get up by night in the depth of winter and tramp off in the cold. Your nets were laid before the creatures were awake, and your tracks completely covered. You even had birds of your own, trained to serve you and decoy their kin, while you yourself lay in hiding, seeing yet unseen, and you had learned by long practice to jerk in the net before the birds could fly away.

Or you might be out after hares, and for a hare, you had two breeds of dogs: one to track her by scent because she feeds at dusk and hides by day, and another to cut off her escape and run her down because she is so swift. Even if she escaped these, she did not escape you; you knew all her runs and hiding places, and there you would spread your nets so that they were barely visible. The very haste of her flight would fling her into the snare. To make sure of her, you had men placed to keep a lookout and pounce on her immediately. There you were at her heels, shouting and scaring her out of her wits, so she was caught from sheer terror, and there lay your men, as you had taught them, silent and motionless in their ambush.

I say, therefore, that if you chose to act like this against human beings, you would soon have no enemies left to fight, or I am much mistaken. And even if the need should arise for you to do battle on equal terms in open field, even then, my son, the skills you have studied so long, which teach you to outsmart your opponent, will still be powerful. Among them are all the practices that have trained the bodies and fired the courage of your men, making them adept in every craft of war. One thing you must always remember: if you wish your men to follow you, they expect you to plan for them.

Leaders Plan Ahead

Effective leaders must always anticipate future needs and challenges, never becoming complacent or careless. Whether planning for day or night operations, navigating different terrains, or preparing for various types of engagements, meticulous preparation is crucial. Cyrus's father advises constant vigilance and strategic planning; emphasizing the importance of understanding both one's own movements and those of the enemy. This proactive approach helps avoid pitfalls and seize opportunities, ensuring that leaders can guide their troops successfully through any situation.

Hence, you must never know a careless mood; if it is night, you must consider what your troops shall do when it is day; if day, how the night should be spent. For the rest, you do not need me to tell you now how you should draw up your troops or conduct your march by day or night, along broad roads or narrow lanes, over hills or level ground, or how you should encamp and post your guards, or advance into battle or retreat before the foe, or march past a hostile city, or attack a fortress or withdraw from it, or cross a river or pass through a narrow pass, or guard against a cavalry charge or an attack from lancers or archers, or what you should do if the enemy comes into sight when you are marching in a column, and how you are to take up position against him, or how to deploy into action if you are in line and he attacks you from the flank or rear, and how you are to learn all you can about his movements while keeping your own as secret as possible. These are matters on which you need no further word of mine; all that I know about them, you have heard a hundred times, and I am sure you have not neglected any other authority you thought you could rely on. You know all their theories, and you must apply them now, according to circumstances and your needs.

But," he added, "There is one lesson that I want to impress on you, and it is the greatest of them all. Observe the sacrifices and pay heed to the omens. When they are against you, never risk your army or yourself, for you must remember that men undertake enterprises based only on probability, without real knowledge of what will bring them happiness.

You can learn this from all life and history. How often have cities been persuaded into war by advisers thought to be the wisest men, only to be utterly destroyed by those they attacked? How often have statesmen helped to raise a city or a leader to power, and then suffered the worst at the hands of those they exalted? Many who could have treated others as friends and equals, giving and receiving kindnesses, have chosen to use them as slaves, and then paid the price. Many, not content to enjoy their share of good, have been driven by the desire to control everything and lost everything they once possessed. And many have won the very wealth they prayed for, only to find destruction through it.

So little does human wisdom know how to choose the best, as helpless as a man who could only draw lots to decide what to do. But the gods, my son, who live forever, know all things— the past, the present, and the future, and all that shall come from these. To us mortals who ask their counsel and whom they love, they will show signs to tell us what we should do and what we should leave undone. Nor should we think it strange if the gods do not give their wisdom to all men equally; they are not compelled to care for men unless they choose to do so."

BOOK II

The Reorganization
of the Army

II.1

Cyrus Prepares for Battle
Strengthening Forces and Leadership

Summary

This chapter recounts Cyrus's journey to Media, where he meets his uncle, Cyaxares, to prepare for battle. Cyrus brings 30,000 men and is informed by Cyaxares of the advancing enemy forces, which include tens of thousands of soldiers from various regions. Recognizing their numerical disadvantage, Cyrus proposes arming the Persian soldiers with superior equipment for close combat. He motivates his troops through speeches, emphasizing equal honor for equal effort, and sets up contests to foster excellence. Cyrus ensures unity by having his men live and train together, promoting discipline and mutual respect. Through these efforts, he prepares his forces for the upcoming battle, instilling a strong sense of duty and readiness.

Preparation and Strategic Planning: Equipment and Training

Effective leadership, whether in an army or a corporation, requires meticulous preparation and strategic planning. Leaders must understand the capabilities and limitations of their team, just as Cyrus did when assessing the Persian troops and their equipment. Recognizing when additional resources are needed and adapting strategies accordingly is crucial. Clear communication, realistic assessments of the competition, and innovative thinking are essential, whether arming troops for battle or equipping a team for a major project. Just as Cyrus proposed arming the Persians with breastplates and swords for close combat, corporate leaders must be ready to shift tactics to leverage their strengths and address weaknesses, ensuring their team is prepared for any challenge.

As they walked and talked, Cyrus and his father, Cambyses, traveled until they reached the border. There, a good omen appeared: an eagle flew on their right and led the way. They prayed to the gods and heroes of the land to show them favor and grant them safe entry, and then they crossed the boundary. When they were across, they prayed again for the gods of Media to receive them graciously. After praying, they hugged each other as father and son do, and Cambyses turned back to his city, while Cyrus continued to his uncle Cyaxares in Media.

When Cyrus finished his journey and met Cyaxares, they greeted each other warmly as relatives. Cyaxares asked him how many soldiers he had brought. Cyrus answered, "I have 30,000 men with me, who have served you as mercenaries before, and more fresh troops are coming from the Peers of Persia."

Cyaxares asked, "How many more?"

Cyrus replied, "Their numbers might not please you, but remember, our Peers, though few, easily rule the many Persians. Do you need us, or was it a false alarm and the enemy is not advancing?"

Cyaxares said, "The enemy is indeed advancing, and in full force."

Cyrus asked, "How do you know?"

Cyaxares replied, "Many deserters have come to us, and they all tell the same story in different ways."

Cyrus said, "So we must prepare for battle?"

Cyaxares answered, "Yes, we must."

Cyrus asked, "But you haven't told me the size of their forces or ours. I want to know so we can plan."

Cyaxares said, "Listen, then. Croesus the Lydian is coming with 10,000 horsemen and over 40,000 archers and soldiers. Artamas, the governor of Greater Phrygia, is bringing 8,000 horsemen and 40,000 soldiers. Aribaius, the king of Cappadocia, is bringing 6,000 horsemen and 30,000 soldiers. Aragdus the Arabian has 10,000 horsemen, 100 chariots, and countless slingers. It's unclear if the Hellenes in Asia will join, but the Phrygians from the Hellespont are mustering under Gabaidus with 6,000 horsemen and 40,000 soldiers. The Carians, Cilicians, and Paphlagonians may not join, but the Lord of Assyria and Babylon will likely bring at least 20,000 horsemen, 200 chariots, and thousands of foot soldiers, as he has done before."

Cyrus responded, "So, you estimate the enemy has about 60,000 horsemen and 200,000 archers and soldiers. What about our numbers?"

Cyaxares answered, "We can provide over 10,000 horsemen and around 60,000 archers and soldiers. From our neighbors, the Armenians, we expect 4,000 horsemen and 20,000 foot soldiers."

Cyrus said, "So, our cavalry is less than a third of theirs, and our infantry is less than half."

Cyaxares asked, "Do you think the Persian force you brought is too small?"

Cyrus replied, "We'll decide later if we need more men. First, tell me how the different troops fight."

Cyaxares said, "Both their troops and ours use bows and javelins."

Cyrus replied, "If that's the case, skirmishing at long range will be the strategy."

Cyaxares agreed. Cyrus continued, "In that case, the larger force will win because even if equal numbers fall on both sides, the smaller force will tire first."

Cyaxares said, "Then we must ask Persia for more troops, as Media's defeat would affect Persia too."

Cyrus replied, "Even if every Persian came, we couldn't outnumber the enemy."

Cyaxares asked, "What else can we do?"

Cyrus answered, "I would arm every Persian like our Peers at home, with breastplates, shields, and swords or battle-axes. This will allow us to fight the enemy up close, making it safer for us and harder for them to defend. We Persians will handle those who stand firm, and your cavalry can chase those who flee."

Cyaxares approved of Cyrus's plan and prepared the equipment. By the time the Persian Peers arrived, everything was ready.

Motivation through Inspiring Communication, Dedication and Courage

Effective leaders inspire confidence and dedication by clearly communicating their vision and acknowledging the strengths of their team. Cyrus's speech to his key leaders and soldiers exemplified this by recognizing their past efforts and outlining a path to equality and shared honor. By equipping his men with new armor and responsibilities, he fostered a sense of pride and commitment. Cyrus also emphasized the importance of preparation, training, and competition to enhance skills and discipline. This approach not only motivated individual soldiers but also built a cohesive, high-performing team ready to face any challenge.

Cyrus gathered the Peers and spoke to them: "Friends, when I first saw your light-armed squires facing many enemies, I was worried. But now, seeing you all here, I feel better. Tomorrow, your men will have the same armor as us. You must be brave and lead them well."

The Peers were pleased with Cyrus's words, feeling more confident about the upcoming battle.

One of them said, "Cyrus should speak to our new comrades when they receive their arms. His words will mean more to them, and it will secure their place among the Peers. We still have our duties to motivate our men. We will benefit from their courage."

Cyrus agreed and called a general meeting of the Persian soldiers. He spoke to them: "Men of Persia, you are as strong and brave as we are. You didn't share our rights at home, not because we excluded you, but because you had to find your own livelihood. From now on, I will provide for you. If you wish, you can take our armor, face the same dangers, and earn the same honors."

He continued, "You were trained with bows and javelins, but had less practice than us. Now, with this new armor, we are equals. We will wear breastplates, shields, and carry sabres or battle-axes. With these, we will strike the enemy and not miss. The only difference between us will be our courage. You have as much right to victory as we do."

He ended, "Now you have heard everything. There are your weapons; take them and join us, or remain mercenaries with servant's arms."

Cyrus's words inspired the Persians, and they all took up the new arms, feeling they would be ashamed if they didn't accept equal honor for equal effort.

Before the enemy arrived, Cyrus focused on three tasks: strengthening his men, teaching them tactics, and inspiring their fighting spirit. He asked Cyaxares for assistants to provide for the soldiers, leaving them free to train.

Cyrus stopped training with bows and javelins and had his men perfect their skills with sabres, shields, and breastplates. He wanted them to be ready for close combat and not feel worthless if they didn't protect their comrades.

Believing competition fosters excellence, he set up contests for the soldiers. Each soldier was challenged to be obedient, hardworking, brave, disciplined, skilled in war, and honorable. Leaders were responsible for bringing their men to perfection.

Cyrus announced that the best regiment's brigadier would be promoted to general, the best company's captain to brigadier, the best squad's captain to company captain, and the best five-man squad's captain to ten-man squad captain. The best soldiers would become captains themselves. These officers were honored and served by their subordinates, with greater rewards for greater achievements.

Finally, prizes were announced for the most loyal and diligent units. These prizes were suitable for groups rather than individuals.

Fostering Unity and Discipline, Through Equal Opportunities, Meritocracy, Mutual Respect and Shared Goals

Creating equal opportunities and fostering a sense of unity and mutual respect within a team are essential for building discipline and cohesion. By arranging for equal living conditions and shared spaces, Cyrus ensured that every member felt valued and integrated. This common life promoted mutual respect, reduced misconduct, and strengthened the bonds among team members, enhancing overall discipline and teamwork.

Cyrus arranged for each regiment to have a separate shelter, big enough for all 100 men. This setup ensured everyone was treated equally, fostering unity and preventing any feelings of inferiority. Living together helped the men know each other, creating a common conscience and reducing the likelihood of misconduct.

Cyrus believed the common life would lead to better discipline. Officers could keep their men in order as if marching in single file. This precision would help prevent disorder and restore order if it broke.

Cyrus also knew that living together made men less likely to desert each other. Even animals raised together suffer when separated.

Physical Effort and Workout Before Breakfast

Promoting physical effort and shared training before breakfast builds discipline, health, and teamwork. Cyrus led his men in activities that required exertion, believing this improved their well-being and work ethic. He valued every member equally, ensuring that even servants felt respected and included. This approach not only prepared his men for battle but also fostered a sense of unity and mutual respect, essential for a strong and cohesive team.

Cyrus ensured that no man ate without first working up a sweat. He led hunts, invented games, and conducted work that required effort. He believed this regimen improved their appetite, health, and work ethic, making them gentler towards each other. Shared training increased their courage.

Cyrus's quarters were large enough to entertain guests. He invited brigadiers, company captains, smaller squad leaders, and sometimes even private soldiers. Occasionally, he invited entire squads, companies, or regiments, honoring those who undertook special tasks. There was no distinction between the food served to him and his guests.

Cyrus insisted that army servants be treated equally with soldiers, valuing their loyalty, intelligence, and readiness to serve. He believed they should possess qualities of the "better classes" and never despise their work, seeing all tasks as fit for them.

Through these measures, Cyrus prepared his men for battle, instilling discipline, unity, and a strong sense of duty.

II.2

The Lively Banquet
Conversations on Equality and Merit

Light-Hearted Conversations and Humor Raise the Morale of the Troops

It was always Cyrus's goal, when he and his soldiers ate together, to make sure the conversation was lively and elegant while also being beneficial for those listening. So one day, he steered the talk to the following topic: "Do you think, gentlemen," he said, "that our new comrades seem lacking in some ways because they haven't been trained like us? Or will they prove to be our equals in everyday life and on the battlefield when we face the enemy?"

Hystaspas responded: "I don't know what kind of warriors they will be, but I can say some of them are quite difficult in private life. Just the other day," he continued, "Cyaxares sent a gift of sacrificial meat to every regiment. There was enough meat for three servings each, and the servant started with me. So, when he came back, I told him to start at the other end of the table and serve the company in that order.

But then someone in the middle yelled out, 'Equality indeed! There's not much of it here if we in the middle are never served first!' It annoyed me that they thought they were being treated worse, so I called him up to sit beside me. He did so quickly, but when the dish came to us, we found only a few scraps left. At this, my man got very upset and grumbled, 'Just my luck! To be invited now and never before!'

I tried to comfort him. 'Never mind,' I said, 'soon the servant will start with us, and then you can take the biggest piece.' Just then, the third and last course came around, and he took his helping. But he thought the piece was too small and put it back, intending to pick another. The server, thinking he didn't want any more, moved on to the next man before he could take his second slice.

At this, our friend got so upset that he knocked over the gravy, the only thing left to him. The captain next to us saw this and laughed, and," said Hystaspas, "I started coughing to hide my own laughter. That, Cyrus," he said, "is a portrait of one of our new comrades as best as I can draw it."

Humor and friendly conversations, at the right time, is motivating.

Work-related conversations can be tough and stressful. Great leaders take the opportunity of a coffee break, a dinner, or even a short casual interaction to create a relaxed atmosphere, build rapport, and show their human side, which is crucial for team building and unity. Using light-hearted conversations and humor to raise morale is an effective leadership strategy. Leaders who create a positive and enjoyable environment help their team bond and reduce stress, making them more resilient and motivated. Cyrus exemplified this by engaging his soldiers in lively banter during a banquet. He steered the conversation to humorous anecdotes, which not only entertained but also fostered camaraderie among his troops. This approach helped to build a sense of unity and kept the soldiers' spirits high, proving that a leader who can bring joy and laughter to their team can enhance overall morale and effectiveness.

Teaching New Soldiers to Respect Hierarchy and Obedience

The description, as expected, was met with laughter, and then another brigadier spoke up: "Well, Cyrus," he said, "our friend here has certainly met a rude fellow: my experience is different. You remember how you told us to teach our men the lessons we learned from you? Well, I went and started instructing one of my companies. I placed the captain in front with a fine young man behind him, and the others in the order I thought best; I stood facing them and waited until the right moment, then gave the order to advance.

But my young man got in front of the captain and marched ahead of the troop. I shouted, 'What are you doing?' 'Advancing as you ordered,' he said. 'I never ordered you to advance alone,' I replied, 'the order was for the whole company.' He turned to the ranks and said, 'Don't you hear the officer? The orders are for everyone to advance!' The others marched past their captain to me.

Of course, the captain called them back, and they began to grumble: 'Which of the two do we obey? One tells us to advance, the other won't let us move.'

I had to explain that no one in the rear was to move until the front rank man led off: they only had to follow the man in front.

Just then, a friend came by, going to Persia, asking for a letter I had written home. So I turned to the captain, who knew where the letter was, and asked him to fetch it. Off he ran, and my young man followed him, with armor and all. The rest of the company thought they had to follow too, and they brought the letter back in style. That is how my company carries out your instructions."

He paused, and everyone laughed heartily at the armed escort for the letter. Then Cyrus spoke: "Thank goodness! These new friends of ours are wonderful! So grateful for any kindness, you can win them over with a dish of meat! And so obedient, they follow orders before understanding them! I can only hope for an army like them."

He joined in the laughter but turned it into praise for his new recruits. Then one of the company, a brigadier named Aglaïtadas, who was somewhat sour-tempered, asked: "Cyrus, do you really believe these stories?" "Certainly," he replied, "why would they lie?" "Why," Aglaïtadas repeated, "to raise a laugh and boast like impostors."

Cyrus cut him off, "Hush! You mustn't use such harsh words. An impostor claims to be richer or braver than he is and undertakes what he can't do for personal gain. But someone who brings joy to his friends, not for profit or harm, should be called a man of taste and wit."

This was Cyrus's defense for the merrymakers. And the officer who started the jest turned to Aglaïtadas and said: "Just think, sir, if we had tried to make you cry! What would you have said then? Even now, when we only want to amuse you, you shame us."

"And isn't the shame justified?" Aglaïtadas replied. "Making someone laugh is less valuable than making them cry. Tears teach self-control, learning, and righteousness. But what do your mirth-makers do? Do smiles make a man a better leader or citizen? Can he learn from a grin?"

But Hystaspas responded: "Take my advice, Aglaïtadas, save your sorrow for our enemies: make them sit in grief, and give us, your friends, some laughter. You must have plenty of it since you don't waste it on yourself or anyone else. So don't be stingy now, and give us a smile."

"I see," said Aglaïtadas, "you want to make me laugh, don't you?" But the brigadier interjected, "Then he is a fool for trying: one might strike fire from you, but not a laugh."

At this, everyone laughed, and even Aglaïtadas smiled. Cyrus, seeing this, said: "Brigadier, you are wrong to corrupt such a serious man, making him laugh when he opposes gaiety."

Integrating New Hires into Group Culture for Cohesion and Respecting

Incorporating group culture into new hires' training is vital for cohesion and respect. Effective leaders ensure that newcomers align with the team's values, norms, and hierarchy.

Cyrus exemplified this by teaching his new soldiers the importance of following orders and understanding their roles. He used practical drills to instill respect for the chain of command, reinforcing group culture and ensuring operational efficiency. This approach not only educated the recruits but also strengthened the entire unit's discipline and unity.

True Equality Is Not Equal Distribution but Merit-Based Rewards.

So they talked and joked. Then Chrysantas began a new topic. "Cyrus," he said, "and gentlemen, I see that within our ranks are men of all kinds, some better and some worse, yet if we win anything, everyone wants an equal share. To me, nothing is more unfair than treating the good and bad equally."

"Perhaps," said Cyrus, "we should bring this to the army council and ask if we should share equally or reward according to merit."

"But why," asked Chrysantas, "not just issue an order like in the competitions?"

"Doubtless," Cyrus replied, "but this is different. The troops might feel that all they win belongs to them in common, but they know that I had the command from the start and could appoint judges as I wished."

"Do you really think," asked Chrysantas, "the army will agree to give up equal shares so the best men get the most?"

"Yes, I do," said Cyrus, "because we will argue for it and because it's too base to deny that those who work hardest deserve the most. Even the worst must admit the brave should gain the most."

Cyrus wanted this resolution for the sake of the Peers. They would be better if judged by their deeds and rewarded accordingly. Now was the right time to raise the question, with the Peers resenting being equal to common people. Everyone agreed that the question should be raised, and all should argue for it.

One brigadier smiled and said: "I know one man who will agree that not everything should be shared equally."

"Who?" another asked. "He is in our quarters," said the first, "and always wants the lion's share."

"Of everything?" said a third. "Of work too?" "Oh, no!" said the first, "you caught me. When it comes to work, he will give up his share without complaint to anyone."

"For my part," said Cyrus, "I think idlers should be removed if we want obedience and energy in our men. Most soldiers will follow the lead: they will seek nobility if their leaders are noble, but baseness if they are base. Too often, the worthless find more friends. Vice, with her gifts, wins many hearts, but Virtue, climbing the steep path, struggles to attract followers when their comrades call them down the easy way.

There are degrees of evil: some are just lazy drones, but others are greedy and lead in villainy, showing that rascality has benefits. Such people must be removed entirely. We should not only fill their places with our fellow citizens but also choose the best from all mankind. Just as we select the best horses from any stock, we should choose those who will increase our power and honor. No chariot can travel fast if the horses are slow, and no house can stand if the household is evil: better empty walls than traitors.

And be sure, my friends, removing the bad brings benefits beyond their absence: those left are purified, and the worthy cling to virtue when they see the dishonor of wickedness."

So Cyrus spoke, and his words were praised by all, and they set out to do as he advised. But then Cyrus started joking again. He saw a captain with a very ugly companion and called out: "How now, Sambulas? Have you adopted the Greek fashion? Will you roam the world with this lad because there is none so fair?" "By heaven," answered Sambulas, "you are not far wrong. It brings me great joy to look at him," he said. Hearing this, all the guests turned to look at the young man's face. But when they saw how unattractive he was, they couldn't help but burst out laughing. "Oh my goodness, Sambulas, tell us about the brave act that brought you two so close! How did he win your heart?" they asked.

"Alright, listen closely," he replied, "and I'll tell you the whole truth. Every time I call him, whether it's morning, noon, or night, he comes to me right away. He has never made an excuse or been too busy to come. And he always comes running, not walking. Whatever task I've given him, he has done it immediately and with all his energy. He has made all the junior officers under him into perfect examples of hard work; he shows them through actions, not just words, what they should strive to be."

"And so," said another guest, "for all these qualities, you honor him with the kiss of kinship?" But the unattractive young man interrupted, "Not at all! He doesn't really love working. And kissing me, if it came to that, would be more effort than all his duties combined."

Fair Leadership Ensures Equality of Opportunities, Not Outcomes

Effective leadership recognizes that true equality doesn't mean equal distribution but rewarding individuals based on merit. This approach fosters motivation and drives excellence within a team.

For instance, Cyrus understood that giving equal shares to all, regardless of their contribution, would demotivate high performers.

Instead, he proposed to the army council that rewards should be based on merit, ensuring that those who worked the hardest and demonstrated the most skill received the greatest rewards. This policy encouraged everyone to strive for excellence, knowing their efforts would be recognized and rewarded appropriately.

Grit, Training, and Motivation
Three Pillars to a Team's Success

Rewarding Bravery and Merit to Encourage Best Efforts

So the time passed in the general's tent, shifting from serious to lighthearted, until finally, the third toast was made, and everyone prayed to the gods, saying, "Grant us all that is good." Then they all broke up and went to sleep.

The next day, Cyrus gathered the soldiers together and spoke to them: "My men," he said, "my friends, the day of battle is near, and the enemy is close. The rewards of victory, if we win—and we must believe we will win and make it so—will be the enemy himself and all his possessions. If the enemy wins, then all our goods will be theirs.

So I want you to remember this: when those who join together for war understand that unless everyone does their part with enthusiasm, nothing good will come of it; there, we can expect great success. For there, nothing that needs to be done will be left undone. But if each person thinks, 'My neighbor will work and fight, even if I fail,' then disaster is near for everyone, and no one will escape.

This is how God has ordered it: those who do not work for their own salvation are given into the hands of others to rule over them. Now I ask anyone here," he added, "to stand up and say whether he believes that virtue will grow best among us if the person who works the hardest and takes the greatest risk gets the highest honors. Or should we believe that cowardice makes no difference since we all share equally?"

Then Chrysantas, one of the nobles, stood up. He was a wise man but not strong in body. He spoke like this: "I don't think, Cyrus, that you really believe cowards should get the same share as the brave. No, you wanted to test us to see if anyone would dare to claim an equal part in all the rewards won by the bravery of others, even though he did nothing courageous himself.

I, myself," he continued, "am neither fast nor strong, and on the day of battle, I know I won't be first, second, hundredth, or even thousandth. But I know that if our strong men do their best, I too will receive some part of the blessings we win. But if cowards rest and the good and brave lose heart, I fear I will get a larger portion of something bad rather than good."

Chrysantas finished speaking, and then Pheraulas stood up. He was a common man but well known and liked by Cyrus from their days at home: a respectable-looking man with a noble spirit. He spoke next.

Rewarding Performance to Motivate Your Team

Effective leadership ensures that bravery and merit are recognized and rewarded, fostering a culture of excellence and motivation. Leaders should create a system where contributions are acknowledged based on their impact and effort, not just uniformly distributed. In Cyropaedia, Cyrus proposes rewarding soldiers based on their performance and bravery, rather than giving equal shares to all. This approach motivates each soldier to strive for excellence, knowing their efforts will be recognized and rewarded, thereby enhancing the overall effectiveness and morale of the group.

Ensuring Preparedness Through Training and Discipline

"Cyrus, friends, and Persians, I believe we all start equal today in this race for valor. We are trained the same, treated as equals, and fight for the same rewards. We are all told to obey our leaders, and those who obey the best are honored by Cyrus. Valor is no longer just for the noble class; it's the greatest prize for any man.

Today, we face a battle where no one needs to teach us how to fight; we know it naturally, like a bull knows how to use its horns or a horse its hooves. Animals know how to defend themselves without being taught. I remember, as a child, I instinctively knew how to protect myself from a blow: using my fists if I had nothing else. No one taught me, in fact, they punished me for it, but I did it anyway because it was natural.

Today, we fight in this natural way: energy, not skill, is needed, and it will be glorious to compete with our noble Persian friends. We must remember that we all have the same prizes, but the stakes are different: our noble friends give up a life of honor, while we escape from a life of toil and disgrace.

What excites me most, friends, is that Cyrus will be our judge: someone who gives fair judgments. He loves a brave man as much as he loves his own soul. I've seen him give more to a valiant man than he keeps for himself.

I know our noble friends pride themselves on their training in hunger, thirst, cold, and nakedness, but we were trained by Necessity, the best and strictest teacher. Our friends learned endurance by carrying weapons, tools designed to be as light as possible, but Necessity made us carry heavy burdens.

Today, these weapons feel like wings to me rather than weights. I'm ready, Cyrus, to fight and will ask for no more than I deserve. And you," he said to the common men, "you should enter the battle and compete with these noble warriors: today is our day."

Pheraulas's words were supported by many others. It was decided that each man should be honored according to his merits and that Cyrus would be the judge. So the matter was settled, and all was well.

Ensuring Preparedness Through Training and Discipline

Effective leadership involves rigorous training and discipline to ensure all team members, regardless of their background, are prepared and can contribute effectively. Leaders must establish comprehensive training programs that instill the necessary skills and discipline in their teams. Cyrus focuses on equipping his soldiers with the proper training and discipline, ensuring they are ready for battle. By doing so, he ensures that every soldier, whether newly recruited or seasoned, can perform their duties effectively, thereby enhancing the unit's overall cohesion and effectiveness.

Boosting Team Morale Through Competitive Camaraderie

Cyrus then hosted a banquet with a certain brigadier and his regiment as the main guests. Cyrus had noticed the officer one day during a drill; he had split the ranks into two groups, ready for a mock battle. They wore armor and carried light shields, with some using stout fennel staves and others picking up clods of earth to use as weapons.

When ready, the officer gave the signal, and the mock battle began. The earth clods hit shields and armor, but when they got close, the stave-wielders struck at thighs, hands, and legs, or backs and shoulders, laughing and enjoying the mock fight. Then they switched roles, and the others had their turn with the staves.

Cyrus admired the officer's creativity and the soldiers' discipline. He enjoyed watching the exercise and the fun the men had. He was pleased with the results, which favored the Persian fighting style. He invited them all to dinner then and there.

At the feast, many guests had bandages on their hands and legs. Cyrus asked what happened, and they explained they had been bruised by the clods of earth. He asked, "At long range or close quarters?" They said long range, and the stave-wielders said the close quarters were more fun. But those who had been hit protested that being clubbed at close range was not fun, showing their bruises.

They laughed about it, and the next day, the plain was filled with similar mock battles whenever the army had free time.

Another day, Cyrus saw a brigadier marching his regiment back from the river to their quarters. They marched in single file on his left, and at the right moment, he ordered the second company to line up beside the first, then the third, and then the fourth. When all were lined up, he ordered, "Companies in twos," and then "Companies in fours," until they reached the tent doors, where they halted and reformed into a single file, entering the tent in order and sitting down to eat.

Cyrus admired the quiet instruction and care the officer showed and invited him and his regiment to dinner in the royal tent.

It happened that another brigadier was among the guests and said to Cyrus, "Will you never invite my men to dinner? Every day, morning and evening, we do the same drills. After meals, we practice retreating in reverse order, so everyone knows how to fall back in good order. We march east and west, leading in turns, to learn to obey commands whether I'm at the front or rear."

"Do you always do this?" asked Cyrus.

"Yes," he answered, "as regularly as our meals."

"Then I invite you all to dinner for three reasons: you practice both forms of drill, you do it morning and evening, and you train your bodies and souls. Since you do it twice a day, you deserve dinner twice."

"Not twice in one day," begged the officer, "unless you can give us two stomachs each."

So the conversation ended. The next day, Cyrus kept his word and invited the regiment to dinner, and again the day after. When the other regiments heard about it, they began doing the same drills.

Strengthening Bonds Through Gaming

Leaders know that creating a positive atmosphere through gaming-like competition, camaraderie, and humor can significantly boost team morale and strengthen bonds among members. Cyrus cleverly integrated these elements into military training by organizing mock battles and competitive drills that felt more like games than rigorous exercises. This approach not only made the activities entertaining but also encouraged soldiers to engage more fully, fostering resilience and unity within the group. Just as in modern competitive entertainment, the combination of fun, rivalry, and teamwork led to improved performance and a stronger sense of belonging among his men.

Strategic Maneuvers and Diplomacy
A Tale of Cyrus and Cyaxare

Substance over Superficiality

One day, as Cyrus was holding a review, a messenger came from Cyaxares to tell him that an embassy from India had just arrived and to bid him return with all haste. "And I bring with me," said the messenger, "a suit of splendid clothes sent from Cyaxares himself: my lord wishes you to appear in all possible splendor, for the Indians will be there to see you."

At that, Cyrus commanded the brigadier of the first regiment to draw up to the front with his men behind him on the left in single file and to pass the order on to the second regiment, and so on throughout the army. Officers and men were quick to obey; so in no time, the whole force on the field was drawn up, one hundred deep and three hundred across, with their officers at the head.

When they were in position, Cyrus bade them follow his lead, and off they went at a good pace. However, the road leading to the royal quarters was too narrow for them to pass with such a wide front, so Cyrus sent word along the line that the first detachment, one thousand strong, should follow as they were, then the second, and so on to the last. As he gave the command, he led on without a pause, and all the detachments followed in due order, one behind the other.

But to prevent mistakes, he sent two gallopers up to the entrance with orders to explain what should be done if the men were unsure. When they reached the gates, Cyrus told the leading brigadier to draw up his regiment around the palace, twelve deep, with the front rank facing the building. This command was to be passed on to the second regiment, and the second to the third, and so on till the last.

While they were doing this, he went in to Cyaxares himself, wearing his simple Persian dress without any pomp. Cyaxares was pleased with his quickness but troubled by the plainness of his attire. He said to him, "What is the meaning of this, Cyrus? How could you show yourself like this to the Indians? I wished you to appear in splendor: it would have honored me for my sister's son to be seen in great magnificence."

But Cyrus replied, "Would it have honored you more if I had put on a purple robe, bracelets on my arms, and a necklace around my neck, and then come to you after a long delay? Or as now, when to show you respect I obey you quickly and bring you this large and fine force, even though I wear no ornament but the dust and sweat of speed? I make no display except to show you these men who are as obedient to you as I am." Such were the words of Cyrus, and Cyaxares felt they were just, so he sent for the Indian ambassadors immediately.

The Importance of Swift Obedience

Leaders know that creating a positive atmosphere through gaming-like competition, camaraderie, and humor can significantly boost team morale and strengthen bonds among members. Cyrus cleverly integrated these elements into military training by organizing mock battles and competitive drills that felt more like games than rigorous exercises. This approach not only made the activities entertaining but also encouraged soldiers to engage more fully, fostering resilience and unity within the group. Just as in modern competitive entertainment, the combination of fun, rivalry, and teamwork led to improved performance and a stronger sense of belonging among his men.

Diplomacy and Justice Are Vital in Resolving Conflicts.

When they entered, they gave this message: "The king of the Indians asks what is the cause of the strife between the Assyrians and the Medes. When we have heard you," they said, "our king bids us go to the Assyrians and put the same question to them. In the end, we are to tell you both that the king of the Indians, after enquiring into the justice of the case, will support the one who has been wronged."

To this, Cyaxares replied: "Then take this answer from me: we do the Assyrians no wrong nor any injustice whatsoever. Now go and make an inquiry of them if you wish and see what answer they will give." Then Cyrus, who was standing by, asked Cyaxares, "May I also say what is on my mind?" "Speak," answered Cyaxares. Then Cyrus turned to the ambassadors and said, "Tell your master, unless Cyaxares thinks otherwise, that we are ready to do this: if the Assyrians lay any injustice to our charge, we choose the king of the Indians himself to be our judge, and he shall decide between us."

With that, the embassy departed. When they had gone, Cyrus turned to his uncle and began, "Cyaxares, when I came to you, I had little wealth of my own, and of the little I brought with me, only a small amount is left. I have spent it all on my soldiers. You may wonder at this," he added, "since you have supported them, but believe me, the money has not been wasted: it has all been spent on gifts and rewards for the soldiers who deserved it.

"I am sure," he added, "if we need good workers and good comrades in any task, it is better and more pleasant to encourage them with kind words and deeds than to drive them with penalties. If it is for war that we need such reliable helpers, we can only win the men we want with kind words and deeds. Our true ally must be a friend and not a foe, one who can never envy the prosperity of his leader nor betray him in times of trouble.

"This is my belief, and since it is so, I know we need money. But to look to you for everything, when I know you already spend so much, would be wrong in my eyes. I only ask that we take counsel together to prevent the failure of your funds. I know that if you gained great wealth, I would be able to help myself in need, especially if I used it for your advantage.

"I think you told me the other day that the king of Armenia has begun to despise you because he hears we have an enemy, and therefore he neither sends you troops nor pays the tribute that is due." "Yes," answered Cyaxares, "that is his trick. I cannot decide whether to march on him at once and try to subdue him by force, or let the matter be for now, fearing to add to our enemies." Then Cyrus asked, "Are his dwellings strongly fortified, or could they be attacked?" And Cyaxares answered, "The actual fortifications are not very strong: I made sure of that. But he has the hill country where he can retreat and be safe for the moment, knowing that he is out of reach with everything he can take there unless we are prepared to lay siege, as my father once did."

Diplomacy and Justice

Diplomacy and justice are key to resolving conflicts effectively. When Indian ambassadors inquired about the conflict between the Assyrians and Medes, Cyaxares and Cyrus emphasized their commitment to fairness. Cyaxares asserted their innocence, and Cyrus suggested that the Indian king act as a neutral judge if needed. This demonstrated their respect for impartiality. Afterward, Cyrus discussed the importance of motivating soldiers through rewards rather than punishment and the need for financial resources, suggesting they address the Armenian king's failure to pay tribute to strengthen their position without overburdening Cyaxares.

Strategic Planning

Cyrus said, "If you are willing to send me with a moderate force of cavalry—I will not ask for many men—I believe, with heaven's help, I could compel him to send the troops and the tribute. I even hope that in the future he may become a firmer friend than he is now." Cyaxares said, "I think they are more likely to listen to you than to me. I have heard that his sons were your companions in the hunt when you were boys, and possibly old habits will return, and they will come to you. Once they were in our power, everything could be done as we desire." "Then," said Cyrus, "this plan of ours should be kept secret, shouldn't it?" "No doubt," answered Cyaxares. "In that way, they would be more likely to fall into our hands, and if we attack them, they would be taken unprepared."

"Listen then," said Cyrus, "and see what you think of this. I have often hunted the border between your country and Armenia with all my men, and sometimes I have taken horsemen with me from our comrades here." "I see," said Cyaxares, "and if you chose to do the same again, it would seem natural, but if your force was obviously larger than usual, suspicion would arise at once." "But it is possible," said Cyrus, "to make an excuse that would be believable for us and for them too if any rumor reached them. We might say that I intend to hold a splendid hunt and might ask you openly for a troop of horse."

"Excellent!" said Cyaxares. "And I shall refuse to give you more than a certain number, saying that I wish to visit the outposts on the Syrian side. And as a matter of fact," he added, "I do wish to see them and put them in as strong a state as possible. Then, as soon as you have started with your men and marched, let us say, for a couple of days, I could send you a good number of horse and foot from my own detachment. When you have them at your back, you could advance at once, and I will follow with the rest of my men as close as possible, to appear in time of need."

So, Cyaxares proceeded to gather horse and foot for his own march and sent provision wagons forward to meet him on the road. Meanwhile, Cyrus offered sacrifices for the success of his expedition and found an opportunity to ask Cyaxares for a troop of his junior cavalry. But Cyaxares would only spare a few, though many wished to go. Soon afterward, he started for the outposts himself with all his horse and foot, and then Cyrus found the omens favorable for his enterprise and led his soldiers out as if he meant to hunt.

He was scarcely on his way when a hare started up at their feet, and an eagle, flying on the right, saw the creature as it fled, swooped down, struck it, bore it aloft in its talons to a cliff nearby, and killed it there. The omen pleased Cyrus well, and he bowed in worship to Zeus the King and said to his company, "This shall be a truly noble hunt, my friends, if God so wills."

When he came to the borders, he began the hunt in his usual way, with the mass of horse and foot going ahead in rows like reapers, beating out the game, with picked men posted at intervals to receive the animals and give chase. They took great numbers of boars, stags, antelopes, and wild asses: even today, wild asses are plentiful in those parts.

When the chase was over, Cyrus had reached the frontier of the Armenian land, and there he made the evening meal. The next day he hunted until he reached the mountains which were his goal. There he halted again and made the evening meal. At this point, he knew that the army from Cyaxares was advancing, and he sent a secret message to them, telling them to stay about eight miles off and take their evening meal there to maintain secrecy. When their meal was over, he told them to send their officers to him, and after supper, he called his own brigadiers together and addressed them:

"My friends, in the past, the Armenian was a faithful ally and subject of Cyaxares, but now, seeing an enemy against us, he shows contempt: he neither sends troops nor pays tribute. He is the game we have come to catch, if we can. This, I think, is the way. You, Chrysantas, will sleep for a few hours, and then take half the Persians with you, make for the hill country, and seize the heights where we hear he takes refuge when alarmed. I will give you guides.

The hills, they say, are covered with trees and scrub, so we may hope you will escape unseen: still, you might send a few scouts ahead, disguised as a band of robbers. If they come across any Armenians, they can either capture them to prevent them from spreading the news, or scare them away so they won't realize your whole force is coming and only think it's a pack of thieves.

That is your task, Chrysantas, and now for mine. At daybreak, I shall take half the foot soldiers and all the cavalry and march straight to the king's residence. If he resists, we must fight; if he retreats across the plain, we must chase him down; if he makes for the mountains, then it will be your job to ensure none of them escape.

Think of it as a hunt: we down below are the beaters rounding up the game, and you are the men at the nets. Just remember, the earths must all be stopped before the game is up, and the men at the traps must be hidden, or they will turn back the fleeing quarry.

One last word, Chrysantas: you must not act now as I have seen you do in your passion for the chase: do not stay up all night without sleep, you must let all your men have the rest they need. Nor must you—just because you scour the hills in the hunt without a guide, following the quarry and changing course wherever it leads—you must not now plunge into the wildest paths: you must tell your guides to take you by the easiest road unless it is much longer. In war, they say, the easiest way is the quickest. And once more, because you can race up a mountain yourself, you should not lead your men at a run; match your pace to the strength of all. Indeed, it would be good if some of your best and bravest men fell behind now and then to encourage the slower ones: it would quicken everyone's pace to see them racing back to their places past the marching files."

Chrysantas listened, and his heart beat high at the trust placed in him. He took the guides and gave the necessary orders for those who were to march with him, then he lay down to rest. When all his men had the sleep he thought sufficient, he set out for the hills.

At daybreak, Cyrus sent a messenger to the Armenian with these words: "Cyrus bids you see to it that you bring your tribute and troops without delay." "And if he asks you where Cyrus is, tell the truth and say I am on the frontier. If he asks whether I am advancing myself, tell the truth again and say that you do not know. And if he inquires how many we are, ask him to send someone with you to find out."

Having so instructed the messenger, he sent him on, thinking this more courteous than attacking without warning. Then he drew up his troops in the best order for marching, and, if necessary, for fighting, and set forth. The soldiers were ordered not to harm anyone, and if they met any Armenians, they were to tell them not to be afraid, but to open a market wherever they wished and sell meat or drink as they chose.

Strategic Leadership and Planning: Balancing Diplomacy and Preparedness

To achieve successful outcomes in leadership, strategic planning, clear communication, and the ability to maintain a balance between diplomacy and military readiness are crucial. Cyrus exemplified this by organizing a covert operation against the Armenian king, who had neglected to provide the required troops and tribute. By disguising his military advance as a hunting expedition, Cyrus maintained the element of surprise, coordinated seamlessly with Cyaxares, and gave clear, detailed instructions to his officers, ensuring the operation's success. This approach highlights how leaders can use strategic foresight and effective communication to manage complex situations, ensuring that all team members are aligned with the mission's objectives. In a modern organizational context, this can be likened to a leader preparing a team for a major project by carefully planning, maintaining confidentiality, and providing clear, actionable guidance, all while balancing the need for diplomacy and assertiveness.

BOOK III

The Conquest
of Armenia and Scythia

III.1.

Cyrus and the Trial of the Armenian King

Communication and Transparency

> Effective leaders must communicate openly and truthfully, as demonstrated by Cyrus's emphasis on honesty during the king's trial. Transparency fosters trust and ensures that actions are justified and understood. It helps in maintaining the integrity and respect of the leader among followers.

Thus, Cyrus made his preparations. But when the Armenian heard what the messenger had to say, he was terrified: he knew he was wrong in neglecting the tribute and withholding the troops, and he was especially afraid it would be discovered that he was fortifying his palace. *[Editor's note: By "the Armenian", the author most likely refers to King Artavasdes of Armenia, father of Tigranes]* Therefore, with much fear, he began to gather his own forces, and at the same time, he sent his younger son, Sabaris, into the hills with the women, including his wife, his elder son's wife, and his daughters, taking their best ornaments and furniture with them and an escort to guide them.

Meanwhile, he sent a party to find out what Cyrus was doing and organized all the Armenian contingents as they arrived. But soon, other messengers arrived, saying that Cyrus himself was near. Then his courage failed him; he didn't dare to fight and withdrew. When the recruits saw this, they fled, each man trying to save his own property. When Cyrus saw the plains full of people running and riding everywhere, he sent out messengers privately to explain that he had no quarrel with anyone who stayed quietly in their homes, but if he caught anyone fleeing, he would treat them as an enemy. Thus, the greater part were persuaded to remain, though some retreated with the king.

But when the escort with the women came upon the Persians in the mountains, they fled with cries of terror, and many of them were taken prisoners. In the end, the young prince himself was captured, along with the king's wife, his daughters, his daughter-in-law, and all the goods they had with them. When the king learned what had happened, scarcely knowing where to turn, he fled to the summit of a certain hill. Cyrus, when he saw it, surrounded the spot with his troops and sent word to Chrysantas, telling him to leave a force to guard the mountains and come down to him. So, the mass of the army was collected under Cyrus, and then he sent a herald to the king with this question:

"Son of Armenia, will you wait here and fight with hunger and thirst, or will you come down into the plain and fight it out with us?" But the Armenian answered that he wished to fight with neither.

Cyrus sent again and asked, "Why do you sit there, then, and refuse to come down?"

"Because I don't know what to do," answered the other.

"It is simple enough," said Cyrus, "come down and take your trial."

"And who shall try me?" asked the king.

"He," answered Cyrus, "to whom God has given the power to treat you as he wishes, without a trial at all."

Thereupon the Armenian came down, yielding to necessity, and Cyrus took him and all that he had and placed him in the center of the camp, for all his forces were now at hand.

Valuing and Transforming Followers

A good leader recognizes the potential for growth and transformation in their followers, even when they have erred. Tigranes' argument for his father's reformation highlights the importance of giving individuals the chance to learn from their mistakes. This approach can strengthen loyalty and commitment.

Meanwhile, Tigranes, the elder son of the king, was on his way home from a far country. In the old days, he had hunted with Cyrus and been his friend, and now, when he heard what had happened, he came forward just as he was. But when he saw his father and mother, his brother and sisters, and his own wife all held as prisoners, he could not keep back the tears. But Cyrus gave him no sign of friendship or courtesy, and only said, "You have come in time; you may be present now to hear your father tried."

With that, he summoned the leaders of the Persians and the Medes, and any Armenian of rank and dignity who was there, nor would he send away the women as they sat in covered carriages, but let them listen too.

When all was ready, he began: "Son of Armenia, I would advise you, in the first place, to speak the truth, so that at least you may avoid what deserves the utmost hate: beyond all else, be assured, lying openly destroys the sympathy between man and man.

Moreover," he said, "your own sons, your daughters, and your wife are well aware of all that you have done, and so are your own Armenians who are here: if they see that you say what is not true, they must surely feel that out of your own lips you condemn yourself to suffer the utmost penalty when I learn the truth."

"Nay," answered the king, "ask me whatever you will, and I will answer truly, come what may."

"Answer then," said Cyrus, "did you once make war upon Astyages, my mother's father, and his Medes?"

"I did," he answered.

"And were you conquered by him, and did you agree to pay tribute and furnish troops whenever he required, and promise not to fortify your dwellings?"

"I did," he said.

"Why is it, then, that today you have neither brought the tribute nor sent the troops, and are building forts?"

"I set my heart on liberty: it seemed to me so fair a thing to be free myself and to leave freedom to my sons."

"And fair and good it is," said Cyrus, "to fight for freedom and choose death rather than slavery. But if a man is defeated in war or enslaved by any other means and then attempts to rid himself of his lord, tell me yourself, would you honor such a man as upright and a doer of noble deeds, or would you, if you got him in your power, punish him as a criminal?"

"I would punish him," he answered, "since you drive me to the truth."

"Then answer me now, point by point," said Cyrus. "If you have an officer and he does wrong, do you let him remain in office, or do you set up another in his place?"

"I set up another."

"And if he has great riches, do you leave him all his wealth, or do you make him a beggar?"

"I take away from him all that he has."

"And if you found him deserting to your enemies, what would you do?"

"I would kill him," he said: "why should I die with a lie on my lips rather than speak the truth and die?"

At this, his son tore his garments and threw the tiara from his brows, and the women lifted up their voices in wailing and tore their cheeks, as though their father was already dead and they themselves were undone. But Cyrus told them to be silent and spoke again.

"Son of Armenia, we have heard your own judgment in this case, and now tell us, what ought we to do?"

But the king sat silent and perplexed, wondering whether he should ask Cyrus to put him to death or act against the rule he had set for himself.

Then his son Tigranes turned to Cyrus and said, "Tell me, Cyrus, since my father is in doubt, may I give advice in his place and say what I think is best for you?"

Now Cyrus remembered that, in the old hunting days, he had noticed a certain wise man who went about with Tigranes and was much admired by him, and he was curious to know what the youth would say. So he readily agreed and told him to speak his mind.

"In my view," said Tigranes, "if you approve of all that my father has said and done, certainly you ought to do as he did. But if you think he has done wrong, then you must not copy him."

"But surely," said Cyrus, "the best way to avoid copying the wrongdoer is to practice what is right?"

"True enough," answered the prince. "Then by your own reasoning, I am bound to punish your father, if it is right to punish wrong."

"But would you want your vengeance to do you harm instead of good?"

"No," said Cyrus, "for then my vengeance would fall upon myself."

"Even so," said Tigranes, "and you will do yourself the greatest harm if you put your own subjects to death just when they are most valuable to you."

"Can they have any value," asked Cyrus, "when they are caught doing wrong?"

"Yes," answered Tigranes, "if that is when they turn to good and learn sobriety. For it is my belief, Cyrus, that without this virtue all others are in vain. What good will you get from a strong man or a brave man if he lacks sobriety, no matter how good a horseman he is, no matter how rich, no matter how powerful in the state?

Strategic Mercy and Practical Wisdom

Cyrus demonstrates the strategic use of mercy and practical wisdom by considering the broader impact of his actions. Rather than seeking vengeance, he looks for ways to turn adversaries into allies, ensuring long-term stability and support. This lesson shows the power of mercy coupled with strategic thinking in leadership.

"I take your meaning," answered Cyrus; "your father, you would have me think, has been changed in this one day from a fool into a wise and sober-minded man?"

"Exactly," said the prince. "Then you would call sober-mindedness a condition of our nature, such as pain, not a matter of reason that can be learned? For certainly, if he who is to be sober-minded must learn wisdom first, he could not be converted from folly in a day."

"Nay, but, Cyrus," said the prince, "surely you yourself have known one man at least who out of sheer folly has set himself to fight a stronger man than he, and on the day of defeat his senselessness has been cured. And surely you have known a city that has marshaled her battalions against a rival state, but with defeat, she changes suddenly and is willing to obey and not resist?"

"But what defeat," said Cyrus, "can you find in your father's case to make you so sure that he has come to a sober mind?"

"A defeat," answered the young man, "of which he is well aware in the secret chambers of his soul. He set his heart on liberty, and he has found himself a slave as never before: he had designs that needed stealth and speed and force, and not one of them has he been able to carry through. With you, he knows that design and fulfillment went hand in hand; when you wished to outwit him, outwit him you did, as though he had been blind and deaf and dazed; when stealth was needed, your stealth was such that the fortresses he thought his own you turned into traps for him; and your speed was such that you were upon him from miles away with all your armament before he found time to muster the forces at his command."

Understanding True Defeat and Submission

> Recognizing a stronger adversary can lead to true submission and respect, more effectively than physical defeat. This understanding fosters voluntary obedience and genuine loyalty.

"So you think," said Cyrus, "that just knowing someone is stronger than himself is enough to make a man come to his senses?"

"I do," answered Tigranes, "and it's more effective than just being defeated in battle. For someone beaten by force may think that with more training, he can fight again. Cities that are captured may hope to fight back with allies one day. But when we meet people who are better than us and we recognize it, we are ready to follow them willingly."

"You think," said Cyrus, "that bullies and tyrants can't recognize the self-controlled, thieves can't see the honest, liars can't recognize the truth-speakers, and unjust people can't see the upright? Hasn't your own father lied and broken his word with us, even though he knew we kept every part of our agreement with Astyages?"

"Ah," replied the prince, "knowing alone won't make a man change. He must face consequences like my father does today."

"But," answered Cyrus, "your father hasn't suffered yet: though he fears he might suffer greatly."

Power of Fear over Punishment

Fear can be a stronger motivator than punishment. People subdued by fear are often more compliant and less likely to rebel, compared to those who merely face physical consequences.

"Do you think," asked Tigranes, "that anything can control a man more than fear? Even those beaten in war may fight again, but those terrified can't even look at their conquerors, even when comforted."

"Then you believe," said Cyrus, "that fear controls more than suffering?"

"Yes," answered Tigranes, "and you know it's true: fear of banishment, defeat in battle, or shipwreck can make men unable to eat or sleep, while the exiled, defeated, or enslaved may eat and sleep better. Think of those who, out of fear of capture and death, have killed themselves. Fear, the greatest horror, can completely control the soul. And think of my father now, whose fears are for us all, not just himself."

Cyrus said, "Today, it may be as you say: but I think the same man can be arrogant in good fortune and submissive in defeat: free him, and he'll return to his arrogance."

"I don't deny it, Cyrus," said the prince. "Our actions make us suspect: but you can put guards in our land, control our strongholds, and take pledges. Even so, we won't resent it, knowing it's our fault. But if you give control to others, they might mistrust you and not be true friends, or you may avoid their hostility and fail to check their arrogance, needing to control them even more later."

Value of Voluntary Service and Friendship

Genuine service and friendship, rooted in mutual respect and goodwill, are more valuable and effective than forced compliance. Leaders should seek to inspire loyalty and cooperation through positive relationships.

"Nay, by the gods," cried Cyrus, "I wouldn't enjoy those who serve out of necessity. Only if I see friendship or goodwill in their duty, I could forgive their faults rather than accept grudging service from those who hate me."

Tigranes answered, "You speak of friendship, but can you find greater friendship than with us?"

"Surely I can," he answered, "with those who haven't been enemies, if I choose to help them as you'd have me help you."

"But now, can you find anyone you can help as much as my father? If you let a man live who's never wronged you, will he be grateful? If he keeps his children and wife, will he love you more than someone who deserved to lose them? If he stays on the throne of Armenia, will he suffer like we would? The one who fears loss the most will be most grateful for the gift. If you want things settled here, think: will peace be with a new ruler or the familiar house? If you need a large force, who can handle it better than the experienced general? If you need money, who knows the resources better? As a friend," he added, "if you discard us, you harm yourself more than my father could."

Such were the pleadings of the prince, and Cyrus, as he listened, was overjoyed, for he felt he would accomplish all he promised Cyaxares; his own words came back to him, "I hope to make the Armenian a better friend than before."

Then he turned to the king and said, "Son of Armenia, if I were to listen to you, tell me, how large an army would you send and how much money for the war?"

The king replied, "I'll tell you my power, and you can take what men you choose, leaving the rest to guard the country. And with the money: you should know our total wealth, and take what you need."

Cyrus said, "Tell me truly: how great is your power and wealth?" The Armenian replied: "Our cavalry is 8,000 strong and our infantry 40,000; our wealth, including my father's treasures, is over 3,000 talents."

Cyrus, without more ado, said, "Of your whole army, give me half, since your neighbors the Chaldaeans are at war with you: for the tribute, instead of fifty talents, you shall give twice as much to Cyaxares for default; and lend me another hundred for myself, and I promise, if God wills, to repay you with greater gifts, or the full amount if I can; and if not, you may blame my ability, not my will."

The Armenian cried, "By all the gods, Cyrus, don't say that, or you'll dishearten me. Look on all I have as yours, what you leave and what you take."

"So be it then," answered Cyrus, "and to ransom your wife, how much would you give?"

"All that I have," said he.

"And for your sons?"

"For them too, all that I have."

"Good," answered Cyrus, "but isn't that already twice what you have? And you, Tigranes," said he, "how much to redeem your bride?"

The newly-wed youth, whose wife was dear to him, said, "I'd give my life to save her from slavery."

"Take her then," said Cyrus, "she's yours. She's never been a prisoner since her husband never deserted us.

70

And you, son of Armenia," he said to the king, "take your wife and children home, with no ransom, so they won't feel like slaves. But now, stay and eat with us, and go where you wish afterwards."

So the Armenians stayed. After the evening meal, Cyrus asked Tigranes, "Where is that friend who used to hunt with us, whom you admired so much?"

"Don't you know," he said, "my father put him to death?"

"And why?" said Cyrus, "what fault did he find in him?"

"He thought he corrupted me," said the youth; "yet he was gentle and brave, with a beautiful soul. When he died, he told me, 'Don't be angry with your father, Tigranes, for killing me. He acts not from malice, but ignorance; and sins of ignorance are unintentional.'"

Cyrus said, "Poor soul! I grieve for him."

The king defended himself: "Remember, Cyrus, a man kills another with his wife not just for turning her to folly, but for robbing her love. I was jealous of that man who seemed to steal my son's reverence."

"May the gods be merciful!" said Cyrus, "you did wrong, but it's human. And you, Tigranes," he said to the son, "forgive your father."

So they talked in friendliness and kindness, befitting a time of reconciliation; then father and son, with their dear ones, drove away rejoicing.

When they were home, they all praised Cyrus: his wisdom, endurance, gentleness, stature, and beauty. Tigranes asked his wife, "Did Cyrus seem so beautiful to you?" She answered, "Ah, my lord, he wasn't the man I saw." "Who was it then?" asked Tigranes. "He," she answered, "who offered his own life to free me from slavery."

So they delighted together as lovers will, after all their sufferings.

The next day, the king of Armenia sent gifts to Cyrus and all his army, ordered his contingent to be ready in three days, and brought Cyrus twice the amount he had named. But Cyrus took only what he fixed, giving the rest back to the king, asking whether he or his son would lead the force. The father said it was Cyrus's choice, but the son said, "I won't leave you, Cyrus, even if I must carry baggage to follow you." Cyrus laughed and said, "What will you take to let us tell your wife you've become a baggage-bearer?" "She won't need to be told," he answered, "I'll bring her with me, so she can see what her husband does." "Then it's high time," said Cyrus, "you got your baggage ready." "We'll come," he said, "in good time, with whatever baggage my father gives."

So the soldiers were the guests of Armenia for the day and rested for the night.

III.2

Strategic Diplomacy and Military Fortification

Strategic Use of Speed and Surprise

> Swift and decisive action, particularly in military contexts, can lead to significant advantages. This is highlighted by Cyrus's decision to seize the Chaldaean hills quickly to prevent the enemy from organizing their defenses.

But on the following day, Cyrus took Tigranes and the best of the Median cavalry, along with chosen followers of his own, and scoured the entire country to decide where to build a fort. He stopped at the top of a mountain pass and asked Tigranes where the heights were from which the Chaldaeans descended when they came to plunder. Tigranes showed him. Then Cyrus asked if the mountains were completely uninhabited. "No," said the prince, "there are always men on the lookout who signal to the others if they see anything." "And what do they do," Cyrus asked, "when they see the signal?" "They rush to the rescue as quickly as they can," he said. Cyrus listened and looked, and he saw that large areas were desolate and untilled because of the war. That day they returned to camp, had their supper, and slept.

The next morning, Tigranes appeared with all his baggage ready for the march, accompanied by 4,000 cavalry, 10,000 bowmen, and as many targeteers. As they marched, Cyrus offered a sacrifice, and finding that the omens were favorable, he called together the leaders of the Persians and the chief captains of the Medes and spoke to them:

"My friends, there lie the Chaldaean hills. If we could seize them and set up a garrison to hold the pass, we could compel both the Chaldaeans and Armenians to behave properly. The omens are favorable; and in such work, speed is our best ally. If we reach the heights before the enemy can gather, we may take the position without a fight, facing only a few weak and scattered forces. Steady speed is all I ask for, and nothing could be easier or less dangerous. To arms then! The Medes will march on our left, half the Armenians on our right, and the rest in the front to lead the way, with the cavalry in the rear to push us forward and let none of us give way."

With that, Cyrus led the advance, the army following in column. When the Chaldaeans saw them coming up from the plain, they signaled to their fellows until the heights echoed with answering shouts, and the tribesmen gathered on every side. Then Cyrus sent word along his lines, "Soldiers of Persia, they are signaling us to hurry. If we reach the top before them, all they can do will be in vain."

The Chaldaeans were said to be the most warlike of all the tribes in that country, each armed with a shield and two javelins. They fought for pay wherever needed, partly because they were natural warriors and partly because of poverty; their country was mountainous with little fertile land.

As Cyrus and his force neared the head of the pass, Tigranes, marching at his side, said, "Do you know, Cyrus, that we will soon be in the thick of the fight ourselves? Our Armenians will never stand the charge." Cyrus acknowledged this and immediately sent word for the Persians to be ready to give chase as soon as they saw the Armenians feign flight and draw the enemy within reach.

They marched with the Armenians in front, and the Chaldaeans, who had gathered, waited until they were almost upon them and then charged with a tremendous shout. The Armenians, as usual, turned and ran. But in the midst of the pursuit, the Chaldaeans met new opponents coming up the pass, armed with short swords. Some were cut down before they could retreat, others were captured, and the rest fled. In moments, the heights were taken. From the top of the pass, Cyrus and his staff looked down and saw the Chaldaean villages with people fleeing from the nearest houses.

Soon the rest of the army came up, and Cyrus ordered them all to take their morning meal. Afterward, seeing that the lookout position was strong and well-supplied with water, he began fortifying it and told Tigranes to send for his father with all the carpenters and stonemasons he could bring. While a messenger went to the king, Cyrus did all he could with what he had.

Win-Win Negotiation

Balancing power and addressing the needs and concerns of different parties through negotiation is crucial. Cyrus demonstrates this by negotiating with the Chaldaeans and Armenians to secure peace and cooperation.

Meanwhile, they brought up the prisoners, all bound in chains and some wounded. Seeing their plight, Cyrus ordered the chains removed and called for surgeons to treat their wounds. He told them he came not to destroy them or wage war against them, but to make peace between them and the Armenians. "I know," he said, "before we took your pass, you didn't want peace. Your land was safe, and you could raid the Armenians. But now you can see how things stand today. I will let you all go home free and allow you and your fellows to decide whether to have us as enemies or friends. If you choose war, come armed next time, but if you choose peace, come unarmed and welcome. I will ensure your well-being if you are my friends."

Hearing this, the Chaldaeans thanked him and went home. Meanwhile, the Armenian king, receiving Cyrus's call and hearing the situation, gathered his workmen and came quickly. When he saw Cyrus, he said, "Ah, my lord, how blind we mortals are! We see so little of the future and take on so much! I sought freedom and made myself a slave, and now, when we thought we were utterly undone, we find a safety we never had. Those who troubled us are taken as I wished. I assure you, Cyrus, I would have paid what you took from me many times over to dislodge the Chaldaeans. The things of worth you promised have been delivered, and we are deeply in your debt for many kindnesses. We would be ashamed not to repay them, for we could never fully repay such a benefactor."

The Armenian gave his thanks.

Then the Chaldaeans returned, begging Cyrus for peace. Cyrus asked, "Do you seek peace today because you think it's safer than war now that we hold these heights?" The Chaldaeans agreed. "Good," he said. "And what if there were other benefits to peace?" "We would be even more pleased," they said. "Is there any reason for your poverty besides the lack of fertile soil?" They said no. "Would you pay the same dues as the Armenians if you could cultivate as much of their land as you wanted?" The Chaldaeans agreed if they could rely on fair treatment. "Would you like your idle land tilled and productive, with workers paying you customary dues?" the Armenian king asked. "Yes," he said, "so much so that I would pay a large sum for it. It would greatly increase my revenue."

"And you, Chaldaeans, with your splendid mountains, would you let the Armenians use them for pasture if the graziers paid you fairly?" "Yes," they said, "it would be profitable without effort." "Son of Armenia," Cyrus said, "would you use this land for grazing if paying a small sum to the Chaldaeans brought you a greater return?" "Right willingly," he said, "if my flocks could feed safely." "Would they not be safe enough," suggested Cyrus, "if this pass were held for you?" The king agreed.

But the Chaldaeans cried, "We couldn't safely till our fields, much less theirs, if the Armenians held the pass." "True," answered Cyrus, "but what if we Persians held the pass?" "Then all would be well," they said. "It would be ill for us," the Armenian said, "if these neighbors held the post, especially now that it's fortified."

Creating Alliances and Leveraging Resources

Forming alliances and making strategic use of available resources, including human resources, strengthens a leader's position. Cyrus's willingness to employ Chaldaean freebooters and his strategic approach to securing funds from the Indian king exemplify this lesson.

Cyrus said, "I won't give the pass to either of you. We Persians will guard it, and if either of you injures the other, we will side with the sufferers." Both parties applauded, agreeing that only this could ensure lasting peace. They exchanged pledges, agreeing that both nations would be free and independent, with common rights of marriage, tillage, pasture, and mutual help in war. The treaty holds to this day between the Chaldaeans and Armenia. Once peace was made, both parties began building their common fortress, working together.

When evening fell, Cyrus invited them all as guests to his board, saying they were already friends. At supper, a Chaldaean told Cyrus that while most of his people would be satisfied, some lived as freebooters and couldn't learn to farm, being used to living by plunder or as mercenaries, often for the king of India or Astyages. Cyrus suggested they serve him instead, promising to pay as well as anyone. The Chaldaeans agreed, predicting many volunteers.

This pleased everyone. Remembering that Indian ambassadors had visited the Medes and their enemies, Cyrus wanted them to hear of his achievements. He asked the Armenians and Chaldaeans to send guides with his ambassadors to India to request more money for wages and rewards for his soldiers. He preferred not to burden his friends but hoped to receive as much as the Indian king would give. His messenger would say: 'Son of India, my master needs more money. He expects another Persian army,' which Cyrus confirmed. 'If you can send my master all you have, he will ensure you see your kindness as well-placed.' He asked the Armenians and Chaldaeans to instruct their envoys accordingly, aiming to either secure funds or owe the Indian king no gratitude.

Cyrus spoke, convinced the Armenian and Chaldaean ambassadors would speak well of him. Then, as it was time, they ended the meeting and rested.

III.3

Preparations, Rituals and Motivational Speech Before the Attack

Recognize and Reward Loyalty and Service

Leaders should recognize and reward the loyalty and service of their followers. Acknowledging contributions and distributing rewards ensures that every member feels valued and motivated, strengthening the entire team.

The next day, Cyrus sent his messenger with instructions, and the Armenians and Chaldaeans sent their own ambassadors. They chose men who would help Cyrus the most and speak well of his deeds. Cyrus stationed a strong garrison in the fort, stocked it with supplies, and left a Mede officer in command to please Cyaxares. Then he headed home, taking not only his troops but also the forces provided by the Armenians and a selected group of Chaldaeans who considered themselves the strongest. As he descended from the hills into the cultivated land, all the Armenians came out to meet him. They were happy that peace was made and brought their best offerings, driving their most valued animals before them. The king was pleased, thinking Cyrus would enjoy the honor shown by the people. Last came the queen with her daughters and younger son, bearing many gifts, including the golden treasure Cyrus had refused before. But Cyrus said, "No, don't make me a mercenary. Take this treasure back, spend it on equipping your son for war, and buy things that bring joy and beauty into your lives."

With that, he rode away, escorted by the king and his people, who praised him as their savior and hero until he left their land. The king sent a larger army with Cyrus than ever before, as peace was now secure at home. Cyrus gained not only the money he took but also immense goodwill from the people. He encamped on the borders of Armenia for the first night, then sent the army and money to Cyaxares the next day, while he went hunting with Tigranes and the best of the Persian force. When Cyrus returned to Media, he gave gifts of money to his chief officers to reward their subordinates, believing that if each division was commendable, the whole army would be strong. He secured valuable items for the campaign and distributed them among the most deserving, knowing that every gain for the army was an enhancement for himself. At every distribution, he addressed the officers, emphasizing that blessings were won through toil, vigilance, speed, and unwavering resolve against foes.

Foster Unity Through Shared Goals and Challenges

Leaders can foster unity by presenting shared goals and challenges. By encouraging teamwork and emphasizing the importance of collective success, leaders can keep rivalry under control and build a stronger, more cohesive group.

As he saw his men were strong, bold, skilled, and disciplined, Cyrus desired to act against the enemy, aware that delay could ruin the best-prepared forces. He noticed jealousy among soldiers and wanted to lead them into enemy territory quickly, believing that common dangers would foster comradeship and eliminate envy. He assembled his force in battle array, making a show of perfection to inspire them, and ordered his officers to motivate their men for action, planning to present themselves at Cyaxares' gates the next morning.

Seize the Initiative and Maintain the Element of Surprise

Effective leaders seize the initiative and maintain the element of surprise. By acting decisively and unpredictably, leaders can keep their adversaries off balance and enhance their chances of success.

The next morning, they assembled at the meeting place, and Cyrus addressed Cyaxares, suggesting that since their preparations were complete, they should not wait for the enemy to invade but should attack on enemy soil. This would prevent damage to their own territory, allow them to sustain themselves on enemy resources, and boost their soldiers' morale. Cyaxares agreed, and they made final preparations, praying to the gods for favor and guidance. With favorable signs and the army ready, Cyrus invaded enemy land, offering sacrifices and seeking the gods' favor. They marched a short distance, set up camp, and captured much spoil, finding abundant supplies while waiting for the enemy. News of the enemy's advance soon came, and Cyrus told Cyaxares they must face the enemy, showing no fear but eagerness for battle. They marched forward, careful with their meals and fires to deceive the enemy, while the Assyrians entrenched their position.

The two armies drew closer, and the Assyrians fortified their camp. Cyrus took cover behind villages and hills to surprise the enemy. The first night passed with only guards posted. The next day, the Assyrians stayed within their lines, while Cyrus and Cyaxares prepared for battle. Seeing no movement, Cyaxares suggested marching to the enemy's breastworks to show readiness to fight, but Cyrus protested, believing it would reveal their numbers and embolden the enemy. Instead, he argued for catching the enemy by surprise. Cyrus then spoke to his men, saying they should not reveal themselves prematurely, as the enemy would despise their smaller numbers. He believed the enemy was uncertain and should remain so until the right moment. He emphasized that a sudden confrontation would catch the enemy off guard, fulfilling their long-held desire for battle. Cyrus insisted that they maintain their advantage by not revealing their strength until they could strike decisively, thus ensuring the enemy would be caught off guard and unprepared for the full force of their attack.

Setup Leadership Events to Coach and Empower the Direct Reports

A true leader organizes leadership events that are sometimes ceremonial. Leaderships events are meant to inspire, motivate, train and empower the leadership team, so that they can do the same with their own teams. This sets expectation and builds trust and unity, essential for achieving common goals.

So Cyrus spoke, and Cyaxares and the others were convinced, and waited. In the evening, they ate their meal, posted their guards, lit watch-fires in front of their outposts, and then went to sleep. Early the next morning, Cyrus put a garland on his head and went out to offer a sacrifice. He sent word to all the Persian leaders to join him, wearing garlands like his. After the ritual, he called them together and said, "Gentlemen, the soothsayers tell us, and I agree, that the gods show us through the signs in the sacrifices that a battle is near. They assure us of victory and promise us safety.

"I would be ashamed to give you advice at this moment or tell you how to act. We have all been raised in the same way, learned the same lessons, and practiced them daily. You could teach others just as well. But you might not have noticed one thing, so I ask you to listen. Our new comrades, the men we want to make our peers, need to be reminded of the terms on which Cyaxares has kept us and our daily discipline, the goal for which we asked their help, and the race in which they promised to be our friendly rivals. Remind them also that today will test the worth of every man.

For those who learn late in life, it is no surprise if they occasionally need a reminder. It is good if they show themselves to be good men and true with a little help. Moreover, while you help them, you will be testing your own abilities. He who can strengthen another in such a crisis can have confidence in his own strength. Someone who keeps his ideals to himself and is content with that should remember that he is only half a man. Another reason I do not speak to them myself but ask you to do so is that I want them to try to please you. You are closer to them than I am, each of you to the men in your own division. If you show yourselves to be brave, you will teach them courage and others as well, by deeds and words."

With that, Cyrus dismissed them, telling them to eat breakfast and make a libation, then take their places in the ranks, still wearing their garlands. As they left, he summoned the leaders of the rearguard and gave them his instructions: "Men of Persia, you have been made leaders and chosen for special duties because we think you equal to the best in other matters and wiser than most due to your age. The post you hold is just as honorable as those who form the front. From your position in the rear, you can spot the brave fighters, and your praise will make them even more courageous. If any man is tempted to give up, your eyes will be on him, and you will not allow it.

Victory will mean even more to you than to the others because of your age and the weight of your equipment. If the men in front call on you to follow, answer readily and show them that you can keep up with them. Shout back to them and tell them to lead on faster. Now, go back, eat your breakfast, and then join your ranks with the rest, wearing your garlands on your heads."

Inspire and Motivate Your Team By Reminding Their Mission

A leader must inspire and motivate their team to face challenges head-on. By reminding them of what they are fighting for, leaders can instill a sense of purpose and determination. This drive is crucial for overcoming obstacles and achieving victory.

Thus, Cyrus and his men prepared. Meanwhile, the Assyrians took their breakfast, then boldly marched out and formed up in an impressive order. The king himself organized them, driving past in his chariot and encouraging his troops. "Men of Assyria," he said, "today you must show your bravery. Today you fight for your lives and your land, the land where you were born and the homes where you were raised, and for your wives and children, and all the blessings that are yours. If you win, you will keep them all safely as before. But if you lose, you must surrender them to your enemies.

Fight, therefore, and do battle as though you were in love with victory. It would be foolish for her lovers to turn their backs to the enemy, becoming blind, handless, and helpless. A fool runs away because he longs to live, but he must know that safety comes to those who conquer, but death to those who flee. Fools are those who seek riches but are ready to admit defeat. The victor keeps his possessions and wins those of his enemies. The conquered lose themselves and everything they own."

Thus spoke the king of Assyria. Meanwhile, Cyaxares sent a message to Cyrus, saying that the moment for attack had come. "Although," he added, "there are only a few of them outside the trenches, by the time we advance, there will be enough. Let us not wait until they outnumber us, but charge now while we are confident we can defeat them easily."

But Cyrus answered, "Unless we conquer more than half their number, they will say we attacked when they were few because we were afraid of their full force. They will not feel truly beaten, and we will have to fight another battle. They might make a better plan than today, delivering themselves into our hands one by one, to fight as we choose."

So the messengers took back his reply. Meanwhile, Chrysantas and other leaders brought Assyrian deserters to Cyrus. Cyrus, as a general would, questioned the fugitives about the enemy's actions. They told him that the Assyrians were marching out in force, and the king himself had crossed the trenches and was organizing his troops, addressing them in stirring words. Then Chrysantas turned to Cyrus and said, "What if you also summon our men while there is still time and inspire them with your words?"

But Cyrus answered, "Do not worry about the Assyrian's speeches. No words are so fine that they can turn cowards into brave men on the day they hear them, nor make good archers out of bad, nor skilled spearmen, nor good riders, nor teach men to use their arms and legs if they have not learned before."

"But," replied Chrysantas, "could you not make the brave men braver still and the good better?"

"What!" cried Cyrus, "can one speech fill a man's soul with honor and uprightness on the same day? Can it protect him from all that is base, make him endure every toil and danger for the sake of glory, and make him believe it is better to die with a sword in hand than to escape by running away? If such thoughts are to be ingrained in men, we must start with the laws. They must ensure that the righteous can expect a life of honor and freedom, while the bad face humiliation, suffering, and a life that is no life at all.

Then we should have tutors and governors to instruct, teach, and train our citizens until they believe that the righteous and honorable are the happiest of all men, and the bad and infamous are the most miserable. This is what our men must feel if they are to show that their training can overcome their fear of the enemy. Surely, if in the moment of attack, amid the clash of arms, when long-learned lessons seem forgotten, any speaker could make warriors on the spot, it would be the easiest thing in the world to teach men the highest virtue. For my part, I would not trust our new comrades, whom we have trained ourselves, to stand firm today unless they saw you at their side to set an example and remind them if they forget. As for undisciplined men, I would be astonished if any speech, however splendid, could encourage bravery in their hearts more than a well-sung song could make a musician of a man with no music in his soul."

While they were speaking, Cyaxares sent another message, saying that Cyrus was wrong to delay and should advance against the enemy quickly. Cyrus sent back word through the messengers, "Tell Cyaxares again, there are still not enough of them for our needs. Tell him this so that everyone can hear. But add that if he wishes, I will advance at once."

Trust in Preparation and Discipline

Preparation and discipline are the bedrock of successful leadership. A well-prepared and disciplined team can face any challenge with confidence and effectiveness. Leaders must ensure their team is always ready to act decisively and efficiently.

So saying, and with a prayer to the gods, he led his troops into battle. Once they began the advance, he quickened the pace, and his men followed in perfect order, steadily, swiftly, joyously, filled with competition, hardened by toil, trained by long discipline, every man in the front a leader, and all alert. They had learned the lesson that it was always safest and easiest to meet enemies up close, especially archers, javelin-men, and cavalry.

While they were still out of range, Cyrus sent the watchword along the lines, "Zeus our help and Zeus our leader." As soon as it was returned to him, he started the battle hymn, and the men took up the hymn devoutly in one mighty chorus. For at such times, those who fear the gods have less fear of men. When the chant was over, the Persian leaders went forward side by side, shining, noble, disciplined, a band of gallant comrades. They looked into each other's eyes, called each other by name, with many a cheerful cry, "Forward, friends, forward, gallant gentlemen

" The rear ranks heard the call and sent back a ringing cheer, telling the front to lead on. The whole army of Cyrus was filled with courage, zeal, strength, hardiness, comradeship, and self-control, more terrifying to an enemy than anything else.

On the Assyrian side, those in the front who fought from chariots, as soon as the mass of the Persian force drew near, leapt back and drove to their main body. The archers, javelin-men, and slingers let fly long before they were in range. As the Persians steadily advanced, stepping over the spent missiles, Cyrus called to his men, "Forward now, bravest of the brave! Show us your pace!" They caught the word and passed it on, and in their eagerness and passion for the fight, some leaders broke into a run, and the whole phalanx followed at their heels. Cyrus himself gave up the regular march and dashed forward at their head, shouting, "Brave men to the front! Who follows me? Who will lay the first Assyrian low?" At this, the men behind took up the shout till it rang through the field like a battle-cry: "Who follows? Brave men to the front!"

Thus the Persians closed. But the enemy could not hold their ground; they turned and fled to their entrenchments. The Persians swept after them, many a warrior falling as they crowded in at the gates or tumbled into the trenches. In the rout, some of the chariots were carried into the fosse, and the Persians sprang down after them and slew man and horse where they fell. Then the Median troopers, seeing how matters stood, charged the Assyrian cavalry, who swerved and broke before them, chased and slaughtered, horse and rider, by their conquerors.

Meanwhile, the Assyrians within the camp, though they stood upon the breastworks, had neither wit nor power to draw a bow or fling a spear against the destroyers, dazed as they were by their panic and the horror of the sight. Then came the tidings that the Persians had cut their way through to the gates, and at that, they fled from the breastworks. The women, seeing the rout in the camp, fell to wailing and lamentations, running hither and thither in utter dismay, young maidens, and mothers with children in their arms, rending their garments and tearing their cheeks and crying on all they met, "Leave us not, save us, save your children and yourselves!" Then the princes gathered the trustiest men and stood at the gates, fighting on the breastworks themselves, and urging their troops to make a stand. Cyrus, seeing this and fearing that if his handful of Persians forced their way into the camp, they would be overpowered by numbers, gave the order to fall back out of range. Then was shown the perfect discipline of the leaders; they immediately obeyed the order and passed it on at once. When they were all out of range, they halted and reformed their ranks, better than any chorus could have done, every man knowing exactly where he should be.

BOOK IV

The Capture
of the Assyrians

IV.1

Cyrus's Relentless Ambition
Beyond the Battle to Win the War

Show Gratitude and Recognize Contributions

> Praise, empower and publicly express gratitude to your team members, acknowledging their roles in achieving victory, and when appropriate, promote them on the spot. This recognition boosts morale and encourages continued loyalty and effort from the troops. By valuing each person's contribution, the leader fosters a strong sense of unity and motivation.

Cyrus waited with his troops for the enemy to come out and fight again. When the enemy did not move, he moved his soldiers back and set up camp. He posted guards and sent scouts ahead. Then he gathered his warriors and spoke to them.

"Men of Persia," Cyrus said, "I first want to thank the gods of heaven with all my heart. I know you also thank the gods, for we have won safety and victory, and it is right to be grateful. Next, I want to praise all of you. This great work was done because of you all. I will learn what each man did from those who know, and I will do my best to give each man his due, in words and actions."

"I do not need anyone to tell me about Chrysantas' bravery. He was next to me in battle, and I saw him act as I believe you all did. When I called him to retreat, he was about to strike down an Assyrian, but he heard my voice and immediately obeyed. He passed the word along the lines and led his division out of danger before the enemy could attack. He and his men came out safely because he learned to obey."

"Some of you are wounded, and when I learn how you were wounded, I will give my opinion on your bravery. I already know that Chrysantas is a true soldier and a sensible man, able to command because he can obey. I am now putting him in charge of a thousand troops, and I will not forget him when the gods give me more blessings."

"Remember today's lesson. Think about whether cowardice or courage saves a man in war, whether fighters or shirkers have a better chance, and what joy victory brings. You can decide this today because you have just experienced it. With these thoughts, you will become braver and better."

"Now rest, knowing you have done your duty bravely and steadily. Eat your meal, make your offerings, sing the victory song, and be ready for the next command."

After saying this, Cyrus mounted his horse and rode to Cyaxares. They rejoiced together as victors do. He checked if anything was needed there and then rode back to his troops. They ate their evening meal, set the guards, and Cyrus slept with his men.

Seize Opportunities and Encourage Initiative

Cyrus urges his officers to take advantage of the enemy's retreat, highlighting the importance of acting decisively and taking initiative. He recognizes the value of pursuing the enemy to secure further victories and resources. Encouraging proactive behavior among his leaders ensures they capitalize on favorable situations.

Meanwhile, the Assyrians found their king and many nobles dead and lost hope. Many deserted during the night. Fear spread to Croesus and the allies, seeing danger everywhere and knowing the leading nation had suffered a mortal blow. They decided to abandon their camp at night.

At dawn, Cyrus saw the deserted camp and led his Persians inside. They found the enemy's supplies: sheep, goats, cattle, and wagons full of goods. Cyaxares and his Medes followed, and they all had breakfast there.

After the meal, Cyrus called his officers and said, "We are missing a great opportunity by not pursuing the enemy. They have fled from their fortress; they will not face us on open ground. They are beaten and will not dare to fight us again. The bravest are dead, and the cowards will not fight."

One officer asked, "Why not pursue them now if we are so certain of victory?"

Cyrus replied, "We do not have the horses. The enemy's best fighters are on fast horses. We can make them flee, but we cannot catch them."

The officers suggested, "Let's tell Cyaxares."

Cyrus agreed, "If we do, we all need to go together so Cyaxares sees this is everyone's wish."

They went to Cyaxares, who felt some jealousy that the Persians suggested this first but also thought it might be wiser to avoid more risks. He was enjoying his victory and saw his Medes were doing the same. He replied, "My nephew, you Persians believe in not overindulging in pleasures. The greater the joy, the more important self-control is. Our current fortune should be guarded carefully to ensure lasting peace. If we chase every victory, we risk losing everything.

"If our enemies were weaker, it might be safe to pursue them. But we only fought a small part of their forces. If we push them too hard, we might drive them to be brave out of necessity. They are desperate to save their families and might fight fiercely if cornered. Yesterday they hid in a fort and let us choose our battles. But in open ground, they could surround us. Besides, I do not want to disturb my Medes from their well-deserved rest."

Delegate Authority and Trust Your Team

> Cyrus demonstrates effective leadership by delegating tasks and trusting his team to carry out important missions. He empowers his officers to rally troops and make strategic decisions, showing confidence in their abilities. This delegation not only distributes responsibility but also strengthens the overall effectiveness of the leadership structure.

Cyrus responded, "I do not want to force anyone. Let those who are willing follow me. We will not pursue the main force but will target stragglers. We came a long way to help you; it is only fair you let us take something back."

Cyaxares agreed, "If anyone wants to follow you, they can. Take someone to carry my commands."

Cyrus chose a Mede who had claimed kinship with him before. Cyaxares told this officer to relay the message that anyone willing could follow Cyrus. The officer, eager to help, assured Cyrus he would bring others to join him.

With Cyaxares' support, the officer went to the Medes, urging them to follow Cyrus, praising him as the bravest, noblest, and best of men, and a hero from a divine lineage.

IV.2

Allies in the Making
Cyrus and the Hyrcanians

Summary

In this chapter, while Cyrus is occupied with various matters, two ambassadors from the Hyrcanians arrive, seeking to revolt against their Assyrian overlords. The Hyrcanians, who live primarily on horseback and have been harshly used by the Assyrians, see an opportunity for freedom due to the Assyrian army's recent defeat and the resulting chaos. They offer to ally with Cyrus, providing crucial intelligence and guidance. Cyrus, recognizing the strategic advantage, agrees and secures their loyalty with a pledge. He quickly organizes his forces, including Persians, Medes, and the newly allied Hyrcanians, to pursue the retreating Assyrians. The chapter details the preparation, the swift nighttime march, and the resulting disarray and flight of the Assyrian forces upon encountering Cyrus' army at dawn. Through strategic planning and fostering trust among his allies, Cyrus strengthens his position and readies his troops for further victories.

Value of Strategic Alliance

Cyrus recognizes the importance of forming alliances with the Hyrcanians, who are familiar with the Assyrians and are eager to revolt. By promising them equality and trust, he secures their cooperation. Effective leaders identify potential allies, understand their needs, and create partnerships that benefit both parties.

While Cyrus was occupied with these matters, two ambassadors arrived from the Hyrcanians by some strange chance. These people, neighbors of the Assyrians, were few in number and were under Assyrian control. But they seemed then, as they do now, to live on horseback. Because of this, the Assyrians used them like the Lacedaemonians used the Skirites, for every hard task and danger, without sparing them. At that moment, they had ordered the Hyrcanians to provide a rear-guard of a thousand men and more, to handle any attacks from behind.

The Hyrcanians, being at the back, had put their wagons and families in the rear, as most tribes in Asia take their households with them on the march.

But when they thought about the bad treatment they received from the Assyrians, and saw the fallen king, the defeated and panicked army, the disheartened allies ready to desert, they saw it as a good time to revolt, if the Medes and Persians would join them. So they sent an embassy to Cyrus, as his name was famous after the recent battle.

They told him why they hated the Assyrians and that if he attacked now, they would be his allies and guide him. They also gave a full account of the enemy's actions, eager to get Cyrus moving.

Cyrus asked, "Do you think we can catch the Assyrians before they reach their fortresses? We see it as a great misfortune that they escaped us." (He said this to make his listeners think highly of him and his friends.)

"You will certainly catch them," they replied, "and that by tomorrow if you hurry: they move slowly because of their numbers and wagons, and since they did not sleep last night, they have only gone a little way and are now camped for the evening."

"Can you guarantee what you say is true?" asked Cyrus.

"We will give you hostages," they said; "we will ride off at once and bring them back tonight. You, on your side, should call the gods to witness and give us your pledge, so we can assure our people."

Cyrus gave them his pledge that if they kept their promise, he would treat them as true friends and followers, equal to the Persians and Medes. To this day, Hyrcanians are treated with trust and hold positions equal to high-ranking Persians and Medes.

Decisive and Timely Action

When the opportunity arises, Cyrus acts swiftly by organizing his forces and marching quickly to surprise the enemy. This decisive action prevents the enemy from regrouping and demonstrates the power of acting promptly and strategically. Leaders must be ready to make quick decisions and act on opportunities to gain an advantage over the competition.

Cyrus and his men ate supper and, while it was still daylight, he led his army out, making the two Hyrcanians wait to go with them. The Persians were all with him, and so was Tigranes with his men, along with Median volunteers who joined for various reasons.

Some were childhood friends of Cyrus, others had hunted with him and admired his character, some were grateful because he lifted their fears, others were hopeful, believing great things awaited the brave and fortunate Cyrus. Others remembered his upbringing in Media and wanted to repay his kindnesses; many recalled favors he had won for them from his grandfather through his goodness; and many, hearing about the Hyrcanians leading them to treasures, joined out of simple greed.

So they marched out, with all the Persians and most of the Medes, except those with Cyaxares, who stayed behind. The rest went out with joyful faces and eager hearts, following Cyrus willingly, out of gratitude.

Once they were in the field, Cyrus thanked the Medes, praying that the gods guide them all and give him the power to reward their zeal. He said that the infantry would lead, and they would follow with the cavalry, and when the column halted, they should send gallopers for orders.

He asked the Hyrcanians to lead the way, but they said, "Aren't you going to wait for the hostages? Then you could start with our pledges."

But he replied, "If I'm not mistaken, we hold the pledges in our hearts and hands. We believe that if you are true to us, we can help you, and if you betray us, you won't have us at your mercy; God willing, we'll hold you at ours. But since your people follow the Assyrians, point them out so we can spare their lives."

The Hyrcanians, impressed by his confidence, led the way, losing their fear of the Assyrians, Lydians, and their allies, now worried only that Cyrus might think them insignificant.

As night fell, a strange light shone in the sky, filling Cyrus and his men with awe and courage. Marching swiftly, they covered a long distance quickly, and by morning they were close to the Hyrcanian rear-guard.

When the guides saw it, they told Cyrus those were their men, recognized by the number of fires and their position in the rear.

Cyrus sent a guide to tell them to come out with raised right hands if they were friendly. He also sent one of his own men to say, "However you approach us, so will we Persians behave." One messenger stayed with Cyrus, while the other rode ahead.

Cyrus halted his army to see what the tribe would do, and Tigranes and the Median officers asked for orders. Cyrus explained that the nearest troops were Hyrcanians, and one of the ambassadors and a Persian were going to tell them to come out with raised right hands if friendly. "If they do," he added, "welcome them at your posts and encourage them, but if they draw swords or try to escape, make an example of them: leave no one alive."

The Hyrcanians, overjoyed at the message, galloped to Cyrus with raised right hands as instructed. The Medes and Persians welcomed and encouraged them.

Cyrus spoke: "Hyrcanians, we have shown our trust in you, and you must trust us. Now, tell me, how far are the Assyrian headquarters and main body?" "About four miles away," they replied.

"Forward then," said Cyrus, "Persians, Medes, and Hyrcanians. I now call you friends and comrades. Remember, if our hands or hearts fail, we face disaster: our enemies know why we are here. But if we fight with all our strength, we'll catch them like runaway slaves, some on their knees, others fleeing, unable to defend themselves. They are already beaten and will see us before they expect, unprepared and terrified."

"If we want to live in peace and happiness, let's not give them time to plan or defend themselves, but appear as a storm of shields and weapons."

"You Hyrcanians will lead as a screen, with us behind you. As soon as I engage, you must give me a squadron of horse for use while waiting at the camp."

"I advise the older men and officers to ride in close order to keep ranks against the enemy; let the younger men chase and kill; our safest plan is to leave as few enemies alive as possible."

"If we win," he added, "beware of the lust for plunder that has ruined many conquerors. A plunderer is no longer a man, but a porter, easily treated as a slave."

"Remember, nothing brings more gain than victory; the victor takes all: people, wealth, land. Focus on victory; if the plunderer is defeated, he loses everything. Also, regroup by daylight, as we won't admit anyone in the dark."

He sent them to their stations, telling them to pass down his orders. They advanced, Hyrcanians leading, Cyrus in the center with his Persians, and cavalry on either flank.

At daybreak, the enemy saw them: some stared, some realized the truth, calling and shouting, unfastening horses, gathering goods, tearing what they needed from beasts of burden, arming, harnessing horses, leaping on horseback, helping women into carriages, seizing valuables, burying treasures, or fleeing headlong. Many different reactions, but none stood to fight: they perished without resistance.

Croesus, king of Lydia, had sent his women ahead at night for a cool journey, following with his cavalry. The Lord of Hellespontine Phrygia did the same. When they heard from fleeing soldiers, they fled with the rest.

The kings of Cappadocia and Arabia, not far off, stood their ground but were unprepared and cut down by the Hyrcanians. Most fallen were Assyrians and Arabians, taking no precautions in their land.

The victorious Medes and Hyrcanians chased the enemy, while Cyrus made his remaining cavalry circle the camp, cutting down anyone with weapons. He sent a herald to those remaining, ordering horsemen, targeteers, and archers to disarm, leaving horses in stalls: disobedience meant death, with Persian troops standing guard.

Weapons were brought and burned.

Cyrus remembered his troops had no food or drink and knew they needed provisions quickly. Officers who prepare quarters and supplies would likely be left behind, delayed by packing.

He proclaimed all stewards should present themselves, or the oldest in each tent must take their place; disobedience would be punished severely. Stewards followed their masters' example and obeyed. Cyrus ordered those with more than two months' rations to sit, then those with one month's rations. Very few were left standing.

Building Trust and Loyalty

Cyrus gains the loyalty of the Hyrcanians by treating them as equals and giving them a clear role in the mission's success. By fulfilling his promises and showing trust in his allies, he ensures their dedication and support. Effective leadership involves building trust through integrity, shared goals, and recognizing the contributions of all team members.

He addressed them: "If you dislike hard blows and want gentle treatment, double the meat and drink in every tent, with everything needed for a fine meal. The victors will expect a feast. Welcome them well."

The stewards eagerly complied. Cyrus then spoke to his officers: "Friends, we could take the best food and wine for breakfast, but helping our allies will strengthen us more. If we neglect those fighting for us, they'll see us as weak and selfish. The true feast is to meet the needs of those who took risks and worked hard, ensuring they have all they need when they return, bringing more joy than mere food."

"Even without their example, this isn't the time for gluttony or drunkenness. We aren't done yet; dangers remain. We have many more enemies than ourselves, who must be guarded and used for supplies. Our cavalry isn't back; we must consider their loyalty upon return."

"Gentlemen, avoid food and drink that cause sleep and stupor."

"This camp has vast treasures, but taking what we want isn't as valuable as proving our justice to allies, binding them closer."

"Let Medes, Hyrcanians, and Tigranes distribute the spoils, and be content with a smaller share to keep their loyalty."

"Selfishness may bring temporary riches, but letting go of vanity secures lasting wealth for us and our kin."

"At home, we trained to master our appetites for moments like this. Where better to show our discipline?"

Hystaspas the Persian supported him: "Cyrus, it would be shameful if we fasted while hunting but succumbed to temptation when great wealth is at stake. This wouldn't honor our race."

All approved. Cyrus said: "Since we agree, each of you give me five trustworthy men to check supplies, praising the diligent and punishing the neglectful more severely than their masters."

They handled these matters accordingly.

IV.3

Strategic Reorganization
The Birth of Persian Cavalry

Summary

The Medes and Hyrcanians return to the camp with captured supplies and women, showcasing their success in battle. Cyrus feels envious and believes his own group has underperformed. He addresses his officers, highlighting the need for Persian cavalry to secure their own victories and match their allies' capabilities. Cyrus proposes using captured horses and gear to train their cavalry, arguing that adults can learn to ride as well as boys. The officers agree, and preparations begin to form a Persian cavalry. Spoils are divided fairly among the troops and allies. Cyrus sends a messenger to Persia to request additional troops and supplies, while also maintaining communication with Cyaxares. He plans to release surrendered prisoners to encourage further surrenders and keep the land populated. The chapter concludes with organizing the camp, distributing horses, and setting up defenses for future engagements.

Ambitious Vision and Strategic Adaptation

Cyrus demonstrates ambition by recognizing the need for Persian cavalry to match the successes of the Medes and Hyrcanians. He observes their effective use of cavalry and seizes the opportunity to propose a similar strategy, showing that a leader should be forward-thinking and willing to adapt for faster growth and success.

But it didn't take long for some of the Medes to return: one group had caught up with the wagons that had gone ahead, seized them, and brought them back to the camp, loaded with everything an army might need. Another group had captured the covered carriages carrying the women, the wives or concubines of the Assyrian nobles, who were taken along because of their beauty.

To this day, Asian tribes always take their most precious belongings with them on campaigns. They say it helps them fight better, feeling they must protect their treasures with all their heart. This might be true, but it could also be because they desire pleasure.

Observing and Learning from Others

> By closely watching the Medes and Hyrcanians, Cyrus identifies their strengths and realizes the importance of cavalry in achieving victory. This lesson emphasizes that leaders should continuously analyze the performance of competitors and allies, adopting and improving upon effective strategies and equipment to stay competitive and successful.

When Cyrus saw the feats performed by the Medes and the Hyrcanians, he almost blamed himself and his followers. He felt that while others had risen to the occasion, shown their strength, and won their prizes, he and his men had stayed behind like lazy people. It was quite a sight to see the victors returning, driving their spoils before them, showing off to Cyrus, and then rushing off again in search of more, following their instructions.

Despite his envy, Cyrus carefully set aside all their booty. Then he called his officers together and, standing where everyone could hear, he spoke:

Building and Empowering Teams

> Cyrus's decision to form a Persian cavalry by using captured resources and training his own men highlights the importance of building and empowering new teams. A leader should capitalize on available opportunities to create and develop teams, ensuring they are well-equipped and trained to enhance overall organizational effectiveness and growth.

"My friends, we can all agree that if the spoils now on display were ours to keep, every Persian would become wealthy, and we, who earned these prizes, would get the most. But I don't see how we can claim such rewards without having our own cavalry.

Think about it," he continued, "we Persians have weapons to defeat the enemy at close quarters, but when we do, how can we catch and kill horsemen, archers, or light-armed troops if we can only pursue them on foot? Why should they fear us when they know we are as harmless as tree stumps in an orchard?

As it stands, our cavalry thinks every gain belongs as much to them as to us, perhaps even more. For now, we must accept this situation. But if we had a cavalry force as good as our allies', it would be clear to all that we could handle the enemy ourselves, just as we do now with their help. They might become less arrogant, and we would be less dependent on them.

Empowerment and Team Building

Cyrus emphasizes the importance of forming a well-trained and equipped cavalry. By recognizing the potential in his own men and encouraging them to learn new skills, he demonstrates how leaders should empower and build effective teams to enhance organizational capabilities.

So, no one would disagree that having Persian cavalry would make a big difference for us, but the question is, how do we get it? Let's consider: we have hundreds of captured horses with their bridles and gear, and all the equipment needed for a mounted force, like breastplates and spears. What else do we need? It's clear we need men.

But we already have men under our command. Nothing is more ours than ourselves. Some might say we lack the necessary skill. True, but those who have the skill now also had to learn it at some point. You might object that they learned as boys.

Maybe so, but are boys better at learning than grown men? Who can handle heavy tasks better, boys or men? Besides, we have an advantage over other pupils: we don't need to learn the bow or javelin as boys do; we already know those skills. We haven't spent our time farming, crafting, or managing households. We've had the leisure to focus on war—it has been our life.

Moreover, riding is not like other war exercises that are useful but unpleasant. Riding a horse is surely more enjoyable than walking on foot. And think of the speed—you can quickly join a friend or catch your prey, whether it's a man or a beast. And it's so convenient! Whatever weapon you carry, your horse helps bear the load. 'Wear arms' and 'bear arms' mean the same thing on horseback.

To address the worst case, suppose we face some risk before becoming adept riders and find we're neither proper infantry nor cavalry. This could be a danger, but we can always turn back into infantry. I don't propose we unlearn foot soldier skills by learning to ride."

Cyrus spoke, and Chrysantas rose to support him, saying:

"I don't just want to be a horseman; I believe that once I can ride, I will feel like I'm flying. Right now, when I race, I'm happy if I can beat a rival or get close enough to hit my target. But as a horseman, I can catch my man as far as I see him, or come up with the beasts I chase and take them down myself or spear them as if they were standing still. When hunter and prey are racing side by side, it's as if neither is moving.

I've always envied the centaur—if only he had the intelligence and skill of a man, combined with the speed and strength of a horse, to catch and defeat all before him. I will have these powers once I become a rider. My human wits will provide forethought, my hands will wield weapons, and my horse's legs will follow the foe and overthrow them. I won't be tied to my steed like the centaur, which I think is a great improvement. The centaur couldn't use human inventions as a horse, and couldn't enjoy horse pleasures as a man.

But I, once I learn to ride, will do all the centaur can and more. I can dismount, dress like a human, dine, and sleep in my bed. I will be a centaur that can be taken apart and put together again. I'll have another advantage: the centaur had only two eyes and ears, but I'll watch with four eyes and listen with four ears. A horse often sees and hears things before its rider and gives warning. So, please write my name down among those who want to ride."

"And ours too," they all cried, "ours too, in heaven's name!"

Cyrus then spoke: "Since we all agree, let's make a rule that anyone receiving a horse from me will be considered disgraceful if seen walking, whether on a long or short journey."

Everyone agreed, and that's why, even today, no Persian noble would willingly be seen on foot.

IV.4

A Strategy of Smart Conquest

Securing Stability of the Conquered Territories through Fair Integration

Cyrus demonstrates a strategic approach to conquering new territories by focusing on the development and prosperity of the land with its own people. By ensuring that the prisoners and inhabitants feel safe and secure under his rule, he effectively eliminates resistance and encourages surrender. His fair treatment of those who surrender and his promise of protection and continuity in their daily lives integrate the conquered people into a larger nation. This approach not only stabilizes the newly acquired territory but also promotes its growth and prosperity, showcasing Cyrus's intelligence in fostering a unified and thriving realm.

While they were debating, the Median cavalry and the Hyrcanians came galloping home, bringing men and horses from the enemy, sparing those who surrendered. Cyrus's first question was if everyone was safe, and when they said yes, he asked about their achievements. They proudly told their exploits in detail.

Cyrus listened with a smile, praised them, and said, "I see you've done great deeds. You look taller, fairer, and more impressive than before."

He then asked how far they had gone and if the land was inhabited. They said they had traveled far, found the land full of sheep, goats, cattle, horses, and rich in corn and everything good.

Cyrus said, "We must become masters of this land and ensure the people don't run away. A well-populated country is valuable, but a deserted one becomes barren. You've rightly killed the defenders, but you've spared those who surrendered. If we let these men go, it would be best for us. We won't need to guard or feed them, and their release will encourage more prisoners to surrender. If the inhabitants see their fellows alive and free, they'll be more likely to stay and obey than fight. That's my view, but if anyone has a better idea, let him speak."

Everyone approved of the plan. Cyrus then called the prisoners and told them:

"Gentlemen, your lives are safe because of your obedience today. If you continue this way, no harm will come to you. You won't have the same ruler, but you'll live in the same houses, farm the same land, and live with your families as before. You won't have to fight anyone, and if any wrong is done to you, we'll fight for you. Bring us your weapons, and you'll have peace and our promises. If you don't, expect war immediately. If anyone helps us, we'll treat him as a friend and benefactor. Make this known among your people. If some want to comply but others stop them, lead us against those obstructing you, and you'll be their masters."

The prisoners agreed and promised to follow his instructions.

IV.5

Building A Unified Community Through Fairness

Summary

Cyrus organizes a communal meal for his allies—the Medes, Armenians, and Hyrcanians—in the newly conquered Assyrian territory, ensuring that everyone is well-provisioned. He assigns guards to prevent theft and potential escapes. Meanwhile, Cyaxares, the king of the Medes, becomes enraged upon discovering that his troops and Cyrus have left him behind and sends a messenger demanding their return. Cyrus reassures his allies, sends for reinforcements from Persia, and discusses the fair distribution of spoils. He also emphasizes the need to integrate captured resources and manpower into their forces, ultimately strengthening their position in the newly acquired territory.

Ensuring Fair Distribution to Build a Community with Mutual Trust

Cyrus emphasizes fair distribution of resources among his allies to foster a sense of community and teamwork. By treating the Medes and Hyrcanians as equals, he builds mutual trust and cooperation, essential for unifying diverse groups into the Persian Empire. This approach not only secures loyalty but also promotes a cohesive and harmonious integration of different nations into one.

When they left, Cyrus told the Medes and Armenians, "It's time to eat. We have prepared food and drink for you. Send us half of the bread you've baked; there's enough for both of us. But don't send any relish or drink, we have enough."

He then told the Hyrcanians to take their friends to their quarters, the officers to the largest tents, and the rest where they thought best. The Hyrcanians could dine where they liked, their quarters were intact, and everything was prepared for them.

Cyrus also said, "We Persians will guard the camp outside during the night, but you must watch over the inside and keep your weapons ready. Our messmates are not yet our friends."

So, the Medes and Tigranes' men cleaned up, put on clean clothes, and dined. They sent half the bread to the Persians but no relish or wine, thinking Cyrus had a store because he said they had enough. But Cyrus meant the hunger and the river's water.

Cyrus and his men ate, and at night he sent them out in groups to lie in ambush around the camp, forming a double guard against attack and preventing theft. Many tried to escape, but all were caught. Cyrus let the captors keep the treasures but had the thieves executed, making theft rare in the future.

The Persians passed their time this way, while the Medes feasted, made music, and enjoyed themselves with plenty of food and drink. Cyaxares, the Median king, got drunk with his officers to celebrate their good fortune. Hearing the noise, he thought most Medes had stayed behind, but their servants were the ones celebrating with food and wine from the Assyrian camp.

When it was day and no one came to the palace except last night's guests, and Cyaxares saw the camp deserted, he was furious at Cyrus and his men for leaving him. Enraged, he ordered one of his staff to take his troopers and deliver a message to Cyrus and his men, demanding the Medes return immediately, whether Cyrus agreed or not.

The messenger asked, "How shall I find them, my lord?"

Cyaxares replied, "As Cyrus found those he sought."

The messenger said, "I heard that some Hyrcanians who revolted from the enemy guided him."

Cyaxares was even angrier, knowing Cyrus didn't tell him, and urgently demanded the Medes return, threatening the officer if he failed.

The officer, regretting not going with Cyrus himself, set off with a hundred troopers. They took a wrong turn and only reached the Persians at midnight after encountering retreating Assyrians and forcing them to guide them. They found the camp but were not let in until dawn by Cyrus's pickets.

At dawn, Cyrus summoned the Persian priests, called Magians, and asked them to choose the offerings due to the gods for their blessings. He then called the Peers together and said:

"Gentlemen, God has blessed us with many things, but we Persians are too few to guard them. If we can't protect our gains, they will fall back into other hands. If we leave some to guard them, we will be seen as weak. One of you must go to Persia immediately, explain our needs, and request an army to secure the empire of Asia.

Turning to one of the Peers, he said, "You, as the eldest, go and tell them what we need. Tell my father how much to send home as an offering to the gods and ask the magistrates how much is due to the state. Send commissioners to watch and help us. Prepare your baggage and take your company as an escort. Farewell."

With that, he turned to the Medes, and the messenger from Cyaxares delivered the king's angry message, demanding the Medes return immediately, even if Cyrus wished them to stay. The Medes were silent, torn between disobeying the summons and fearing Cyaxares's wrath.

Cyrus spoke: "Herald and sons of the Medes, I understand Cyaxares's fear, knowing so little of what we've done. But when he learns of our victory, his fear will vanish. We haven't deserted him on this crucial day; we're defeating his enemies. We acted with his consent, not without it. I'm sure his anger will fade when he knows the truth. For now," he said to the messenger, "rest, you've had a hard task. And we," he told the Persians, "must prepare for an enemy who will either fight or surrender. Let's get ready in our best form, which might bring us more than we expect. And you," he said to the Hyrcanian chieftain, "arm your men and then come back to me."

The Hyrcanian did so, and Cyrus said, "Son of Hyrcania, I'm pleased with your friendliness and wisdom. Our interests align; the Assyrians hate you more than me now. We must ensure our allies stay with us and gain more. The Mede messenger wants to recall our cavalry, but we need to make him want to stay. Give him a good time, and I'll offer him better work. Talk to him about our great expectations, then report back to me."

The chieftain took the Mede to his quarters, and the Persian messenger presented himself, ready for the journey. Cyrus instructed him to tell the Persians all that had happened and gave him a letter to Cyaxares. "I'll read it to you so you can answer any questions."

Diplomatic Communication and Conflict Resolution

Cyrus shows diplomatic skill by addressing Cyaxares's anger and concerns through a carefully crafted letter. He reassures Cyaxares of their actions and future plans, highlighting the importance of clear communication and negotiation in resolving conflicts and maintaining strong alliances.

The letter said: "Cyrus to Cyaxares, greeting. We haven't deserted you; no one is abandoned when their enemies are defeated. The further we are from you, the more secure you are. It's not the friend nearby who keeps you safe but the one who drives enemies away. Remember what I've done for you before blaming me. I brought allies, not just those you asked for, and now you demand they all return, leaving them no choice. Yesterday, I felt gratitude to you and them, but today you make me wish to repay only those who followed me. Still, I'm sending for more troops and instructing them to serve you if needed. I advise you, though younger, not to retract gifts or use threats. For us, we'll rejoin you once we've secured more blessings for both. Farewell."

"Deliver this to Cyaxares, and answer any questions based on it. Remember, speed is important," said Cyrus, giving him the letter and sending him off.

Cyrus then reviewed his fully armed troops: Medes, Hyrcanians, Tigranes' men, and Persians. Some local people were bringing in horses or surrendering arms. Cyrus ordered the javelins piled up and burned after his troops took what they needed. He told the owners to stay with their horses until further orders. Then he called the Hyrcanian and cavalry officers and said:

"My friends, I call you often because our situation is new and needs adjustment. We have much spoil and prisoners guarding it, but we don't know what belongs to whom. The guards can't be exact in their duties without knowing them. To fix this, you must divide the spoil. Some have fully supplied tents; they must now care for their property. Others need more supplies, which you must provide. There's more than enough, I'm sure. The enemy had plenty for our small numbers. Some treasurers from the Assyrian king and others told me they have gold coins from certain tributes. Announce that this deposit must be delivered to you, scare those who don't comply, and distribute the money. Mounted men should get two shares for every foot soldier's one, and keep the surplus for purchases. In the camp market, ensure fair trade; hucksters must be allowed to sell and bring more goods."

The officers quickly issued the proclamations. But the Medes and Hyrcanians asked Cyrus, "How can we distribute the spoil alone, without your men and you?"

Cyrus replied with a question, "Do you think we must all handle every detail together? Can I never act for you, and you for me? That would only create trouble and reduce results. Look, we Persians guarded the booty for you, and you believe we did well. Now you can distribute it, and we'll trust you to be fair.

There's another benefit I'd like us all to have. We have many horses now and more coming in. If left riderless, they'll be a burden. But if we mount riders on them, we'll be free of the trouble and stronger. If you have other men you'd prefer to share the danger, give the horses to them. But if you want us to fight by your side, give the horses to us. Today, when you rushed into danger alone, we feared for you and felt ashamed not to be there. But with horses, we can follow you closely. If mounted, we'll be more effective, or we can dismount and march as infantry. We can always find someone to hold our horses."

They answered, "Cyrus, we don't have men for these horses ourselves, and even if we did, we wouldn't go against your wish. Take them and use them as you think best."

Cyrus replied, "I will, gladly, and may good fortune bless us all. You in your spoil distribution and us in our horsemanship. First, set apart offerings for the gods as our priests prescribe, then choose gifts for Cyaxares."

They laughed and said they'd choose him fair women. "So be it," said Cyrus, "fair women and anything else you please. After that, make sure our friends among the Medes who followed us willingly have no reason to complain about their share. The Medes must honor our first allies, making them glad they chose us. Also, give a share to the messenger from Cyaxares and his retinue, persuading him to stay with us. Tell him I'd like him to stay and explain things better to Cyaxares. As for my Persians, we'll be content with what's left. We're used to simple living, and you'd laugh at us in grand attire, just as you will when you see us on horses or, rather, falling off them."

They left, laughing about the riding, and Cyrus called his officers to distribute the horses and gear equally among the divisions. He issued another proclamation inviting any slave from the Syrians, Assyrians, or Arabians who was a Mede, Persian, Bactrian, Carian, Cilician, Greek, or other nationality to come forward and declare themselves.

Many came forward eagerly, and Cyrus selected the strongest and fairest, told them they were now free, and would bear arms. He provided them with shields and light swords to follow the troopers, ensuring they received supplies like his own Persians. Persian officers, wearing corslets and carrying lances, were to appear on horseback, starting with himself, each appointing another Peer to lead the infantry.

IV.6

An Alliance for Vengeance
Gobryas and Cyrus

Summary

An old Assyrian prince named Gobryas visits Cyrus, seeking vengeance for his son's murder by the new Assyrian king, who is his enemy. Gobryas offers his fortress, land, tribute, and military support in exchange for Cyrus' help. Cyrus accepts, promising to avenge Gobryas' son. After their agreement, Gobryas departs, leaving a guide for Cyrus. Meanwhile, the Medes and Hyrcanians organize resources, with offerings for the gods, provisions for the campaign, and fair distribution of wealth.

A Prince's Plea: Seeking Justice for a Fallen Son

> The story illustrates the value of creating win-win deals in leadership. When Cyrus asks Gobryas what he will gain in return for avenging his son, it emphasizes the importance of mutually beneficial arrangements. Leaders who seek partnerships where both parties benefit can secure loyalty and achieve long-term success through balanced and reciprocal agreements.

While they were dealing with these matters, an old Assyrian prince named Gobryas appeared before Cyrus, riding a horse with a group of mounted soldiers behind him, all armed as cavalry. The Persian officers assigned to collect the weapons asked them to hand over their lances to be burned with the rest, but Gobryas said he wanted to see Cyrus first. So the adjutants brought him in, but made his escort stay where they were.

When the old man stood before Cyrus, he immediately began to speak: "My lord, I am an Assyrian by birth; I have a strong fortress in my land, and I rule over a large domain; I command two thousand three hundred cavalry, all of whom I offered to the king of Assyria; if he ever had a friend, it was me. But he has fallen by your hands, a brave man, and his son, who is my worst enemy, now reigns in his place. So I have come to you, begging at your feet. I am ready to be your servant and ally, and I beg you to avenge me. You yourself will be like a son to me, for I have no male children left.

The son I had, my only son, was beautiful and brave, my lord, and loved and honored me as a father wishes to be loved. The king, my old master, sent for my son, intending to give him his daughter in marriage; and I let my boy go, with high hopes and a proud heart, thinking he would return as the king's son-in-law. The prince, who is now king, invited him to go hunting, and challenged him to do his best, thinking he was the better horseman. They hunted together as friends, and when a bear appeared, they both chased it. The king's son threw his javelin but missed, while my son threw his and killed the bear.

The prince was deeply hurt but hid his anger. Soon after, they chased a lion, and again the prince missed, but my son hit it and killed it, proudly saying, 'See, I have shot twice and killed both times!' This made the prince so jealous that he grabbed a spear from one of his followers and killed my son, my only son, my beloved, taking his life.

I, who thought to welcome a bridegroom, instead carried home a corpse. I, an old man, buried my son, who had just begun to grow a beard, my brave, well-loved boy. His killer acted as if he had killed an enemy, showing no remorse, and offered no honor to my son's memory. Yet his own father pitied me and shared my grief.

If my old master were still alive, I would never have come to you to harm him; I received many kindnesses from him and did many services for him. But now that his kingdom has passed to my son's murderer, I can never be loyal to him, and he could never see me as a friend. He knows how I feel about him and how I now live in mourning, growing old in loneliness and sorrow.

If you can take me in and give me hope of avenging my son, I would feel young again, I wouldn't be ashamed to live, and when I die, it would not be in utter misery."

Cyrus replied: "Gobryas, if your heart is truly with us as you say, I accept you as my suppliant, and with the help of the gods, I promise to avenge your son. But tell me," he added, "if we do this for you, and allow you to keep your fortress, land, arms, and power, how will you serve us in return?"

The old man replied: "My fortress will be yours whenever you visit; the tribute I used to pay to Assyria will be paid to you; and whenever you go to war, I will join you with my men. I also have a daughter, a beloved maiden ready for marriage; I once thought she would marry the current king, but she begged me not to give her to her brother's murderer, and I agreed. Now, I will place her in your hands, to treat as I will treat you."

So Cyrus said, "On the faith that you have spoken truly and with sincere intent, I take your hand and give you mine; let the gods be witnesses." After this, Cyrus allowed the old man to leave in peace without surrendering his weapons, and then asked how far away he lived, saying, "I plan to visit you." Gobryas replied, "If you leave early tomorrow, you can stay with us the next day."

With that, Gobryas departed, leaving a guide for Cyrus.

Then the Medes presented themselves; they had set aside offerings for the gods as the Persian priests directed, and they had chosen for Cyrus the finest of all the tents and a lady from Susa, said to be the most beautiful woman in all Asia, along with two highly skilled singing girls. The second-best choice was for Cyaxares, and they took for themselves all they needed for the campaign, since there was plenty of everything.

The Hyrcanians had what they wanted too and shared equally with the messenger from Cyaxares. The remaining tents were given to Cyrus for his Persians; and the coined money was collected and divided as soon as it was all gathered.

BOOK V

The Decision to
March Against Babylon

V.1

The Influence of Emotions and the Importance of Self-Discipline

Summary

Cyrus and his troops set up camp in Assyria after capturing the Assyrian army. He asks loyal guards to protect the portion of the spoils set aside for Cyaxares and generously offers his own share to those who would enjoy it most. A Mede asks for one of the singing girls, and Cyrus gladly gives her to him. Cyrus assigns his childhood friend Araspas to guard a noble lady from Susa, whose husband is away on a mission in Bactria. Araspas describes the lady's extraordinary beauty, but Cyrus avoids seeing her to remain focused on his duties. Despite Araspas's belief that love is voluntary, he eventually falls in love with the lady. Cyrus then reassures his allies and Medes, expressing his gratitude and commitment, and they vow to stay and follow him.

Controlling one's Emotions

> Emotions can influence judgment and behavior. Leaders avoid getting emotionally involved. They need self-discipline to remain focused on one's duties and responsibilities and avoid emotional distractions. Cyrus doesn't want to see the beautify Panthea, to avoid distraction.

These were the actions they took and the words they spoke. Then Cyrus asked them to guard the portion chosen for Cyaxares, picking those most loyal to their lord. He said, "I gladly accept what you have given me, but I want those who would enjoy it the most to use it."

One of the Medes, who loved music, said, "Cyrus, last night I listened to the singing girls you now own. If you give me one, I would prefer being on this campaign to staying at home."

Cyrus replied, "I'll gladly give her to you. I'm more thankful you asked than you are for receiving, as I am eager to please you all."

So, this man took his prize. Then Cyrus called Araspas the Mede, his childhood friend. Cyrus had given him a Median cloak when he returned to Persia from his grandfather's court. Now, he asked Araspas to take care of the tent and the lady from Susa. [*Editor's note: Although the author doesn't mention her name here, we'll see that this lady is the beautiful Panthea.*]

She was the wife of Abradatas, a Susian. When the Assyrian army was captured, her husband was away on a mission to Bactria for his master, who was a friend of the Bactrian king. Cyrus asked Araspas to guard the lady until her husband could take her back.

Araspas replied, "Have you seen the lady you want me to guard?"

"No, I haven't," said Cyrus.

"But I have," said Araspas. "I saw her when we chose her for you. At first, we didn't notice her in the tent as she sat on the ground with her maids, dressed like them. But when we looked closely, we saw she stood out, even though she was veiled and looking down.

"When we asked her to stand, all her maids stood with her. We saw she was taller, nobler, and more graceful than the others, and her beauty shone through her simple clothes. We saw big tears falling from her veil to her feet.

"One of us said, 'Take comfort, lady. Your husband was brave and handsome, but we've chosen a man who is just as good in looks, mind, and power; we believe Cyrus is more admirable than anyone, and you will be his from now on.' But when she heard that, she tore her veil and cried, while her maids wept with her.

"We saw her face, neck, and arms, and I tell you, Cyrus, I and all who saw her thought there was no woman in Asia as beautiful as she. You must see her yourself."

"I shouldn't," said Cyrus, "if she's as beautiful as you say."

"Why not?" asked the young man.

"Because," said Cyrus, "if her beauty convinces me to see her today when I'm very busy, I fear I'd neglect my duties to gaze at her forever."

The young man laughed and said, "Do you think beauty can make a man do wrong against his will? If beauty worked that way, everyone would feel its power equally.

"Fire burns everyone equally because that's its nature, but beauty is different; one person loves it, another doesn't, and not everyone loves the same thing. Love is voluntary; people love what they choose. Brothers don't love their sisters that way, nor fathers their daughters. Respect and law control passion.

"But if a law said, 'Don't eat and you won't starve; don't drink and you won't thirst; cold won't bite in winter nor heat inflame in summer,' we couldn't follow it because we naturally feel these needs. Love is voluntary; people love what they choose, just like they choose clothes or shoes."

"Then," said Cyrus, "if love is voluntary, why can't someone stop loving when they want to? I've seen people in love, suffering and enslaved by those they love, wishing to be free but unable to escape. They are like slaves, doing anything for their beloved, even when it doesn't make sense. They don't try to run away but guard their 'tyrants' so they don't leave."

The young man replied, "True, some are like that, but they are worthless scamps. Though they wish to die to end their misery and have many ways to escape life, they don't. These people are ready to steal but aren't forced to; they choose to, and we blame them, not pity them. Beautiful people don't force others to love them; it's the scoundrels who lack self-control and blame love. Honorable men, even if they desire gold, fine horses, or beautiful women, don't take them against their principles.

"I've seen this lady, and she's very beautiful, but here I am, still your trooper, doing my duty."

"I don't deny it," said Cyrus, "but you probably left in time. Love takes a while to seize someone. You can touch fire briefly and not get burned; it takes time to catch. That's why I avoid playing with fire or looking at beauty. If you listen to me, don't let your eyes linger on her too long; beauty can ignite love from afar."

"Don't worry," said the young man, "I could look forever and not do anything dishonorable."

"Good answer," said Cyrus. "Guard her well. She might be useful to us all one day."

With that, they parted. But after seeing the lady's beauty and grace every day, and thinking she noticed his care, and her attendants attending to his needs, love took over his heart. It wasn't surprising.

Meanwhile, Cyrus wanted the Medes and allies to stay willingly, so he called their leaders and spoke:

"Medes and gentlemen, I know you didn't join me for money or to serve Cyaxares; you came for me. You marched with me at night and faced danger to honor me. I am grateful for your kindness, but I can't repay you now. I won't say, 'If you stay, I'll repay you,' as it would sound like bribery. Instead, even if you leave today, I'll still honor you and remember you in my good fortune.

"I can't leave; I promised the Hyrcanians, and I won't betray them. I am also bound to Gobryas, who offered us his resources, and I won't make him regret it. Most importantly, I respect the gods too much to abandon the blessings they've given us. This is my duty; you must decide yours and tell me."

The first to speak was a Mede who had claimed kinship with Cyrus. "Listen to me, king! For king I see you as by nature; like the bee king whom all bees follow willingly. Wherever he goes, they follow, never leaving him, wanting his rule. Our men feel the same for you. When you left for Persia, we all wanted to follow until Astyages stopped us. When you returned for aid, we saw your friends flock to you. When you started this campaign, the Medes joined you eagerly.

"Now we feel safe in enemy lands with you, but without you, we'd fear returning home. Others will speak for themselves, but I and my men will stand by you. We won't tire of your company and will endure your benefits."

Then Tigranes said, "Don't be surprised, Cyrus, if I'm silent. My soul is ready to follow your commands."

The Hyrcanian chieftain said, "If the Medes leave today, it must be some evil force, as no one would retreat when the enemy is fleeing and surrendering, especially with such a great leader who serves us so selflessly."

The Medes cried, "You led us out, Cyrus, and you must lead us home when the time comes."

Cyrus prayed aloud, "O mighty Zeus, help me to be more generous and kinder to my friends."

Then he ordered the rest of the army to set up outposts and take care of their own matters, while the Persians took their tents and divided them among their cavalry and infantry. They arranged for stewards to bring what they needed and groom their horses so they could focus on the war. That's how they spent the day.

V.2

The March to Gobryas' Fortress
A Test of Loyalty and Strategy

Summary

Cyrus leads his army to Gobryas' fortress, where they find it well-defended and stocked with supplies. Gobryas invites Cyrus inside, offering him riches and his daughter's hand in marriage in exchange for avenging his son's death. Cyrus accepts the gifts as a dowry for Gobryas' daughter and promises to seek justice. They plan a march towards Babylon, considering alliances with other enemies of the Assyrians. Gobryas shares the cruelty of the Assyrian king, and Cyrus strategizes to confront Babylon directly. The chapter highlights themes of loyalty, honor, and military strategy.

Trust and Loyalty

A leader must build and maintain trust and loyalty among their followers. Cyrus demonstrates this by keeping his promises to Gobryas, reinforcing their faith in his leadership. Trust is crucial for securing alliances and motivating people to support the leader's vision and goals. Loyalty fosters a strong, cohesive team ready to face challenges together.

The next day, they started their journey to Gobryas. Cyrus rode at the front with his new Persian cavalry, which had two thousand riders, followed by more troops carrying shields and swords, and the rest of the army marched behind them. The cavalry were instructed to make sure their attendants knew they would be punished if they fell behind the rear-guard, went ahead of the group, or strayed to the sides.

By the evening of the second day, they reached Gobryas' castle. They saw it was very strong and prepared for a serious defense. They also noticed large herds of cattle and many flocks of sheep and goats gathered near the castle walls for protection.

Gobryas sent a message to Cyrus, asking him to look around and find the easiest way to approach the castle. He also asked Cyrus to send his most trusted Persians inside the fortress to see what was inside and report back.

Cyrus, wanting to check if the citadel could be attacked if Gobryas turned out to be untrustworthy, rode around the walls and found them strong everywhere. The messengers who went inside returned, saying there were enough supplies to last a generation.

Gobryas' Offer and Cyrus's Response

While Cyrus was thinking about this, Gobryas came out with all his men, bringing wine, corn, barley, and driving oxen, goats, and pigs—enough to feed the whole army. His stewards started distributing the supplies and serving a feast. Gobryas then invited Cyrus to enter the castle now that the garrison had left, taking any precautions he thought necessary. Cyrus agreed and sent scouts and a strong detachment in before entering the palace himself. Once inside, he opened the gates and called for his friends and officers.

When they joined him, Gobryas brought out golden cups, pitchers, goblets, ornaments, and countless gold coins, along with many beautiful things. Finally, he brought out his daughter, tall and fair, still mourning her brother. Gobryas said to Cyrus, "I give you all these riches and my daughter, to deal with as you see fit. We ask you to avenge my son and her brother."

Cyrus replied, "I promised before that if you were loyal to me, I would avenge you, and today I renew that promise to your daughter. With God's help, I will fulfill it. As for these gifts," he added, "I accept them and give them as a dowry for your daughter and whoever marries her. But I will take only one precious thing with me, something so valuable that if I traded it for all the wealth in the world, I wouldn't be as happy."

Gobryas wondered what this rare thing could be, thinking it might be his daughter. "What is it, my lord?" he asked. Cyrus answered, "A man may hate injustice and lies, but if no one offers him great wealth or power or beautiful children, he can't show what kind of man he really is. You have given me everything today: this fortress, treasures, your power, and your worthy daughter. This shows everyone that I cannot betray my friend or act unrighteously for wealth. This is your gift to me, and as long as I am known as a just man, I will never forget it and will repay you with honor."

"Do not doubt," he added, "that you will find a worthy husband for your daughter. Among my friends, there are many good men, and one of them will marry her. They will not admire you more because of your gifts, but they will envy me and hope to prove their loyalty to their friends and never yield to enemies. They would never sacrifice virtue for wealth. This is the nature of some of the men here."

Gobryas smiled. "By heaven, show me these men, and I would ask you for one as my son-in-law." Cyrus said, "You will see them yourself; follow us, and you will recognize them."

Strategic Decisions and Preparation

With these words, he clasped Gobryas' hand and left, his men behind him. Though Gobryas urged him to stay and eat in the citadel, Cyrus preferred to have his meal in the camp and invited Gobryas to join them. There, lying on a couch of leaves, he asked Gobryas, "Tell me, who has the largest store of coverlets, you or each of us?" The Assyrian replied, "You have more than I, more coverlets, more couches, and a larger dwelling-place, for your home is earth and heaven, and every nook can be a bed, and your coverlets are the brushwood and grass of hills and plains."

However, when the meal began, Gobryas saw the poverty of what was served and thought his own men were more generous. But his mood changed as he saw the grace and decorum of the Persians. Not a single trained Persian gaped, snatched at the food, or was so absorbed in eating that they ignored everything else. They prided themselves on showing their good sense and intelligence while eating, just as a perfect rider handles his horse with composure. They believed getting flustered over food and drink was swinish and beastly.

Gobryas also noticed that they only asked pleasant questions and jested kindly. Their mirth was free from rudeness and vulgarity. He was most impressed by their belief that on a campaign, since everyone faced the same danger, no one deserved a larger share than anyone else. They thought it was perfect to ensure their comrades were well-fed for fighting.

When Gobryas got up to leave, he said, "I understand now, Cyrus, why we have more gold, goblets, and wealth, but we are not as valuable as you. We always try to increase our possessions, but you focus on perfecting your souls."

Cyrus replied, "My friend, be here tomorrow with all your cavalry in full armor so we can see your power, and then lead us through your country, showing us who is hostile and who is friendly."

They parted, each attending to their own concerns. The next day, Gobryas appeared with his cavalry and led the way. Cyrus, as a true general, not only supervised the march but also looked for chances to weaken the enemy and strengthen his own forces. He called for the Hyrcanian chief and Gobryas, the two he thought could give him the information he needed.

"My friends," he said, "I think it's right to trust your loyalty and consult you about the campaign. You, even more than I, must ensure the Assyrians do not overpower us. If I fail, I might find a way to escape. But if the king wins, I see nothing but hostility for you."

His companions agreed, saying they understood the facts and were deeply concerned about the outcome.

Cyrus then asked, "Does the king think you alone are his enemies, or do you know of others who hate him too?" The Hyrcanian replied, "The Cadousians are his bitterest foes, and they are numerous and warlike. The Sakians, our neighbors, also hate him because he tried to subdue them."

Cyrus asked, "Do you think they would join us in attacking him?" The Hyrcanian said, "They would be glad to, if they could." "What stops them?" Cyrus asked. "The Assyrians themselves, among whom we are now marching," they replied.

Cyrus turned to Gobryas and asked, "What about the current king? Didn't you say he was very insolent?" Gobryas confirmed, saying the king had given him reason to think so. Cyrus asked, "Did he treat only you this way, or did others suffer too?"

Gobryas explained that many others suffered, but he would mention one young man whose father was more important than Gobryas and who was a friend of the prince. At a drinking party, the king had the young man seized and mutilated because someone praised the boy's beauty and envied his bride. The king now claims it was because the young man tried to seduce his paramour. That young man, now a eunuch, leads his province since his father died.

Cyrus asked, "Do you think he would welcome us if he knew we came to help him?" Gobryas was sure of it but said it was hard to reach him because they would have to march past Babylon.

Cyrus asked, "What's the problem with that?" Gobryas exclaimed, "Babylon can send out an army ten thousand times larger than yours. That's why the Assyrians are less prompt now, because those who have seen your army think it's small and have spread the word. So, I think it would be better to advance carefully."

Cyrus listened and replied, "You are right to urge caution, Gobryas. But I believe the safest route is to march directly to Babylon, the center of the enemy's strength. If they cannot find us and think we disappeared out of fear, their courage will grow. But if we march on, we will find them still mourning their dead, nursing their wounds, and trembling at our daring and their own defeat.

Leading by Example

"Men with courage are unstoppable, but when they lose heart, their numbers make panic worse. Fear spreads among them, growing so great that no leader can calm it or restore confidence. If victory goes to those with the largest numbers, we are in danger. But if battles are won by the quality of the fighters, then take heart. We have more fight in us than they do.

"Our enemies are fewer and weaker than when they fled from us, while we are stronger and more numerous with your men joining us. In the company of conquerors, the hearts of followers are lifted. Remember, the enemy sees us, and seeing us advance will be more alarming than if we wait here. Lead us straight to Babylon."

The March Toward Babylon
Strategies and Alliances

Summary

Cyrus and his troops continue their march, entering Assyrian territory. After raiding the land and gathering spoils, Cyrus proposes giving the surplus to Gobryas, who has been generous to them. Cyrus then sends Gobryas to deliver a message to the Assyrian king, who replies with hostility. Planning a secret alliance, Cyrus collaborates with Gobryas and Gadatas to infiltrate and capture a strategic fortress. As the Assyrian king prepares to retaliate, Cyrus organizes a rapid response to support Gadatas. With meticulous planning and efficient coordination, Cyrus advances his forces towards Babylon, demonstrating strategic brilliance and fostering solid alliances.

Strategic Collaboration and Detailed Planning

Your enemy's enemies may become your friends. Cyrus' actions highlight the importance of strategic collaboration and meticulous planning. By recognizing the enemies of his enemy, Cyrus leverages their hatred of the Assyrian king to form valuable alliances with Gobryas and Gadatas. This demonstrates effective leadership in identifying and utilizing common interests to achieve shared goals. In the business world consider partnering with your main competitor's competitors in pertinent markets or industries.

Entering Enemy Territory

And so the march continued, and on the fourth day, they reached the edge of Gobryas' territory. Since they were now in enemy land, Cyrus changed his formation, taking the infantry under his command with some cavalry to support them, and sending the rest of the mounted troops to scout the area. Their orders were to kill anyone with weapons and drive in the rest, along with all the cattle they could find. The Persians were ordered to join in the raid, and while some came back empty-handed, others brought a lot of loot.

When all the spoils were gathered, Cyrus called the officers of the Medes, the Hyrcanians, and his own Persian leaders, and said:

"My friends, Gobryas has treated us generously and given us many good things. What do you think? After we set aside the usual portion for the gods and a fair share for the army, should we give the rest to him? Wouldn't it be a noble gesture, showing that we want to outdo those who do good to us?"

Everyone agreed enthusiastically, and an officer stood up and said:

"Absolutely, Cyrus, let's do it. I feel that Gobryas might have thought we were poor because we didn't have gold coins or drink from golden cups. But if we do this, he will see that people can be generous without needing gold."

"Alright," said Cyrus, "let's pay the priests, take what the army needs, and then call Gobryas and give him the rest."

So they took what they needed and gave all the remaining spoils to Gobryas.

Gobryas' Message to the Assyrian King

Cyrus then marched towards Babylon, his troops ready for battle. But since the Assyrians didn't come out to meet them, he told Gobryas to ride ahead and deliver this message:

"If the king will come out to fight for his land, I, Gobryas, will fight for him, but if he won't defend his own country, we must surrender to the conquerors."

Gobryas rode just far enough to deliver the message safely. The king sent back a messenger with this reply:

"Your master says to you: 'I regret not killing you when I killed your son. Now, if you want to fight, come back in thirty days. We are not ready yet; we are still preparing.'"

Gobryas replied:

"May your regret never end! I have started to make you suffer since the day you began to regret."

Gobryas brought the king's message back to Cyrus, and Cyrus led his army away, then called Gobryas and said:

"You told me that the eunuch made by the king would be on our side, right?"

"And I am sure he will be," answered Gobryas, "for we have spoken freely many times."

Planning a Secret Alliance

"Then," said Cyrus, "you must go to him when the time is right. Make sure only he knows what he intends, and if he truly wants to be our friend, keep it secret. In war, a man can do his friends more good by pretending to be hostile, or harm his enemies by pretending to be friendly."

"Yes," answered Gobryas, "I know that Gadatas would pay a great price to punish the king of Assyria. But we need to consider what he can do best."

"Tell me," rejoined Cyrus, "you mentioned an outpost built to protect Assyria from the Hyrcanians and Sakians. Could the eunuch be admitted there by the commandant if he came with a force?"

"Certainly," said Gobryas, "if he were as trusted as he is today."

"And he would be trusted," Cyrus continued, "if I attacked his strongholds seriously, and he repelled me forcefully. I could capture some of his men, and he could capture some of mine or some of my messengers sent to those you say are enemies of Assyria. These prisoners would say they were fetching an army to attack the fortress, and the eunuch, hearing their story, could pretend to warn the commandant."

"Undoubtedly," said Gobryas, "if things went that way, the commandant would admit him and even ask him to stay until you withdrew."

"And then," Cyrus added, "once inside the walls, he could give the place to us?"

"We may suppose so," said Gobryas. "He would handle things inside, while you pressured from outside."

"Then go at once," said Cyrus, "and teach him his part. When everything is arranged, come back to me, and offer him the same trust you received from us."

Gobryas hurried away, and the eunuch welcomed him gladly, agreeing to everything and helping to plan. Gobryas returned with news that the eunuch was ready, so Cyrus made his pretended attack the next day and was driven off.

Cyrus' Strategy and the Fortress

But Cyrus also captured a fortress indicated by Gadatas. The messengers he had sent, with specific instructions, fell into Gadatas' hands. Some were allowed to escape to fetch troops and scaling ladders, while the rest were questioned in front of many witnesses. When Gadatas heard their mission, he prepared and set out at night to deliver the news.

He entered the fortress trusted and welcomed as a savior, and for a while, he helped the commandant. But as soon as Cyrus appeared, he took the place with the help of the Persian prisoners he had taken.

Once the fortress was secured, Gadatas went out to Cyrus, bowed, and said, "Cyrus, may joy be yours!"

"Joy is mine already," answered Cyrus, "for you, with God's help, have brought it to me. I value this fortress greatly and am glad to leave it with our allies. And for you, Gadatas, remember that even if the Assyrian has taken away your ability to have children, he hasn't taken your power to make friends. You have made us your friends with this deed, and we will support you as faithfully as sons and grandsons."

So Cyrus spoke. At that moment, the Hyrcanian chief, who had just learned what happened, came running up, grabbed Cyrus' hand, and exclaimed:

"O Cyrus, you are a godsend to your friends! How often I thank the gods for bringing me to you!"

"Then," said Cyrus, "take this fortress and use it well for your nation, our allies, and especially for Gadatas, our friend who won it and gives it to us."

"Once the Cadousians, Sakians, and my people arrive," said the chieftain, "we should call a council to discuss how best to use it."

Cyrus agreed, and when they met, they decided to garrison the post with a combined force from all the allies to keep it friendly and as a bulwark against Assyria.

This decision boosted everyone's enthusiasm, leading the Cadousians to send 20,000 light infantry and 4,000 cavalry, the Sakians 11,000 bowmen, 10,000 on foot and 1,000 mounted, and the Hyrcanians all their reserve infantry and 2,000 cavalry. Previously, most of their cavalry had been left home to support the Cadousians and Sakians against Assyria.

While Cyrus organized everything in the fortress, many Assyrians from the surrounding area brought in their horses and handed over their arms, fearing their neighbors.

Soon after, Gadatas came to Cyrus, saying that messengers reported the Assyrian king was furious about the fortress and preparing to attack his territory. "If you allow me, Cyrus," said Gadatas, "I will try to save my fortresses. The rest is less important."

Cyrus asked, "If you go now, when will you reach home?" Gadatas replied, "In three days, I can have dinner at my house." Cyrus asked, "Do you think the Assyrian will already be there?" Gadatas answered, "Yes, he will hurry while he thinks you are far away."

"And I," said Cyrus, "when could I reach your home with my army?" Gadatas answered, "With your large army, it would take six or seven days."

"Then go quickly," Cyrus said, "and I will follow as fast as I can."

Gadatas left, and Cyrus called all the allied officers, a noble and brave group. Cyrus stood up and said:

"Gentlemen, Gadatas has done deeds worthy of great reward, even before he received anything from us. The Assyrians are now attacking his territory, seeking revenge for the harm they think he has done. They likely believe that if those who join us escape punishment, while their supporters are destroyed, they will lose all their allies.

"Today, we have a chance to do a great deed by rescuing Gadatas, our friend and benefactor. It is just and right to repay his kindness. Additionally, it is in our interest. If people see we repay kindness and punish enemies, many will want to be our friends, and none will want to be our foes.

"But if we abandon Gadatas, how can we expect anyone to help us? How can we respect ourselves? How can we face Gadatas if we, so many and so strong, are less generous than he, one man in a difficult situation?"

Everyone agreed enthusiastically, saying it must be done.

"Alright," said Cyrus, "since we all agree, let each of us choose an escort for our wagons and pack animals. We'll leave them behind with Gobryas in charge. He knows the roads and is skilled. We will advance with our strongest men and horses, carrying three days' provisions. The lighter our gear, the better we'll travel, eat, and sleep on the road.

"Let's arrange the march order. Chrysantas, you lead with your cuirassiers since the road is broad and smooth. Put your brigadiers in the first line, each regiment in file. Close order will make us faster and safer.

"The cuirassiers are our heaviest troops, and if they lead, the lighter troops can follow easily. If the fastest lead at night, the column may fall apart. The vanguard often runs ahead.

"Behind the cuirassiers, Artabazas will follow with the Persian targeteers and bowmen. Then Andamyas the Mede with the Median infantry, Embas and the Armenian infantry, Artouchas with the Hyrcanians, Thambradas with the Sakian foot, and finally Datamas with the Cadousians. Officers will place brigadiers in the first line, targeteers on the right, and bowmen on the left of their squares for best use.

"All baggage-bearers follow in the rear. Officers must ensure everything is ready before sleeping, be on time in the morning, and maintain order on the march.

"Supporting the baggage train will be Madatas the Persian with the Persian cavalry, each regiment in single file. Behind them, Rambacas the Mede and his cavalry, then Tigranes and his men, and the other cavalry leaders. The Sakians follow, and last are the Cadousians with Alkeunas in command, making sure no one falls behind.

"All of you, officers and soldiers, must march in silence. At night, ears are more important than eyes for guidance and information. Any confusion at night is worse than by day and harder to fix. So, maintain silence and order.

"When you plan to rise before dawn, make the night-watches short and numerous so no one suffers from a long vigil before the march. When it's time to start, blow the horn. I expect you all to be ready with everything you need on the road to Babylon, and as each detachment starts, pass the word to those behind."

The officers went to their quarters, talking about Cyrus and his amazing memory, always naming each officer as he assigned their post. Cyrus took special care in this, thinking it odd that a mechanic or physician could name all their tools, but a general couldn't name his officers, the tools he depended on in battle or to inspire and honor.

He believed that personally knowing his men made them more eager to perform noble deeds and avoid disgrace. Cyrus thought it foolish to give orders like "Someone fetch water" or "Someone split wood," where everyone looks at everyone else and no one acts. By naming officers, he ensured responsibility and action.

The army had supper, posted guards, prepared, and rested. At midnight, the horn blew. Cyrus had told Chrysantas he would wait ahead on the road, so he went with his staff and waited until Chrysantas appeared with the cuirassiers. Cyrus gave him the guides, told him to march slowly until receiving a message, as not all troops were on the road yet. Cyrus then took his position, hurrying each division forward and sending messengers to those still behind. Once all were moving, he sent riders to Chrysantas, telling him to advance quickly.

Cyrus then rode to the front, watching the ranks pass. When a division advanced silently and orderly, he complimented them. If there was confusion, he inquired and restored order.

One last precaution: he sent a small, elite infantry group ahead to keep Chrysantas in sight. They were to use their wits and report any concerns to Chrysantas, avoiding unnecessary alarms.

They marched through the night. At dawn, Cyrus ordered most of the cavalry to the front, keeping the Cadousians with their infantry at the rear, needing cavalry support too. The rest of the horsemen went ahead to face the enemy first. In battle, he wanted them ready, and if the enemy fled, he wanted to pursue quickly. He always designated who should chase and who should stay with him, never breaking up the whole army.

Cyrus led the advance, constantly moving, supervising everything, and addressing any issues. Thus, Cyrus and his men marched forward.

[Editor's note: "Assyrians" used here by Xenophon most likely refers to Assyrians as an ethnicity of the ruling powers in that territory, which included the Neo-Assyrian Empire and later the Neo-Babylonian also known as Chaldean Empire, and not the Assyrian dynasty. Babylon was a significant city under the control of these empires. The Assyrian king mentioned in the text would not be a king of the Assyrian dynasty, rather the one who have had authority over Babylon and its surrounding territories at the time of Cyrus' conquests.]

Ambush and Loyalty
The Rescue of Gadatas

Summary

An influential officer in Gadatas' cavalry, seeing his master rebel against Assyria, betrays him by informing the Assyrian king of Gadatas' movements, hoping to gain his possessions. The Assyrians set an ambush, and Gadatas falls into it but is wounded, not killed, and flees towards Cyrus' advancing army. Cyrus confronts the Assyrian forces, routing them and saving Gadatas. Cyrus then cares for the wounded and addresses his troops, emphasizing the need for communication and coordinated action. Gadatas expresses gratitude to Cyrus, offering him gifts and support. Cyrus plans a strategic retreat to avoid Babylon's walls, maintaining order and safety. Ultimately, Cyrus' careful planning and alliances allow him to capture and secure key Assyrian fortresses.

Supporting and Showing Compassion to Allies

Leaders must support their allies, especially when they face internal betrayal or external threats. Cyrus' swift action to rescue Gadatas from the Assyrian ambush demonstrates the importance of standing by allies in times of need. Furthermore, his visit to the wounded Gadatas, showing genuine concern and empathy, highlights the significance of personal connections and compassion in leadership. By protecting and supporting allies, leaders reinforce trust and loyalty within their alliances, ensuring a united and motivated team ready to face challenges together.

There was a powerful officer in the cavalry with Gadatas who, when he saw his master had rebelled against Assyria, thought to himself, "If anything happens to him, I can get all his possessions from the king."

So, he sent a trusted man to find the Assyrian army in Gadatas' territory and tell the king that he could capture Gadatas and all his followers if he made an ambush. The messenger was also to report the strength of Gadatas' forces and to mention that Cyrus was not with him. The officer also revealed the road Gadatas would take. To gain more trust, he sent word to his own people to surrender the castle he commanded in the province to the Assyrian king, along with all it contained, promising to join them himself if he could, or at least to remain loyal to the king.

The messenger rode quickly, met the king, and delivered the message. The king took over the castle and set an ambush with many horsemen and chariots in a group of villages along the road.

When Gadatas approached, he sent scouts ahead. Seeing them, the king ordered a few chariots and horsemen to flee as if they were a small, frightened group. The scouts chased them, signaled to Gadatas, who also pursued them, falling into the trap.

The Assyrians sprang from their ambush when Gadatas was within reach. Gadatas' men, seeing the trap, turned and fled with the Assyrians chasing them. The officer who planned it all stabbed Gadatas in the shoulder, but it wasn't a fatal blow. The traitor then fled to the pursuers and joined the Assyrian king, riding alongside him.

Naturally, the men with slower horses were caught by those better mounted, and the fugitives, exhausted from their journey, were near defeat when they saw Cyrus advancing with his army and found safety, as relieved as shipwrecked sailors reaching port.

At first, Cyrus was astonished but quickly understood the situation. The whole Assyrian cavalry was charging at him, and he met them with his army in perfect order, causing the enemy to flee. Cyrus then ordered his troops to charge while he followed at a safer pace.

The enemy was completely routed: many chariots were captured, some without drivers, others surrounded by Persian cavalry. The officer who attacked Gadatas was among the fallen.

The Assyrian infantry besieging Gadatas' fortress escaped to a stronghold that had revolted from him or reached a significant city where the king and his horsemen had taken refuge.

After this, Cyrus went to Gadatas' territory, ordered the guards for the prisoners, and visited the wounded Gadatas, who came out bandaged. Cyrus said, "I came to see how you were."

Gadatas replied, "I came out to see a man with a soul like yours. I don't know why you helped me as you did, for I had done nothing for you personally. You saved me from death to life just because I had been of some small service to your friends. If I had a son, I don't know if he could be as true a friend as you."

Cyrus answered, "You have overlooked a more wonderful thing, Gadatas."

Gadatas asked, "What could that be?"

"That all these Persians, Medes, Hyrcanians, Armenians, Sakians, and Cadousians are so eager to help you," said Cyrus.

Gadatas prayed aloud, "O Father Zeus, bless them and especially him who made them what they are! Now, Cyrus, to honor these men you praise, take the gifts I bring as their host, the best I have."

He brought out supplies for everyone to make sacrifices and feast in celebration of their victory.

Meanwhile, the Cadousians, always in the rear and unable to join the pursuit, wanted to achieve something on their own. So, their leader, without telling Cyrus, led them on a raid towards Babylon. But as they scattered, the Assyrians attacked in battle order, killing the leader and many men, capturing horses and the spoil they were driving away. The Assyrian king pursued them until he felt safe and then turned back, while the Cadousians found safety in their camp, with the vanguard reaching it late in the afternoon.

Seeing what happened, Cyrus went out to meet them, helping the wounded and sending them to Gadatas for treatment, while he and his Peers helped house the others and provided what they needed. Though it was clear he was upset, he stayed with the attendants and surgeons, ensuring every wounded man was cared for.

The next day, Cyrus summoned all the officers and the Cadousian army and spoke to them:

"My friends and allies, what happened is natural; it is human to err. But we can learn from this mistake that we should never separate a weaker detachment from the main force. If you must march with a small group, communicate with someone who can bring reinforcements. That way, even if you are trapped, your friends can help you and distract the enemy. Separation doesn't mean isolation, and you can still stay united with the main force. But if you act alone, you are no better off than being alone in the field."

"God willing, we will take our revenge soon. After breakfast, we will go to the battlefield, bury our dead, and show the enemy that we are stronger. If they don't come out to fight, we will burn their villages and ravage their land. Go now and eat, but let the Cadousians elect a new leader according to their laws and bring him to me after breakfast."

They did as Cyrus ordered. When they marched out, Cyrus kept the new leader close to him to encourage his men. They buried the Cadousian dead and ravaged the country, then returned to Gadatas' province with supplies taken from the enemy.

Cyrus knew those who joined him near Babylon would suffer unless he was constantly there. So, he sent a message to the king saying he would leave the farmers alone if the Assyrian let those who joined him work in peace. "Remember," he added, "you can only hinder a few of my people, while I can allow a vast territory of yours to be cultivated. The conqueror will reap the crops in war, but if there is peace, it will be you. If any of my people fight you or yours fight me, we must defend ourselves."

When the Assyrians heard this, they urged the king to accept, and he agreed. An agreement was made: peace for the farmers, war for those carrying arms.

Cyrus also invited his supporters among the drovers to bring their herds into his territory and treated the enemy's cattle as booty. This made the campaign more attractive because they lived off the enemy's resources, which lightened the burden of war.

When it was time for Cyrus to leave, Gadatas brought him gifts from his vast estate, including a drove of horses from his own cavalry, whom he distrusted due to the conspiracy. He said, "Cyrus, I give you these horses, and remember that all I have is yours. I have no son to inherit my wealth; when I die, my house will perish with me. I swear by the gods, I have done no injustice or foul deed."

Cyrus, touched by his suffering, said, "I will take the horses and put loyal riders on them to help you and reach my goal of having 10,000 Persian cavalry. But take back the other riches and guard them until I can repay you. I would be ashamed to owe you so much."

Gadatas replied, "I trust you completely, but I cannot guard all this myself. While at peace with the king, my estate near Babylon was prosperous, benefiting from the city without its troubles. But now, with the king as an enemy, we will be attacked and live in fear, surrounded by stronger enemies. My soul couldn't bear my wrongs, so I revolted without thinking of the safest course. I was driven by the dream of vengeance against the wicked king. The king will always find worse villains to aid him, but if a nobler rival appears, he will plot against him too."

Cyrus agreed, saying, "We put a strong garrison in your fortress for safety, and you are now with us, so if the gods favor us, the king will fear you. Bring all you have that is valuable and join our march. You will be of great service to me, and I will help you."

Gadatas asked, "Can I prepare and return before you leave? I want to bring my mother."

"Yes," said Cyrus, "I will wait until you are ready."

So Gadatas, with Cyrus' help, fortified his fortress, gathered his wealth, and brought trusted servants and those he distrusted with their families to ensure loyalty.

Gadatas joined Cyrus, who kept him close to show the roads and resources. When they approached Babylon, Cyrus asked Gobryas and Gadatas if there was another way to avoid the city walls.

Gobryas said, "There are many ways, but I thought you'd want to show your army's size and strength to the king. You approached his walls with a smaller force before, and now, with a larger army, he might think he's unprepared for battle again."

Cyrus replied, "It may seem strange, but marching up to the walls with a smaller force is different from marching past with a larger one. Marching up is done in battle order, and withdrawing safely is planned. Marching past means long, unprotected lines of wagons and baggage, which weakens the fighting men and leaves gaps for the enemy to attack. Keeping distance shows our numbers and strength without exposing our weaknesses. The enemy is less likely to attack unless they think they can win, knowing retreat is difficult."

Everyone agreed with Cyrus, and Gobryas led the army safely by another route. Cyrus strengthened the rear protection as each detachment passed the city, withdrawing safely.

Marching in this order, they returned to their starting point on the Assyria-Media border. Cyrus dealt with three Assyrian fortresses: he captured the weakest by force, and the garrisons of the other two surrendered due to Gadatas' persuasion and the fear of Cyrus.

V.5

Reconciling Leadership and Authority
Cyrus and Cyaxares

Summary

Cyrus, after completing his expedition, invites Cyaxares to the camp to discuss future plans. Cyaxares feels overshadowed and insignificant compared to Cyrus' large following, causing tension between them. Cyrus reassures Cyaxares of his loyalty and recounts his efforts to support him and the Medes. Cyaxares expresses his feelings of dishonor but eventually agrees to reconcile. Their reconciliation brings joy to their followers, and Cyaxares' mood improves as his subjects present gifts, showing their respect. Cyrus focuses on the troops' needs and plans to meet with Cyaxares the next morning to discuss the campaign's future.

Managing Negative Emotions and Reassuring Team Members

Leaders must recognize and address negative emotions within their team, such as feelings of inadequacy or resentment. Cyaxares felt overshadowed and humiliated by Cyrus' success, leading to tension. Leaders need to watch for these negative feelings from peers or team members and manage them effectively. These feelings can include jealousy or resentment when leaders are successful, age-related humiliation when a younger leader outperforms a senior leader, or other insecurities. Cyrus' approach to take Cyaxares aside for an open, heartfelt conversation helped resolve these feelings and restore their relationship. Effective leaders should prioritize open communication and empathy to address and reconcile such issues, ensuring a harmonious and united leadership team.

Cyrus, having completed his expedition, sent a message to Cyaxares urging him to come to the camp to discuss the best use of the captured forts. He also suggested that Cyaxares might review the army and advise on the next steps, or, Cyrus added, "if he prefers, tell him I will come to him and set up camp there."

So, the messenger went with the message, and meanwhile, Cyrus ordered that the Assyrian tent chosen for Cyaxares be furnished as splendidly as possible. He also had the woman and the two singing-girls, who had been set aside for Cyaxares, brought to their quarters.

While they were busy with these preparations, the messenger reached Cyaxares and delivered the message. Cyaxares decided that it was best for Cyrus and his men to stay on the frontier. The forty thousand Persian bowmen and targeteers whom Cyrus had summoned had already arrived.

Watching these soldiers consume the land's resources was challenging enough, and Cyaxares thought he would rather have one group leave before receiving another. The officer in command of the Persian levy, following Cyrus' instructions, asked Cyaxares if he needed the men, and Cyaxares said he did not. Upon hearing that Cyrus had arrived, the Persian commander took his troops and went to join him.

Cyaxares himself waited until the next day and then set out with the Median troops who had stayed behind. When Cyrus heard of his approach, he took his now large Persian cavalry, all the Medes, Hyrcanians, and Armenians, and the best-mounted and best-armed from the rest, and went out to meet Cyaxares to show the power he had gained.

When Cyaxares saw such a large and splendid following with Cyrus, while his own retinue was small and modest, he felt insulted and mortified. When Cyrus dismounted and approached to greet him with a kiss, Cyaxares dismounted but turned his head away and did not kiss Cyrus, tears filling his eyes.

Demonstrating Loyalty and Building Trust

Leaders demonstrate the importance of loyalty and building trust. By clearly communicating his intentions and recounting his supportive actions, Cyrus reassures Cyaxares of his loyalty. This helps to rebuild trust and strengthen their alliance. Leaders should consistently demonstrate loyalty through their actions and maintain transparent communication to build and reinforce trust within their teams and alliances.

Seeing this, Cyrus told the others to stand aside and rest. He then took Cyaxares by the hand, led him under a grove of palm trees, and had the attendants spread Median carpets for them. He made Cyaxares sit down and then sat beside him, saying:

"Uncle, please tell me why you are angry with me. What have you seen that made you feel so bitter?"

Cyaxares replied: "Cyrus, I have always been seen as royal and of royal lineage. My father was a king, and I was considered a king. Now, I see myself here with a small and mean retinue, while you come in splendor and magnificence, followed by the retinue that was once mine and all your other forces. That would be bitter enough from an enemy, but from someone who owes me nothing but kindness, it is unbearable. I would rather be swallowed by the earth than live to see myself so low and my own kinsfolk mock me. Even my own slaves now have more power than I do; they are equipped to harm me more than I could ever repay."

Overcome by emotion, Cyaxares began to weep, so much so that Cyrus' own eyes filled with tears out of pity. After a moment of silence, Cyrus said:

"Cyaxares, what you say is not true, and your thoughts are not right if you believe that because I am here, your Medes are equipped to harm you. I understand your pain, and I will not argue whether you have cause for anger against them. But it is a grave mistake for a ruler to quarrel with all his subjects at once. Widespread anger creates unity among them against you. That's why I didn't send them back without me, fearing your wrath might harm us all. My presence here ensures safety for you. But for you to see me as your enemy is painful when I am doing everything to help you. However, let's not argue pointlessly. Let's see exactly how I have offended you. If I have harmed you, I will admit my fault. But if I haven't, will you not clear me of any wrongdoing?"

"Needs must I," answered Cyaxares.

"And if I have shown zeal in your cause and done my best for you, can I not expect some praise instead of rebuke?"

"That would be fair," said Cyaxares.

"Then," said Cyrus, "let's review what I have done from the beginning. When I became general, you saw your enemies gathering against you and asked Persia for help, praying that I come myself if possible. Didn't I come with the best and bravest I could bring?"

"You did indeed," answered Cyaxares.

"Tell me, did you see any wrong in this? Was it not a service and a kind act?"

"It was kind," said Cyaxares.

"After the enemy came and we had to fight, did you ever see me avoid toil or danger?"

"No," said Cyaxares, "quite the opposite."

"And when, with heaven's help, we won and the enemy retreated, I asked you to pursue them together, to take vengeance and win the spoils together. Did you see any self-seeking in this?"

Cyaxares was silent. Cyrus continued, "If you don't want to answer that, tell me if you felt wronged because when you thought pursuit unsafe, I took the risk and only asked for some of your cavalry? If asking for that was wrong, you must prove it to me."

Cyaxares still kept silent. Cyrus said, "If you won't answer that, tell me if it was wrong when you said you didn't want to stop your Medes' merry-making and send them into danger. Was it wrong for me to ask that those who wished could follow me? And when I got your permission, I persuaded some to join me. Was that wrong?"

"If accepting your gifts is blameworthy, then what is not?" Cyrus asked. "Since we started, have I done anything in secret? Haven't we taken the enemy's camp and killed many of your attackers? Haven't we captured horses and arms and brought the spoils to you or your subjects? Isn't your country growing great and your enemy's land brought low? Are your strongholds not in your power, and your lands restored to you?"

Cyrus paused, and Cyaxares replied, "To call what you have done evil is impossible. But your benefits feel like burdens. I would rather have made my country great by my own power than see it exalted by you. Your deeds are your glory, but they bring dishonor to me. I would rather have given you wealth than receive it from you. Goods given this way leave me poorer. And for my subjects, I suffer more seeing their debt to you. Imagine being in my place. Suppose a friend made your dogs fonder of him than you. Would you be pleased? Or if a friend made your followers prefer him over you, would you be grateful? Or if a friend won your wife's love more than you, would you rejoice? Wouldn't you see it as a great wrong? Now, imagine a friend making your Persians follow him instead of you. Would you call him a friend or a worse enemy than if he killed a thousand of your men?"

Cyaxares continued, "You let me take what I wanted, and you took my power, leaving me desolate. You bring the spoils grandly to my feet, making my country great with my own forces while I have no part in it. I must step in at the end, like a woman, to receive your favors, while in the eyes of all, you are the man, and I am not fit to wear a crown. Are these the deeds of a benefactor? If you were kind as you are kin, you wouldn't rob me of my dignity and honor. What good are broad lands if I am dishonored? I ruled the Medes not because I was stronger, but because they thought our race better."

Cyrus broke in, saying, "Uncle, if I have ever shown you kindness, be kind to me now. Don't blame me anymore. Put me to the test and see how I feel towards you. If my actions have brought you good, then call me your benefactor. If not, blame me as you please."

"Perhaps you are right," answered Cyaxares. "I will do as you wish."

"Then I may kiss you?" said Cyrus.

"Yes, if it pleases you."

"And you will not turn aside as you did just now?"

"No, I will not turn aside."

And he kissed him.

When the Medes, Persians, and all the allies saw this, they were filled with joy. Cyrus and Cyaxares mounted their horses and rode back, with the Medes falling in behind Cyaxares at Cyrus' nod and the Persians behind Cyrus, followed by the others.

When they reached the camp, they brought Cyaxares to the splendid tent, and the appointed attendants made everything ready for him. While waiting for the banquet, the Medes presented themselves, some voluntarily, but most sent by Cyrus. They brought gifts, including a cup-bearer, a cook, a baker, a musician, cups, goblets, and beautiful apparel, almost everything from the spoils they had won. This changed Cyaxares' mood, making him see that Cyrus had not stolen his subjects and that they still respected him.

When it was time for the banquet, Cyaxares invited Cyrus to share it, saying it had been so long since they met. But Cyrus replied, "Don't invite me to the feast, uncle. Our soldiers have high expectations, and it would be wrong for me to neglect them for personal pleasure. If soldiers feel neglected, even the good become faint-hearted, and the bad grow insolent.

You have come a long way, so enjoy the feast and welcome your subjects. Tomorrow morning, our chief officers will come to you to discuss our next steps, whether to continue the campaign or disband the army."

Cyaxares went to the banquet, and Cyrus called a council of his closest and most capable friends. He said, "My friends, thanks to the gods, our prayers are granted. We are now masters of the country, our enemies are defeated, and we grow stronger. If our allies stay with us a little longer, our achievements could be even greater. It's your job, as much as mine, to make them want to stay. Just as the bravest soldier overthrows the most enemies, the best speaker persuades the most people. Convince them not with speeches but by their actions. Study your parts carefully. I will ensure our troops have everything they need before we hold the council of war."

BOOK VI

The Battle with
the Assyrian King

VI.1

Forging Unity
Diverse Allies and Strategic Preparations

Summary

Cyrus met with various groups, including the Cadousians, Hyrcanians, Sakians, Gobryas, and Gadatas, who all urged him to stay. Cyaxares, adorned in splendor, addressed the assembly, asking whether to continue the campaign or disband the army. The allies, including leaders from different regions, unanimously agreed to continue, citing the benefits of their unity and the dangers of separation.

Cyrus proposed securing enemy fortresses to ensure supplies and safety, which the allies supported. Reports indicated that the Assyrian king had fled to Lydia with his treasures, prompting Cyrus to intensify preparations. He reformed the chariot system for better battle effectiveness and gathered more resources.

Cyrus sent Araspas, who had fallen in love with a captive woman, as a spy to Lydia. Panthea, the captive woman, offered to bring her husband, Abradatas, to join Cyrus. Abradatas arrived with his troops, pledged loyalty, and contributed to the war effort. With new resources and strategies, Cyrus prepared for the next phase of the campaign, confident in his growing power and alliances.

The Power of Unity in Leadership

Effective leadership requires recognizing the strength that comes from unity. Cyrus and his allies understood that staying together made them stronger against their enemies. Leaders should foster a sense of solidarity and collaboration among their team members, emphasizing the collective power that can be harnessed when everyone works towards a common goal. By encouraging cooperation and unity, leaders can overcome greater challenges and achieve more significant successes.

The day ended, and they ate supper and went to rest. Early the next morning, all the allies gathered at Cyaxares' gates. While Cyaxares dressed and got ready, hearing that a large crowd was waiting, Cyrus met with the suitors his friends had brought. First came the Cadousians, asking him to stay, then the Hyrcanians, followed by the Sakians. Someone presented Gobryas, and Hystaspas brought in Gadatas the eunuch, who also pleaded for the same thing.

At this, Cyrus, knowing that Gadatas had been fearful for a long time that the army might be disbanded, laughed and said, "Ah, Gadatas, you can't hide it: Hystaspas has bribed you to take this view."

But Gadatas lifted his hands to heaven and swore solemnly that Hystaspas had not influenced him. "No," he said, "it's because I know that if you leave, I am utterly ruined. So I asked Hystaspas if he knew what you planned about disbanding the army."

Cyrus replied, "It would be unfair then to blame Hystaspas."

"Yes, Cyrus, very unfair," said Hystaspas, "because I only told Gadatas that you might not be able to continue the campaign, as your father wanted you home and had sent for you."

"What?" cried Cyrus, "you dared to say that whether I wanted it known or not?"

"Of course I did," he answered, "because I can see you're eager to be home in Persia, the center of attention, telling your father about your deeds."

"Well," said Cyrus, "aren't you longing to go home yourself?"

"No," said the other. "I am not. I plan to stay here and be general-in-chief until I make our friend Gadatas the lord and the Assyrian his slave."

So, half in jest and half in earnest, they bantered each other, and meanwhile Cyaxares finished dressing and came out in great splendor and solemnity, sitting down on a Median throne. When everyone was assembled and silence was proclaimed, Cyaxares said, "My friends and allies, since I am here and older than Cyrus, it seems right that I speak first. The most important question we must discuss is whether to continue the campaign or disband the army. Please share your opinions."

The leader of the Hyrcanians stood up first and said, "Friends and allies, we don't need words when the facts show us the way. We all know that together we give our enemy more trouble than we get, but alone they dealt with us as they liked and we least liked."

Then the Cadousian followed. "The less we talk about breaking up and going home separately, the better. Separation has done us no good, even on the march. My men and I learned this the hard way, as you probably remember."

Next, Artabazus, the Mede who had once claimed kinship with Cyrus, spoke. "Cyaxares, in one way I differ from the previous speakers: they think we should stay to continue the campaign, but I feel like I'm always on campaign at home. I was always out on some expedition because our people were being attacked or our forts threatened, dealing with fears inside and fighting outside, all at my own expense. Now, I occupy the enemy's forts, fear them no more, enjoy their good things, and drink their good wine. Since home means fighting and here means feasting, I am not in favor of breaking up the company."

Then Gobryas spoke. "Friends, I have trusted Cyrus' word and found no fault with him. What he promises, he does. But if he leaves now, the Assyrian will be reprieved and never punished for the wrongs he tried to inflict on you and did inflict on me. I will be punished instead for being your friend."

Strategic Foresight and Adaptability

A good leader must have strategic foresight and the ability to adapt to changing circumstances. Cyrus anticipated the challenges of the upcoming winter and took proactive measures to secure resources and fortify his position. He also innovated by reforming the chariot system to enhance battlefield effectiveness. Leaders should continuously assess their environment, anticipate potential obstacles, and adapt their strategies to ensure success. By being forward-thinking and flexible, leaders can navigate complex situations and maintain a competitive edge.

A good leader must have strategic foresight and the ability to adapt to changing circumstances. Cyrus anticipated the challenges of the upcoming winter and took proactive measures to secure resources and fortify his position. He also innovated by reforming the chariot system to enhance battlefield effectiveness. Leaders should continuously assess their environment, anticipate potential obstacles, and adapt their strategies to ensure success. By being forward-thinking and flexible, leaders can navigate complex situations and maintain a competitive edge.

Finally, Cyrus stood up and said, "Gentlemen, I know that disbanding our forces will decrease our power and increase theirs. If some have given up their weapons, they will soon get new ones. If some have lost their horses, they will replace them. If some have fallen in battle, others, younger and stronger, will take their place. We shouldn't be surprised if they can cause us trouble again soon.

"Why did I ask Cyaxares to debate this question? Because I am afraid of the future. I see opponents we can't fight if we continue as we are. Winter is coming, and though we may have shelter for ourselves, we have nothing for our horses, servants, and the majority of our soldiers, without whom we can't think of a campaign. Our provisions up to our advance line are exhausted, and beyond that, due to the fear we inspire, the locals have hidden their supplies in strong places where they can enjoy them and we cannot reach them.

"Who can wage war with cold and hunger? If our soldiering is to remain as it is, we should disband now and not wait to be driven off by sheer lack of means. But if we wish to go forward, we must take enemy fortresses and secure them. This way, those who can store the most will have the most, and the weaker will suffer siege. Currently, we are like sailors on the ocean: they may sail forever, but the seas they've crossed are no more theirs than those still unsailed. Holding the fortresses will mean the enemy lives in a hostile land while we enjoy halcyon weather.

"Some of you may dread distant garrison duty. If so, put your doubts to rest. We Persians, who must be exiles for now, will take positions nearest to the enemy, while you occupy the land between Assyria and yourselves and cultivate it. If we hold the inner line, your peace won't be disturbed in the outlying parts. The enemy won't neglect the danger at his door to attack you far away."

At this, the whole assembly expressed their eagerness and agreement, and Cyaxares stood up with them. Both Gadatas and Gobryas offered to fortify posts if the allies wished, providing two cities of refuge to start with.

Cyrus, assured of their support, said, "To achieve our goals, we must prepare battering-rams and siege engines, and gather mechanics and builders for our castles." Cyaxares immediately undertook to provide an engine at his own expense. Gadatas and Gobryas each committed to one, Tigranes to another, and Cyrus promised to try for two.

Everyone then set to work finding engineers, artisans, and materials for the machines. Superintendents were appointed from the best-qualified individuals.

Cyrus, knowing this would take time, encamped his troops in the healthiest and easiest-to-supply spot he could find, strengthening natural defenses where necessary. This ensured that the detachment left behind would always be secure, even if he was away with the main force.

He also questioned those familiar with the country to find out where their efforts would be rewarded. He led his men out to forage, securing supplies, maintaining their health and strength, and reinforcing their drill.

During this time, deserters from Babylon and captured prisoners all told the same story: the king had gone to Lydia, taking gold, silver, and treasures. Most soldiers thought he was storing his wealth out of fear, but Cyrus believed he was raising an opponent to face them. Therefore, he pushed preparations vigorously, anticipating another battle. He filled the Persian cavalry to its full complement, acquiring horses from prisoners and friends. He never refused gifts of horses and good weapons.

He also acquired chariots from the enemy and wherever he could find them. He abolished the old Trojan-style charioteering, still used by the Cyrenaeans, which was also practiced by the Medes, Syrians, Arabians, and other Asiatics. He believed the system's flaw was that the best men, in the chariots, could only act at long range, contributing little to victory. Three hundred chariots meant twelve hundred horses and three hundred fighting men, plus the trusted charioteers, another three hundred unable to harm the enemy.

Cyrus replaced this with proper war chariots, with strong wheels for collisions, long axles for stability, and turret-like driver seats built of timber, reaching up to the elbow, leaving room for the driver to manage the horses. The drivers were fully armed, except for their eyes. Iron scythes about two feet long were attached to the axles and under the tree, pointing to the ground for use in a charge. This type of chariot, invented by Cyrus, is still used by the Great King's subjects. He also collected many camels from friends and captured from the enemy.

Cyrus decided to send a spy to Lydia to learn the king's movements and chose Araspas, the officer in charge of the fair lady from Susa. Araspas had fallen in love with his prisoner and tried to make her his lover. She refused, faithful to her husband far away, whom she loved dearly, and didn't accuse Araspas to Cyrus, unwilling to set friend against friend. But when Araspas threatened her with force, she sent her eunuch to tell Cyrus everything.

Cyrus, smiling at the man who boasted of being above love, sent Artabazus with the eunuch to tell Araspas not to use force but to persuade her if he could. Artabazus rebuked Araspas, calling his conduct disgraceful and impious, until Araspas was miserable and ashamed, fearing what Cyrus would do. Cyrus sent for him and said privately, "Araspas, I know you're afraid and ashamed. Be comforted; even the gods are subject to desire. I could tell you what love has made wise men endure. I admitted my weakness in facing loveliness unmoved. I am most to blame for shutting you up with this irresistible power."

Araspas replied, "Cyrus, you are gentle and compassionate, but the world has no pity. They drown me in misery. My enemies rejoice, and my friends advise me to kill myself for fear of you because of my great wrongdoing."

Cyrus said, "Listen: this opinion of you can help me and serve your comrades. If you go to the enemy, pretending to flee from me, they will believe you."

"They will," said Araspas. "Even my friends would believe I ran away."

Cyrus continued, "Then come back with full information about the enemy. They will trust you and show you their plans, so you miss nothing we need to know."

"I will go at once," said Araspas. "They will think I barely escaped punishment from you."

"You can really leave the beautiful Panthea?" Cyrus asked.

"Yes, Cyrus," he answered. "I see now we have two souls. This lesson I learned from the sophist Love. If we had one soul, how could it be both good and evil, desire and not desire the same thing? No, we have two souls: the good soul does good things, and the evil soul does shameful things. Today my good soul conquers, with your help."

"Then go," said Cyrus. "Gain their confidence and tell them what we are doing, but in a way that hinders them. Say we plan to attack their territory at an undecided point; this will prevent them from concentrating their forces. Stay as long as possible; what they do at the last moment is most important for us to know. Advise them on their force disposition, and even if they know you saw their order, they will hesitate to change it. If they do, they will be confused."

Araspas left, gathering his trustiest attendants and saying what was necessary, then departed.

When Panthea heard Araspas had fled, she sent a messenger to Cyrus, saying, "Don't worry about Araspas joining the foe. I will bring you a more trustworthy friend if you let me send for my husband. He will bring all his power. The old king was his friend, but the current king tried to separate us. My husband knows him as a tyrant and would gladly join you."

Cyrus agreed, and Panthea sent word to her husband. When Abradatas received the tokens from his wife and learned the situation, he was overjoyed and set out for Cyrus' camp with a thousand horsemen. Upon reaching the Persian outposts, he sent word to Cyrus, who ordered him taken to Panthea immediately. Husband and wife reunited, and Panthea spoke of Cyrus' nobility, honor, and compassion. Abradatas exclaimed, "How can I repay him for all he has done?"

She answered, "Treat him as he has treated you."

Abradatas went to Cyrus, took his hand, and said, "Cyrus, for your kindness, I give myself to you. I will be your friend, servant, and ally, helping you in any way I can."

Cyrus replied, "I accept your gift, but tonight, sup with your wife. Another day, I will host you and your friends."

Abradatas noticed Cyrus' focus on scythe-bearing chariots, cavalry, and armored war-horses and decided to equip a hundred chariots from his cavalry force. He planned to lead them in a four-poled chariot drawn by eight horses, all protected by bronze chest-plates.

Cyrus got the idea for a chariot with eight poles, drawn by eight yokes of oxen, to carry the lowest compartment of battering engines, standing about twenty-seven feet from the ground. He believed these towers, moving at a fair pace, would be highly useful in battle. The towers had galleries and parapets, each carrying twenty men. Testing it, he found eight yokes of oxen could draw the tower more easily than one yoke could manage ordinary baggage. Satisfied it was feasible, he arranged to use the towers in action, believing that in war, selfishness meant salvation, justice, and happiness.

VI.2

Preparing for Battle Against Lydia with the Help of Indian Spies

Summary

Cyrus receives ambassadors from India, who offer gifts and support from their king. Cyrus tasks three ambassadors with gathering intelligence by pretending to seek an alliance with the Lydians. Meanwhile, Cyrus prepares for war, inspiring his men through hunts, games, and contests, and assembling a formidable force with cavalry, scythed chariots, and camel-mounted archers.

The Indian spies return with news that Croesus, the wealthy king of Lydia, has been chosen as the leader of a massive coalition of forces. Anxiety spreads in Cyrus's camp, but he reassures his generals by reminding them of their past successes. Chrysantas reassures the group, emphasizing the rich rewards awaiting them in Lydia.

Cyrus and his allies agree to march immediately to seize the Lydian supplies. He issues detailed orders for the march, ensuring proper provisions and readiness. With everything in order, Cyrus prepares to offer a sacrifice for a successful journey, and the army readies itself to march, confident in their leader and mission.

Leveraging Allies for Strategic Intelligence

Effective leaders understand the importance of gathering accurate intelligence and leveraging the unique strengths of their allies. By assigning critical tasks to trusted allies, leaders can gather essential information without arousing suspicion. Utilizing fresh perspectives and credible covers, such as allied envoys, enhances the chances of obtaining valuable insights and making informed decisions.

About this time, ambassadors came to Cyrus from India with gifts and a message from their king, saying: "I send you greetings, Cyrus, and I am glad you told me what you need. I want to be your friend and I offer you gifts; if you need anything else, just say the word and it will be yours. I have instructed my men to do whatever you command."

Then Cyrus answered: "This is my command: the rest of you shall stay where you have set up your tents, guard your treasures, and live as you wish. But three of you shall go to the enemy and pretend that you have come to discuss an alliance with your king, and in doing so, learn how things are going, everything they say and do, and bring me word quickly. If you serve me well in this, I shall owe you even more than I owe you for these gifts. Some spies are no better than slaves and cannot find out anything new, but there are others, like you, who can discover undisclosed plans."

The Indians gladly listened and, for the moment, made themselves at home as guests of Cyrus. But the next day, they got ready and set off on their journey, promising to find out as much as they could about the enemy's secrets and bring word back as quickly as possible.

Meanwhile, Cyrus continued his preparations for the war on a grand scale, like someone aiming for a significant achievement. Not only did he carry out all the resolutions of the allies, but he also inspired his friends and followers to compete in arms and equipment, horsemanship, spearmanship, and archery, and in enduring toil and danger.

Cyrus would lead them out to hunt and give special honors to those who excelled in any way. He would encourage the ambition of the officers by praising those who improved their men and by rewarding them in every way he could.

At every sacrifice and festival, he organized games and contests in all martial exercises, giving out prizes to the winners, filling the whole army with enthusiasm and confidence.

By this time, Cyrus had almost everything ready for the campaign except the battering machines. The Persian cavalry was up to its full number of ten thousand men, and the scythed chariots were complete: a hundred of his own and a hundred provided by Abradatas of Susa.

Besides these, there were a hundred of the old Median chariots that Cyrus had persuaded Cyaxares to remodel on his type, giving up the Trojan and Lydian style. The camels were ready too, each carrying two mounted archers.

The bulk of the great army felt almost as though they had already conquered, and the enemy's power was of no concern.

While things were like this, the Indians Cyrus had sent out returned with their report. Croesus had been chosen leader and general-in-chief; a resolution had been passed calling on all the allied kings to bring their entire forces, raise large sums for the war, and spend them on hiring mercenaries and making necessary gifts.

Large numbers of Thracians, armed with short swords, had already been enlisted, and a body of Egyptians were coming by sea, amounting—so the Indians said—to 120,000 men, armed with long shields reaching to their feet, huge spears, and sabers. Besides these, an army was expected from Cyprus, and already present were the Cilicians, men of both Phrygias, Lycaonia, Paphlagonia, Cappadocia, Arabians, Phoenicians, and all the Assyrians under the king of Babylon. Moreover, the Ionians, Aeolians, and nearly all the Hellenic colonists on the coast were compelled to follow Croesus.

Croesus himself had already sent to Lacedaemon to propose an alliance with the Spartans. The army was gathering on the banks of the Pactolus, and they were to move to Thymbrara, the mustering ground for all the Asiatic subjects of the Great King west of Syria, and orders had been issued to open a market there. This report agreed with the accounts given by the prisoners, for Cyrus always made sure to capture men from whom he could get information and sent out spies disguised as runaway slaves.

Maintaining Morale and Perspective

> Successful leaders maintain morale and perspective, especially during times of uncertainty or perceived threats. They address concerns openly, reminding their teams of past successes and the strength of their current position. By reinforcing confidence and focusing on the positives, leaders can prevent fear from spreading and ensure that their team remains motivated and ready to face challenges.

These were the tidings, and when the army heard the news, there was much anxiety and concern, as one might expect. The men went about their work with unusual quietness, their faces clouded over, or gathered in knots and clusters, anxiously asking each other the news and discussing the report.

When Cyrus saw that fear was spreading in the camp, he called a meeting of his generals and all whose dejection might harm the cause and whose confidence might help it. He also sent word that any attendants or any rank and file who wished to hear what he had to say could come and listen. When they met, he spoke as follows:

"My friends and allies, I want to be open about why I called you here. I saw that some of you looked panic-stricken when you heard the enemy's reports. But I am astonished that any of you should be alarmed because the enemy is gathering forces and not reassured by remembering that our own force is much larger than it was when we conquered them before, and far better provided with everything we need, thanks to the heavens.

I ask you how you would have felt if you had been told that a force exactly like ours was marching on us, if you had heard that men who had already conquered us were coming now, carrying their victory in their hearts, and that those who had defeated our bows and javelins were advancing again with ten times as many men?

Suppose you heard that the very men who had routed our infantry once were now coming equipped as before, but this time on horseback, each armed with a stout spear ready to charge? Suppose you heard of chariots made on a new pattern, not kept stationary with their backs to the foe, but with horses shielded by armor, drivers protected by wooden walls, and axles fitted with iron scythes to charge into the enemy ranks?

And suppose you heard they have camels to ride on, each one scaring a hundred horses, and that they will bring towers from which to help their own friends and overwhelm us with volleys of darts so we cannot fight on level ground?

If this were what you heard of the enemy, I ask again, you who are now fearful, what would you have done? You who turn pale when told that Croesus has been chosen commander-in-chief, Croesus who proved more cowardly than the Syrians, and when they were defeated and fled, instead of helping them, took to his heels himself.

We are also told that the enemy does not feel equal to facing us alone and is hiring others to fight for him better than he could himself. I can only say, gentlemen, that if any individual considers our position alarming or unfavorable, he had better leave us and join our opponents; he will do us more good there than here."

Addressing Concerns and Maintaining Focus

Effective leaders address their team's concerns openly and shift their focus towards achievable goals. By understanding and acknowledging their team's initial reactions, leaders can redirect energy from frustration to motivation. Highlighting new opportunities and immediate objectives helps maintain morale and drive action. Leaders ensure preparedness by setting clear expectations and providing detailed plans, emphasizing adaptability and readiness for any challenges ahead.

When Cyrus finished, Chrysantas the Persian stood up and said: "Cyrus, you should not be surprised if some looked troubled when they heard the news. The troubled looks were signs of annoyance, not fear. Just like if a group was expecting breakfast immediately but were told there was business to attend to first, I do not suppose they would be pleased. Here we were, thinking our fortunes were made, and now we are told there is more to do, and of course, we were annoyed, not afraid, but wishing it were all over.

However, since it now seems that Syria is not the only prize—though there is much to be got in Syria: flocks, herds, corn, and palm-trees—Lydia is also a prize, the land of wine, oil, fig-trees, and shores where the sea brings more good things than the eye can see. Once we realize this, our spirits will rise, and we will hasten to lay our hands on the Lydian wealth without delay."

So he spoke, and the allies were pleased and applauded.

"Truly, gentlemen," said Cyrus, "as Chrysantas says, we should march without delay to be ahead of our foes and reach their supplies before they do; the quicker we are, the fewer resources they will have.

That is how I see it, but if anyone has a safer or easier way, let them tell us."

Many speakers followed, all urging an immediate march without opposition, and so Cyrus spoke again:

"My friends and allies, God willing, our hearts, bodies, and weapons are prepared; now we need to gather what we need for ourselves and our animals for at least twenty days. The journey itself will take more than fifteen, and we will find no food along the way; it has been cleared out by us and our foes.

We must collect enough corn, without which we cannot fight or live, and every man must carry enough wine to get used to drinking water, as most of the country will have no wine and the largest supply we could take would not last. To avoid sudden sickness, we must start by taking water with our food: porridge with water, bread soaked in water, and boiled meat in water. We will not miss wine if we drink a little after the meal. Then we can gradually reduce the amount until we become water-drinkers.

Gradual change allows every creature to adapt; God teaches us this by gradually leading us from winter to summer and back again. We should follow God, taking one step at a time until we reach our goal.

Spend on food instead of heavy rugs and coverlets; you will not sleep less soundly for lack of bedclothes. But with clothing, it is different: a man can hardly have too much, whether sick or healthy. For seasoning, take what is sharp, dry, and salted, as such foods are more appetizing and satisfying. And since we may find growing corn in unravaged areas, we should take handmills for grinding, as they are the lightest machines for the purpose.

We must also supply ourselves with medicines—they are small but invaluable if needed. And we need a large supply of straps; everything seems to need a strap, but they wear out and break. Some of you know how to shave spears, so do not forget a plane and a rasp; sharpening a spearhead sharpens the spirit too. And we must take plenty of timber for chariots and wagons, as breakdowns are likely on the road, along with tools for repairs. Each wagon should have a mattock and a shovel, and each beast of burden should carry a billhook and an axe, always useful to the owner and sometimes to all.

The officers of the fighting line must ensure the men under their command have everything they need. Those in charge of the baggage train will inspect the animals and ensure every man is provided. The road-makers will take the soldiers disqualified from serving as javelin-men, bowmen, or slingers: old javelin men with axes, bowmen with mattocks, and slingers with shovels. They will advance in squads in front of the wagons to work on the road as needed, and I will know where to find the men I need.

I also intend to take a corps of smiths, carpenters, and cobblers, men of military age with the proper tools, to supply any need. These men will not be in the fighting line but will have a place where they can be hired. Any huckster wishing to follow the army may do so but will be deprived of all goods if caught selling anything during the fifteen days for which provisions have been ordered; after that, they may sell what they like. Any merchant offering a well-stocked market will receive recompense and honor from the allies and myself. If anyone needs an advance of money for trading, they must send me guarantors who will ensure they march with the army, and then they can draw on our funds.

These are the general orders: if anyone thinks something has been omitted, point it out to me. Now return to your quarters and make your preparations, and I will offer a sacrifice for our journey. When the signs are favorable, we will give the signal, and you must present yourselves, with everything ordered, at the appointed place under your officers. And you, officers, will come to me as a group for final orders when your divisions are in line."

VI.3

Cyrus's Strategic Preparations for Battle Against the Lydians

Summary

Cyrus and his army set out for battle, camping nearby on the first day to address any forgotten supplies. Cyaxares stayed in Media with a third of the Median troops. Scouts reported sighting the Lydian forces, prompting Cyrus to send cavalry to investigate. Captured prisoners revealed that Croesus and his Lydian army were about seven miles away and preparing for battle. Cyrus instructed his troops to eat and then called a meeting with his officers. Araspas, who had been spying, returned with detailed information about the Lydian army's formation. Cyrus outlined his battle strategy, emphasizing the positioning of different units and the importance of readiness. Abradatas volunteered to take the front position against the Egyptians, and after drawing lots, he was given the post. The officers then carried out Cyrus's orders, prepared their positions, and rested for the night.

The Importance of Thorough Preparation

Leaders ensure all aspects of their mission are meticulously planned. Cyrus demonstrated this by organizing his troops, ensuring supplies were readily available, and addressing any potential issues before advancing. By prioritizing readiness and logistics, he minimized risks and maximized his army's efficiency and morale. This preparation included detailed strategies for various scenarios, showcasing the foresight required for successful leadership.

The day ended, and they ate supper and went to rest. Early the next morning, all the allies gathered at Cyaxares' gates.

With these instructions, the army went to make their preparations while Cyrus offered a sacrifice. As soon as the omens were favorable, he set out with his forces. On the first day, they camped as close by as possible so that anything left behind could easily be fetched and any omission readily supplied.

Cyaxares stayed in Media with a third of the Median troops to not leave their own country undefended. Cyrus himself pushed forward with all possible speed, keeping his cavalry in the lead and constantly sending explorers and scouts ahead to some lookout points. Behind the cavalry came the baggage, and on the plains, he had long strings of wagons and beasts of burden, with the main army behind them, so that if any of the baggage train fell back, the officers who caught them up would ensure they did not lose their places in the march.

But where the road was narrower, the fighting men marched on either side with the baggage in the middle, and in case of any block, it was the soldiers' job on the spot to attend to the matter. As a rule, the different regiments would march alongside their own baggage, orders having been given that all members of the train should advance by regiments unless absolutely prevented.

To help matters, the brigadier's own body-servant led the way with an ensign known to his men, so that each regiment marched together, the men doing their best to keep up with their comrades. Thus, there was no need to search for each other, everything was to hand, there was greater security, and the soldiers could get what they wanted more quickly.

After some days, the scouts ahead thought they could see people in the plain collecting fodder and timber, and then they made out beasts of burden, some grazing and others already laden, and as they scanned the distance, they felt sure they could distinguish something that was either smoke rising or clouds of dust; and from all this, they concluded that the enemy's army was not far off.

Whereupon their commander dispatched a messenger with the news to Cyrus, who sent back word that the scouts should stay where they were, on their lookout, and tell him if they saw anything more, while he ordered a squadron of cavalry to ride forward, intercept, if they could, some of the men on the plain and so discover the actual state of affairs.

While the detachment carried out this order, Cyrus halted the rest of his army to make such dispositions as he thought necessary before coming to close quarters. His first order was for the troops to take their breakfast; after breakfast, they were to fall in and wait for the word of command.

When breakfast was over, he sent for all the officers from the cavalry, the infantry, and the chariot brigade, and for the commanders of the battering engines and the baggage train, and they came to him.

Meanwhile, the troop of horse had dashed into the plain, cut off some of the men, and now brought them in captive. The prisoners, on being questioned by Cyrus, said they belonged to the camp and had gone out to forage or cut wood and so had passed beyond their own pickets, for, owing to the size of their army, everything was scarce.

"How far is your army from here?" asked Cyrus.

"About seven miles," they said.

"Was there any talk about us down there?" he asked.

"We should think there was," they answered; "it was all over the camp that you were coming."

"Ah," said Cyrus, "I suppose they were glad to hear we were coming so soon?" (putting this question for his officers to hear the answer).

"That they were not," said the prisoners, "they were anything but glad; they were miserable."

"And what are they doing now?" asked Cyrus.

"Forming their line of battle," they answered; "yesterday and the day before they did the same."

"And their commander?" said Cyrus, "who is he?"

"Croesus himself," said they, "and with him a Greek, and also another man, a Mede, who is said to be a deserter from you."

"Ah," cried Cyrus, "is that so? Most mighty Zeus, may I deal with him as I wish!"

Then he had the prisoners led away and turned to speak to his officers, but at this moment another scout appeared, saying that a large force of cavalry was in the plain.

"We think," he added, "that they are trying to get a sight of our army. For about thirty of them are riding ahead at a good round pace and they seem to be coming straight for our little company, perhaps to capture our lookout if they can, for there are only ten of us there."

At that, Cyrus sent off a detachment from his own bodyguard, bidding them gallop up to the place, unseen by the enemy, and stay there motionless.

"Wait," he said, "until our own ten must leave the spot and then dash out on the thirty as they come up the hill. And to prevent any injury from the larger body, do you, Hystaspas," he said, turning to the latter, "ride out with a thousand horse, and let them see you suddenly, face to face. But remember not to pursue them out of sight, come back as soon as you have secured our post. And if any of your opponents ride up with their right hands raised, welcome them as friends."

Accordingly, Hystaspas went off and got under arms, while the bodyguard galloped to the spot. But before they reached the scouts, someone met them with his squires, the man who had been sent out as a spy, the guardian of the lady from Susa, Araspas himself.

Utilizing Intelligence for Strategic Advantage

Cyrus leveraged intelligence effectively by employing scouts and spies like Araspas to gather detailed information about the enemy. Understanding the exact location, strength, and formation of Croesus's Lydian forces allowed him to make informed decisions. This highlights the value of accurate intelligence in formulating strategies that give a leader the upper hand in any competitive situation.

When the news reached Cyrus, he sprang up from his seat, went to meet him himself, and clasped his hand, but the others, who of course knew nothing, were utterly dumbfounded until Cyrus said: "Gentlemen, the best of our friends has come back to us. It is high time that all men should know what he has done. It was not through any baseness, or any weakness, or any fear of me, that he left us; it was because I sent him to be my messenger, to learn the enemy's doings and bring us word.

"Araspas, I have not forgotten what I promised you, I will repay you, we will all repay you. For, gentlemen, it is only just that all of you should pay him honor. Good and true I call him who risked himself for our good and took upon himself a reproach that was heavy to bear."

At that, all crowded around Araspas, took him by the hand, and made him welcome.

Then Cyrus spoke again: "Enough, my friends, Araspas has news for us, and it is time to hear it. Tell us your tale, Araspas, keep back nothing of the truth, and do not make out the power of the enemy less than it really is. It is far better that we should find it smaller than we looked for rather than strong beyond our expectations."

"Well," began Araspas, "in order to learn their numbers, I managed to be present at the marshalling of their troops."

"Then you can tell us," said Cyrus, "not only their numbers but their disposition in the field."

"That I can," answered Araspas, "and also how they propose to fight."

"Good," said Cyrus, "but first let us hear their numbers in brief."

"Well," he answered, "they are drawn up thirty deep, infantry and cavalry alike, all except the Egyptians, and they cover about five miles; for I was at great pains," he added, "to find out how much ground they occupied."

"And the Egyptians?" Cyrus said, "how are they drawn up? I noticed you said, 'all except the Egyptians.'"

"The Egyptians," he answered, "are drawn up in companies of ten thousand, under their own officers, a hundred deep, and a hundred broad: that, they insisted, was their usual formation at home. Croesus, however, was very loath to let them have their own way in this: he wished to outflank you as much as possible."

"Why?" Cyrus asked, "what was his object?"

"To encircle you, I imagine, with his wings."

"He had better take care," said Cyrus, "or his circle may find itself in the center."

Flexibility and Adaptability in Command

Flexible Leadership: Cyrus's ability to adapt his plans based on new information exemplifies flexible leadership. He adjusted his strategies and positions in response to the scouts' reports and Araspas's intelligence. Leaders must be ready to pivot and modify their plans in the face of changing circumstances, ensuring their team remains effective and can respond to unforeseen challenges.

"But now you have told us what we most needed to know, and you, gentlemen," said he to the officers, "on leaving this meeting, you will look to your weapons and your harness. It often happens that the lack of some little thing makes man or horse or chariot useless. To-morrow morning early, while I am offering sacrifice, do you take your breakfast and give your steeds their provender, so that when the moment comes to strike you may not be found wanting. And then you, Araspas, must hold the right wing in the position it has now, and the rest of you who command a thousand men must do the same with your divisions: it is no time to be changing horses when the race is being run; and you will send word to the brigadiers and captains under you to draw up the phalanx with each company two deep." (Now a company consisted of four-and-twenty men.)

Then one of the officers, a captain of ten thousand, said:

"Do you think, Cyrus, that with so shallow a depth we can stand against their tremendous phalanx?"

"But do you suppose," rejoined he, "that any phalanx so deep that the rear-ranks cannot close with the enemy could do much either for friend or foe?

"I myself," he added, "would rather this heavy infantry of theirs were drawn up, not a hundred, but ten thousand deep: we should have all the fewer to fight. Whereas with the depth that I propose, I believe we shall not waste a man: every part of our army will work with every other.

"I will post the javelin-men behind the cuirassiers, and the archers behind them: it would be absurd to place in the van troops who admit that they are not made for hand-to-hand fighting; but with the cuirassiers thrown in front of them they will stand firm enough, and harass the enemy over the heads of our own men with their arrows and their darts. And every stroke that falls on the enemy means so much relief to our friends.

"In the very rear of all, I will post our reserve. A house is useless without a foundation as well as a roof, and our phalanx will be no use unless it has a rear guard and a van, and both of them good.

"You," he added, "will draw up the ranks to suit these orders, and you who command the targeteers will follow with your companies in the same depth, and you who command the archers will follow the targeteers.

"Gentlemen of the reserve, you will hold your men in the rear, and pass the word down to your own subordinates to watch the men in front, cheer on those who do their duty, threaten him who plays the coward, and if any man shows signs of treachery, see that he dies the death. It is for those in the van to hearten those behind them by word and deed; it is for you, the reserve, to make the cowards dread you more than the foe.

Inspiring Confidence and Delegating Responsibilities

Effective leaders inspire confidence and delegate responsibilities to their subordinates. By trusting his officers with critical tasks and involving them in strategic decisions, a leader fosters a sense of unity and purpose within the team. Cyrus maintained high morale among his soldiers by sharing intelligence, recognizing their efforts, and empowering them to take charge of essential operations. This approach shows that leaders who build trust and cohesion can motivate their team to perform at their best, even in challenging situations.

"You know your work, and you will do it. Euphratus," he added, turning to the officer in command of the artillery, "see that the wagons with the towers keep as close to the phalanx as possible.

"And you, Daouchus, bring up the whole of your baggage train under cover of the towers and make your squires punish severely any man who breaks the line.

"You, Carouchas, keep the women's carriages close behind the baggage train. This long line of followers should give an impression of vast numbers, allow our own men opportunity for ambuscades, and force the enemy, if he tries to surround us, to widen his circuit, and the wider he makes it the weaker he will be.

"That, then, is your business; and you, gentlemen, Artaozus and Artagersas, each of you take your thousand foot and guard the baggage.

"And you, Pharnouchus and Asiadatas, neither of you must lead your thousand horse into the fighting line, you must get them under arms by themselves behind the carriages: and then come to me with the other officers as fully equipped as if you were to be the first to fight.

"You, sir, who command the camel corps will take up your post behind the carriages and look for further orders to Artagersas."

"Officers of the war-chariots, you will draw lots among yourselves, and he on whom the lot falls will bring his hundred chariots in front of the fighting line, while the other two centuries will support our flanks on the right and left."

Such were the dispositions made by Cyrus; but Abradatas, the lord of Susa, cried: "Cyrus, let me, I pray you, volunteer for the post in front."

And Cyrus, struck with admiration for the man, took him by the hand, and turning to the Persians in command of the other centuries said: "Perhaps, gentlemen, you will allow this?"

But they answered that it was hard to resign the post of honor, and so they all drew lots, and the lot fell on Abradatas, and his post was face to face with the Egyptians. Then the officers left the council and carried out the orders given, took their evening meal, posted the pickets, and went to rest.

VI.4

Emotional Farewells Before Battle and Final Preparations

Summary

This chapter focuses on the final preparations before the battle. It highlights the emotional moments between Abradatas and his wife Panthea, showcasing their deep bond and her support. It also emphasizes Cyrus's leadership as he offers sacrifices, ensures his troops are ready, and delivers a motivational speech to his officers, reminding them of their strengths and the importance of unity and confidence. Finally, it sets the stage for the upcoming battle, with the army ready and motivated to face the Lydian army and Croesus.

Personal Sacrifice and Support

> Leaders recognize the impact of personal sacrifices and the value of supportive relationships in motivating and empowering their team. When leaders and their supporters are willing to make personal sacrifices, it fosters a deep sense of commitment and shared purpose, enhancing overall performance and resilience.

But early the next morning, Cyrus offered a sacrifice, while the rest of the army ate their breakfast.

After the libation, they armed themselves, appearing as a great and splendid company in bright tunics, splendid breastplates, and shining helmets.

All the horses had frontlets and chest plates, the chargers had armor on their shoulders, and the chariot horses had armor on their flanks.

The whole army glittered with bronze and looked like a field of flowers with their scarlet colors.

The eight-horse chariot of Abradatas was a marvel of beauty and richness.

Just as he was about to put on the linen corslet of his native land, Panthea came, bringing him a golden breastplate and helmet, along with armlets, broad bracelets, a flowing purple tunic, and a hyacinth-colored helmet plume.

She had made all these in secret, taking the measure of his armor without his knowledge.

When he saw them, he gazed in wonder and said, "Dear wife, did you destroy your own jewels to make this armor for me?"

But she replied, "No, my lord, at least not the richest of them all, for you shall be my loveliest jewel when others see you as I see you now."

As she spoke, she put the armor on him, but despite trying to hide it, tears rolled down her cheeks.

When Abradatas was arrayed in the new armor, he, who had been fair enough to look upon before, now appeared splendid, noble, beautiful, and free, just as his nature was.

He took the reins from the charioteer and was about to set foot on the chariot when Panthea asked the bystanders to withdraw.

She said to him, "My own lord, there is little need to tell you what you already know, yet this I say: if any woman loved her husband more than her own soul, I am of her company.

Why should I try to speak? Our lives say more than any words of mine.

And yet, feeling for you as I do, I swear to you by the love between us that I would rather go down to the grave beside you after a hero's death than live on with you in shame.

I have thought you worthy of the highest and believed myself worthy to follow you.

I remember the great gratitude we owe to Cyrus, who, when I was his captive, chose not to treat me as a slave or dishonor me as a free woman.

He saved me for you as though I had been his brother's wife.

When Araspas, my warder, turned from him, I promised that if he would let me send for you, I would bring him a friend in the other's place, far nobler and more faithful."

As Panthea spoke, Abradatas listened with rapture, and when she finished, he laid his hand upon her head and looked up to heaven.

He prayed aloud, "O most mighty Zeus, make me worthy to be Panthea's husband and the friend of Cyrus who showed us honor!"

Then he opened the driver's seat, mounted the chariot, and the driver shut the door.

Panthea could not take him in her arms again, so she bent and kissed the chariot box.

Then the chariot rolled forward, and she followed unseen until Abradatas turned and saw her.

He cried, "Be strong, Panthea, be of good heart! Farewell, and hurry home!"

Her chamberlains and maidens took her, brought her back to her carriage, laid her down, and drew the awning.

No man, of all who was there that day, had eyes to look on the splendid Abradatas in his chariot until Panthea had gone.

Emotional Intelligence and Motivating Troops

Effective leaders understand and leverage the emotional dynamics within their team to inspire peak performance. Cyrus demonstrates this by acknowledging the emotional farewells between Abradatas and Panthea, recognizing the power of personal bonds and the morale boost they provide. He then channels this into a motivational speech, reminding his troops of their superior training and unity, thus strengthening their resolve and confidence.

Meanwhile, Cyrus found the omens favorable, and his army was already drawn up in the order he had fixed.

He had scouts posted ahead, one behind the other, and then he called his officers together for his final words:

"Gentlemen, my friends and allies, the sacred signs from heaven are as they were the day the gods gave us victory before.

I would call to your minds thoughts to bring you gladness and confidence for the fight.

You are far better trained than your enemies, you have lived together and worked together far longer than they have, and you have won victories together.

What they have shared with one another has been defeat, and those who have not fought yet feel they have traitors to the right and left of them.

Our recruits know that they enter battle in the company of men who help their allies.

Those who trust each other will stand firm and fight without flinching, but when confidence is gone, no man thinks of anything but flight.

Forward then, gentlemen, against the foe; drive our scythed chariots against their defenseless cars, and let our armed cavalry charge their unprotected horse and charge them home.

The mass of their infantry you have met before; as for the Egyptians, they are armed in much the same way as they are marshaled.

They carry shields too big to let them move or see, and they are drawn up a hundred deep, which will prevent all but a few from fighting.

If they count on forcing us back by their weight, they must first withstand our steel and the charge of our cavalry.

If any of them hold firm, how can they fight against cavalry, infantry, and turrets of artillery at once?

Our men on the towers will help us, smiting the enemy until he flees instead of fighting.

If you think there is anything lacking, tell me now; God helping us, we will lack nothing.

If anyone wishes to say anything, let him speak now; if not, go to the altar and pray to the gods to whom we have sacrificed, then fall in.

Let each man say to his own men what I have said to him.

Show the men you rule that you are fit to rule.

Let them see fearlessness in your face, your bearing, and your words."

BOOK VII

The Founding of
the New Persian Empire

VII.1

Cyrus's Strategic Victory Over the Lydian Alliance

Summary

Cyrus and his army prayed and took their positions. He led his forces, including Chrysantas with the cavalry and Arsamas with the infantry, against Croesus and the Lydians, who were allied with the Assyrians and Egyptians. Despite being outflanked, Cyrus noticed the Lydian wings were too far from their center. He instructed his troops to prepare for a concentrated attack. In the ensuing battle, Cyrus's forces, including Abradatas, charged fiercely. Although Abradatas and his men were killed, their sacrifice weakened the Egyptian forces. Cyrus's strategic maneuvers, including using camels to disrupt enemy horses, ultimately led to victory. After the battle, Cyrus offered the surviving Egyptians a chance to surrender and join his forces, which they accepted. The Persian cavalry and scythe-bearing chariots were praised for their effectiveness.

Leading by Example and Maintaining Rituals

Effective leaders lead by example and maintain rituals to inspire and unify their team. Cyrus exemplified this by sharing his breakfast with his men after making a sacrificial offering, demonstrating solidarity and humility. Leaders who participate in shared rituals and visibly commit to their values can foster a strong, motivated, and cohesive team.

So they prayed to the gods and took their places, and the squires brought food and drink to Cyrus and his staff as they stood around the sacrifice.

Cyrus took his breakfast where he stood, after making the offering, sharing what he had with those who needed it.

He poured out the libation, prayed, and then drank, along with his men.

Then he prayed to Zeus, the god of his fathers, to be his leader and helper in the fight, and mounted his horse, telling those around him to follow. [*Editor's note: I believe that Xenophon adapted Cyrus's God to Zeus, since he was writing in Greek, to a Greek audience. My understanding is that for Xenophon, in this context Zeus is synonym to God. Persians were Zoroastrians, the first monotheist religion known until today, and unlike the Greeks' or Egyptions' Gods, Ahura Mazda, Zoroastrians' God, was not represented in any physical shape or form.]*

All his squires were equipped like him, with scarlet tunics, bronze breastplates, and bronze helmets with white plumes, short swords, and a lance of cornel-wood.

Their horses had frontlets, chest-plates, and shoulder armor, all of bronze, and the shoulder-pieces also served as leg-guards for the riders.

The only difference in Cyrus's armor was that it was covered with a golden varnish and shone like a mirror.

As he sat on his horse, gazing into the distance, where he planned to go, a peal of thunder rang out on the right, and he cried, "We will follow thee, O Zeus most high!"

So he set forth with Chrysantas on his right at the head of the cavalry and Arsamas on his left with the infantry.

The word went down the lines, "Eyes on the standard and steady marching."

The standard was a golden eagle with outspread wings, borne aloft on a long spear-shaft, and to this day such is the standard of the Persian king.

Before they came in full sight of the Assyrians, Cyrus halted the army thrice.

When they had gone about two miles or more, they began to see the enemy advancing.

As soon as both armies were in full view of each other, and the Assyrians saw how much they outflanked the Persians on either side, Croesus halted to prepare an encircling movement.

He pushed out a column on the right wing and the left so that the Persian forces might be attacked from every side at once.

Cyrus saw this but gave no sign of stopping; he led straight on as before.

He noticed that the turning point where the Assyrians had pushed out on either flank was an immense distance from their center, and he said to Chrysantas, "Do you see where they have fixed their angle?"

Chrysantas answered, "Yes, I do, and I am surprised; it seems they are drawing their wings too far away from their center."

Cyrus said, "Just so, and from ours too."

Chrysantas asked, "Why are they doing that?"

Cyrus replied, "Clearly, they are afraid we shall attack if their wings are in touch with us while their center is still some way off."

Chrysantas asked, "How can they support each other at such a distance?"

Cyrus answered, "As soon as their wings are opposite our flanks, they will wheel round and then advance at once on every side to set us fighting everywhere at once."

Chrysantas asked, "Do you think the movement is wise?"

Cyrus said, "Yes, it is good enough for what they can see, but for what they cannot, it is worse for them than if they had advanced in a single column."

Cyrus then turned to Arsamas and said, "Advance with your infantry slowly, taking your pace from me. And Chrysantas, march beside him with your cavalry, step for step."

Cyrus added, "I will make for their angle myself, where I propose to join battle, first riding around the army to see how things are with all our men."

Cyrus continued, "When I reach the point, and we are on the verge of action, I will raise the paean, and then you must quicken your pace.

You will know when we have closed with the enemy, the din will be loud enough. At the same moment, Abradatas will dash out upon them; such will be his orders. Your duty is to follow, keeping as close to the chariots as possible. Thus we shall fall on the enemy at the height of his confusion.

God helping me, I shall be with you, cutting my way through the rout by the quickest road I can."

Inspiring Courage and Communicating Clear Expectations

Leaders inspire courage and clearly communicate expectations. The leader motivates their team by framing the battle as a glorious feast and emphasizing the rewards for bravery—wealth, honor, freedom, and glory. They contrast this with the disgrace of cowardice. By speaking directly to his seasoned soldiers and recognizing their previous valor, Cyrus reinforces their confidence and commitment. Leaders provide specific instructions to team leaders, ensuring everyone understands their roles and the battle strategy. Effective leaders inspire their teams by highlighting the significance of their efforts and providing clear, actionable guidance, thus fostering a motivated and well-coordinated force ready to face challenges.

Cyrus sent the watchword down the lines, "Zeus our savior, and Zeus our leader," and went forward.

As he passed between the chariots and the cuirassiers, he would say to some, "My men, the look on your faces rejoices my heart," and to others, "You understand, gentlemen, that this battle is not for the victory of a day, but for all that we have won so far and for all our happiness to come."

Cyrus also said, "My friends, we can never reproach the gods again: today they have put all blessings in our hands. Let us show ourselves good men and true."

He added, "Gentlemen, can we invite each other to a more glorious feast than this? Today all gallant hearts are bidden; today they may feast their friends."

He further said, "You know, I think, the prizes in this game: the victors pursue and smite and slay, and win wealth and fame and freedom and empire. The cowards lose them all. He who loves his own soul let him fight beside me: for I will have no disgrace."

When he met soldiers who had fought for him before, he only said, "To you, gentlemen, what need I say? You know the brave man's part in battle, and the craven's."

When he came to Abradatas, he halted, and Abradatas gave the reins to his charioteer and came up to him, and others gathered around from the infantry and the chariots.

Cyrus said, "God has rewarded you, Abradatas, according to your prayer, you and yours. You hold the first rank among our friends. You will not forget, when the moment for action comes, that those who watch you will be Persians, and those who follow you, and they will not let you bear the brunt alone."

Abradatas answered, "Even so, Cyrus; with us here, all looks well enough, but the state of our flanks troubles me. The enemy's wings are strong and stretch far; he has chariots there and every kind of arm as well, while we have nothing else to oppose him.

If I had not won by lot the post I hold, I would feel ashamed to be here in the safest place of all."

Cyrus replied, "If it is well with you, have no concern for the rest. God willing, I mean to relieve our flanks. But you yourself, do not attack until you see the rout of those detachments that you fear."

So much boasting did Cyrus allow himself on the eve of action, though he was the last man to boast at other times.

"When you see them routed," he said, "you may take it that I am there, and then make your rush. That is the moment when you will find the enemy weakest and your own men strongest.

While there is time, Abradatas, be sure to drive along your front and prepare your men for the charge, kindle their courage by your looks, lift up their hearts by your hopes. Breathe a spirit of emulation into them, to make them prove themselves the flower of the chariot-force. Be assured if things go well with us, all men will say nothing is so profitable as valor."

Abradatas mounted his chariot and drove along the lines to do as Cyrus bade.

Meanwhile, Cyrus went on to the left where Hystaspas was posted with half the Persian cavalry, and he called to him and said, "Hystaspas, here is work to test your pace! If we are quick enough in cutting off their heads, none of us will be slaughtered first."

Hystaspas answered with a laugh, "Leave it to us! We'll see to the men opposite. But set someone to deal with the fellows on our flank: it would be a pity for them to be idle."

Cyrus answered, "I am going to them myself. But remember, Hystaspas, to whichever of us God grants the victory, so long as a single foe is on the field, attack we must, again and again, until the last has yielded."

With that he passed on, and as he came to the flank, he went up to the officer in command of the chariots and said to him, "I intend to support you myself. When you hear me fall on the wing, at that instant do your best to charge straight through your opponents. You will be far safer once outside their ranks than if you are caught halfway."

He went on to the rear and the carriages, where the two detachments were stationed, a thousand horse and a thousand foot, and told Artagersas and Pharnouchus, their leaders, to keep the men where they were.

"When you see me close with the enemy on our right, then set upon those in front of you: take them in flank, where they are weakest, while you advance in line, at your full strength. Their lines, as you see, are closed by cavalry; hurl your camels at these, and you may be sure, even before the fighting begins, they will cut a comic figure."

With all his preparations made, Cyrus rode around the head of his right. By this time Croesus, believing that the center, where he himself was marching, must be nearer the enemy than the distant wings, had the signal raised for them to stop their advance, halt, and wheel around where they were.

When they were in position opposite the Persian force, he signaled for them to charge, and thus three columns came at once against Cyrus, one facing his front and one on either flank.

A tremor ran through the whole army; it was completely enclosed, like a small brick laid within a large one, with enemy forces all around it on every side except the rear: cavalry, heavy infantry, targeteers, archers, and chariots.

Nonetheless, the instant Cyrus gave the word, they swung around to confront the foe.

There was deep silence through the ranks as they realized what they had to face, and then Cyrus, when the moment came, began the battle hymn, and it thundered through the host.

As it died away, the war cry rang out unto the God of Battles, and Cyrus swooped forward at the head of his cavalry, straight for the enemy's flank, and closed with them then and there.

The infantry behind him followed, swift and steady, wave on wave, sweeping out on either side, far outflanking their opponents, for they attacked in line and the foe were in column, to Cyrus's great gain.

A short struggle, and the ranks broke and fled before him headlong.

Artagersas, seeing that Cyrus had engaged, made his own charge on the left, hurling his camels forward as Cyrus had advised.

Even at a distance, the horses could not face the camels: they seemed to go mad with fear, galloping off in terror, rearing, and falling foul of one another: such is the strange effect of camels upon horses.

Thus, Artagersas, with his own troops well in hand, had easy work with the enemy's bewildered masses.

At the same moment, the war chariots dashed in, right and left, so that many, fleeing from the chariots, were cut down by the troopers, and many, fleeing from these, were caught by the chariots.

Abradatas could wait no longer. "Follow me, my friends," he shouted, and drove straight at the enemy, lashing his good steeds forward till their flanks were bloody with the goad, the other charioteers racing hard behind him.

The enemy's chariots fled before them instantly, some not even waiting to take up their fighting men.

But Abradatas drove on through them, straight into the main body of the Egyptians, his rush shared by his comrades on either hand.

What has often been shown elsewhere was shown here: of all strong formations, the strongest is a band of friends.

His brothers-in-arms and his messmates charged with him, but the others, when they saw that the solid ranks of the Egyptians stood firm, swung around and pursued the fleeing chariots.

Meanwhile, Abradatas and his companions could make no further way: there was not a gap through the Egyptian lines on either hand.

They could only charge the single soldiers where they stood, overthrowing them by the sheer weight of horse and chariot, and crushing them and their arms beneath the hoofs and wheels.

Where the scythes caught them, men and weapons were cut to shreds.

In the midst of indescribable confusion, the chariots rocking among the weltering mounds, Abradatas was thrown out, and some of his comrades with him.

There they stood, and fought like men, and there they were cut down and died.

Adaptability, Compassion and Opportunity in Leadership

Effective leaders adapt to new unforeseen situations and changing circumstances. When Cyrus saw the Egyptians forming a defensive circle and suffering heavy losses, he displayed compassion by halting the attack and offering them a chance to surrender honorably, while ultimately making them allies to build, develop and expand the Empire. This act of mercy not only preserved their lives but also won their loyalty, showcasing that effective leaders can combine strategic adaptability with compassion to achieve long-term loyalty and respect from their followers.

The Persians, pouring in after them, dealt slaughter and destruction where Abradatas and his men had charged and shaken the ranks.

Elsewhere, the Egyptians, who were still unscathed, and they were many, moved steadily on to meet them.

There followed a desperate struggle with lance and spear and sword, and still the Egyptians had the advantage because of their numbers and their weapons.

Their spears were immensely stout and long, such as they carry to this day, and the huge shield not only gave more protection than a corslet and buckler but also aided the thrust of the fighter, slung as it was from the shoulder.

Shield locked into shield, they thrust their way forward; the Persians could not drive them back with their light bucklers borne on the forearm only.

Step by step, they gave ground, dealing blow for blow until they came under cover of their own artillery.

Then at last, a second shower of blows fell on the Egyptians, while the reserves would allow no flight of the archers or the javelin-men. At the sword's point, they made them do their duty.

Thick was the slaughter, and loud the din of clashing weapons and whirring darts, and shouting warriors, cheering each other and calling on the gods.

At this moment, Cyrus appeared, cutting his way through his own opponents.

To see the Persians thrust from their position was misery to him, but he knew he could check the enemy's advance most quickly by galloping round to their rear, and thither he dashed, bidding his troops follow, and there they fell upon them and smote them as they were gazing ahead, and there they mowed them down.

The Egyptians, seeing what had happened, cried out that the enemy had taken them in the rear and wheeled around under a storm of blows.

At this, the confusion reached its height, cavalry and infantry struggling together.

An Egyptian fell under Cyrus's horse, and as the hoofs struck him, he stabbed the creature in the belly.

The charger reared at the blow, and Cyrus was thrown.

Then was seen what it is for a leader to be loved by his men.

With a terrible cry, the men dashed forward, conquering thrust with thrust and blow with blow.

One of his squires leapt down and set Cyrus on his own charger.

As Cyrus sprang on the horse, he saw the Egyptians worsted everywhere.

By now, Hystaspas was on the ground with his cavalry, and Chrysantas also.

Still, Cyrus would not allow them to charge the Egyptian phalanx; the archers and javelin-men were to play on them from outside.

Then he made his way along the lines to the artillery, and there he mounted one of the towers to take a survey of the field and see if any of the foe still held their ground and kept up the fight.

But he saw the plain one chaos of flying horses and men and chariots, pursuers and pursued, conquerors and conquered, and nowhere any who still stood firm, save only the Egyptians.

These, in sore straits as they were, formed themselves into a circle behind a ring of steel and sat down under cover of their enormous shields.

They no longer attempted to act, but they suffered, and suffered heavily.

Cyrus, in admiration and pity, unwilling that men so brave should be done to death, drew off his soldiers who were fighting around them, and would not let another man lift a sword.

Then he sent them a herald asking if they wished to be cut to pieces for the sake of those who had betrayed them or save their lives and keep their reputation for gallantry?

They answered, "Is it possible that we can be saved and yet keep our reputation untarnished?"

Cyrus said, "Surely yes, for we ourselves have seen that you alone have held your ground and been ready to fight."

"But even so," said the Egyptians, "how can we act in honor if we save ourselves?"

Cyrus answered, "By betraying none of those at whose side you fought. Only surrender your arms to us and become our friends, the friends of men who chose to save you when they might have destroyed you."

The Egyptians asked, "And if we become your friends, how will you treat us?"

Cyrus replied, "As you treat us, and the treatment shall be good."

They asked again, "And what will that good treatment be?"

Cyrus said, "Better pay than you have had, so long as the war lasts, and when peace comes, if you choose to stay with me, lands and cities and women and servants."

The Egyptians asked if he would excuse them from one duty, service against Croesus. Croesus, they said, was the only leader who knew them; for the rest, they were content to agree.

So they came to terms and took and gave pledges of good faith.

Thus it came about that their descendants are to this day faithful subjects of the king, and Cyrus gave them cities, some in the interior, which are still called the cities of the Egyptians, beside Larissa and Kyllene and Kyme on the coast, still held by their descendants.

When this matter was arranged, darkness had already fallen, and Cyrus drew off his army and encamped at Thymbrara.

In this engagement, the Egyptians alone among the enemy won themselves renown, and of the troops under Cyrus, the Persian cavalry was held to have done the best, so much so that to this day they are still armed in the manner that Cyrus devised.

High praise was also given to the scythe-bearing chariots, and this engine of war is still employed by the reigning king.

As for the camels, all they did was to scare the horses; their riders could take no part in the slaughter and were never touched themselves by the enemy's cavalry. For not a horse would come near the camels.

It was a useful arm, certainly, but no gallant gentleman would dream of breeding camels for his own use or learning to fight on camel-back.

And so they returned to their old position among the baggage train.

The Siege of Sardis and the Lesson of Self-Knowledge

Summary

Cyrus and his army prepared for the night while Croesus and his forces fled to Sardis *[Editor's note: Sardis, the capital of the Lydian empire, was a wealthy and famous ancient city. It is near the modern-day town of Sart in Turkey, in the Izmir region. Lydians were Indo-Europeans, culturally very close to the Greeks].* **The next morning, Cyrus marched to Sardis, setting up a siege sending a group to scale the fortifications, leading to the city's capture. Croesus surrendered and was taken to Cyrus, who decided not to sack the city but instead to collect its treasures peacefully. Croesus reflected on his past actions and the oracle's advice, "Know yourself, Croesus, and you'll find happiness," leading to his realization of his errors. Cyrus showed mercy, restoring Croesus's family and attendants, and kept him as an advisor.**

Balancing Mercy with Justice and Rewarding Loyalty

Effective leaders understand the importance of balancing mercy with justice and recognizing loyalty. While maintaining discipline is crucial, showing mercy can foster loyalty and morale. For example, Cyrus disciplined the Chaldaeans for deserting their posts to pillage but allowed them to atone by returning the loot to the soldiers who stayed and guarded the citadel. This act demonstrated that while he would not tolerate indiscipline, he valued fairness and was willing to forgive and reward those who corrected their mistakes. By ensuring that the disciplined soldiers received the loot, Cyrus reinforced the idea that loyalty and steadfastness are rewarded, promoting a culture of reliability and commitment within his ranks.

Then Cyrus and his men ate their evening meal, set up their guards, and went to sleep. But Croesus and his army fled quickly to Sardis, and the other tribes hurried home under the cover of night as fast as they could.

When morning came, Cyrus marched straight to Sardis. When he reached the citadel, he set up his siege engines and ladders as if preparing for an assault. But that night, he sent a group of Persians and Chaldaeans to climb the fortifications at the steepest point. Their guide was a Persian who had been a slave to one of the garrison soldiers and knew a secret way down to the river that led up to the citadel.

As soon as it was clear that the heights had been captured, all the Lydians fled from the walls and hid wherever they could. At daybreak, Cyrus entered the city and ordered his men to stay in their ranks.

Croesus, who had locked himself inside his palace, called out to Cyrus. Cyrus left a guard around the palace and went to inspect the captured citadel. He found the Persians guarding it in perfect order, but the Chaldaeans had deserted their posts to pillage the town. He immediately summoned their officers and told them to leave his army at once.

"I cannot tolerate undisciplined men taking the best of everything," he said. "You know what rewards were in store for you. I meant to make all who served with me the envy of their fellows, but now you cannot be surprised if you encounter someone stronger than you on your way home."

Fear struck the Chaldaeans, and they begged him to forgive them, promising to return all the loot they had taken. He replied that he had no need of it himself. "But if you want to appease me, give it to those who stayed and guarded the citadel. If my soldiers see that discipline brings rewards, everything will be well with us."

So the Chaldaeans did as he ordered, and those who were faithful and obedient received many good things. Then Cyrus made his troops set up camp in the most convenient part of the town and told them to stay at their posts and have their breakfast there.

After that, he ordered that Croesus be brought to him. When Croesus arrived, he cried, "Hail, Cyrus, my lord and master! Fate has given you that title from now on, and thus must I salute you."

The Importance of Self-Knowledge

A crucial aspect of leadership is understanding oneself, including one's strengths, limitations, and motivations. Self-awareness allows leaders to make informed decisions and avoid overestimating their capabilities. Croesus's reflection on the oracle's advice, "Know yourself, Croesus, and you'll find happiness," highlights this lesson. He admitted that his lack of self-knowledge led him to make poor decisions, such as waging war against Cyrus. By recognizing his limitations and the consequences of his actions, Croesus learned the value of self-awareness in leadership. This conversation with Cyrus underscores the importance of self-knowledge in guiding leaders to make wise, balanced decisions and ultimately find personal and professional fulfillment.

Cyrus replied, "All hail to you as well; we are both men. Now tell me, would you be more willing to advise me as a friend?" Croesus answered, "I would be more than glad to do you any good. It would mean good for me as well."

Cyrus said, "Listen, I see that my soldiers have endured much toil and faced many dangers. Now they believe they have taken the wealthiest city in Asia after Babylon. I do not want them to be cheated of their reward because if they win nothing from their labor, I don't know how I can keep them obedient. But I do not want to give them this city to plunder because it would be utterly destroyed, and in plunder, the worst villains get the most."

Croesus responded, "Let me tell the Lydians that I have won your promise that the city will not be sacked, nor their women and children harmed. In return, my men will willingly bring you everything that is costly and beautiful in Sardis. If I can announce these terms, I am certain that by tomorrow, every treasure will be yours. Furthermore, within a year, the city will overflow with wealth and beauty again. But if you sack it, you will destroy the crafts that create all this wealth."

"You don't need to decide now," he added. "Wait and see what is brought to you. Send your guards to my treasuries with some of my men."

Cyrus agreed to this and then asked, "And now, Croesus, tell me one more thing. How did matters go between you and the oracle at Delphi? It is said that you showed great reverence to Apollo and obeyed him in all things." [*Editor's note: In the Greek mythology, The Oracle of Delphi was a highly respected source of wisdom and prophecy where the priestess Pythia would deliver messages from the god Apollo.*]

Croesus replied, "I wish it had been so, but from the beginning, I acted against him."

Cyrus said, "How can that be? Explain it to me; your words seem strange."

Croesus answered, "In the first place, instead of asking the god for what I wanted, I put him to the test to see if he could speak the truth. This, no man of honor could endure, let alone a god. Those who are doubted cannot love their doubters.

And yet he passed the test. Though I did strange things far from Delphi, he knew them all. So I decided to consult him about my children. At first, he wouldn't answer me, but after many offerings and sacrifices, he finally did. When I asked him how I could have sons, he said they would be born. And so they were, but they brought me no joy. One was dumb his whole life, and the other died young. Crushed by these sorrows, I asked the god how I could live happily for the rest of my days, and he answered:

'Know yourself, Croesus, and you'll find happiness.'

When I heard the oracle, I was comforted. I thought the god had given me an easy task with a great reward. I believed that knowing oneself was simple. And so long as I was at peace, I had no complaints. But when the Assyrian persuaded me to march against you, I faced many dangers, yet I was saved. Once again, I had no complaint against the god because he helped me when I was in over my head.

But later, intoxicated by my wealth and flattered by those who wanted me to lead them, I thought I could be the greatest ruler in the world. I took on the role of general, believing I was born to be a monarch, but I did not know myself. I thought I could fight you, who are from a divine lineage, trained in valor from your youth. My ignorance led to my downfall.

But now, O Cyrus, I know myself. Do you think the god will still speak the truth? Do you think that, knowing myself, I can be happy now? I ask because you have the power to answer best. Happiness is yours to give."

Cyrus answered, "Give me time to deliberate, Croesus. I remember your former happiness and pity you. I give you back your wife and daughters (for I hear you have daughters) and your friends and attendants. They are yours once more, and you can live as you used to. But I must take away your power to wage war."

Croesus cried, "By the gods above, you need not think further. If you do as you say, I will live the life all called the happiest, and I know they were right."

Cyrus asked, "And who lived that life of happiness?"

Croesus replied, "My wife. She shared my luxuries and joys but had no part in the wars and battles. You will provide for me as I provided for her, whom I loved more than anyone else. I must send thank-offerings to Apollo again."

As Cyrus listened, he marveled at Croesus's contentedness. For the future, wherever he went, he took Croesus with him, either because he thought Croesus might be useful or because he felt it was safer that way.

VII.3

The Tragic End of Panthea and Abradatas
A Tale of Love and Loyalty

Summary

Cyrus and his men rested for the night, but the next day he organized the inventory of treasures and the reception of Croesus's wealth. Cyrus noticed Abradatas was missing and learned that he had died in battle. Panthea, Abradatas's wife, had found his body and prepared him for burial. Cyrus, deeply moved, visited the site and mourned with Panthea. He honored Abradatas with a grand funeral and promised to care for Panthea. After Cyrus left, Panthea took her own life beside her husband's body. Her chamberlains, in grief, also killed themselves. Cyrus ensured a magnificent sepulcher was built for them, marking their heroic sacrifice.

Honoring Loyalty and Sacrifice

Great Leaders recognize and honor the loyalty and sacrifices of their followers. This respect fosters a culture of dedication and trust within the team. Cyrus exemplifies this by mourning the death of Abradatas, ensuring he receives a grand and respectful burial, and providing support to Panthea. His actions demonstrate that valuing and acknowledging the contributions and sacrifices of individuals can strengthen the overall morale and commitment of the group.

So they rested for the night. But the next day, Cyrus called his friends and generals together. He told some to make an inventory of their treasures and others to receive all the wealth that Croesus brought in. First, they were to set aside for the gods all that the Persian priests thought fit, then store the rest in coffers, weigh them, and pack them on wagons. The wagons were to be distributed by lot to take with them on the march, so they could receive their proper share at any convenient time.

Then Cyrus called some of his squires and said, "Tell me, have any of you seen Abradatas? I wonder why he, who used to come to me so often, is nowhere to be found."

One of the squires answered, "My lord, he is dead: he fell in the battle, charging straight into the Egyptian ranks. The rest, except for his own companions, swerved before their close array."

The squire added, "We hear that his wife found his body, laid it in her own car, and brought it here to the banks of the Pactolus. Her chamberlains and attendants are digging a grave for him on a hill. She has dressed him in his finest clothes and jewels, and she is seated on the ground with his head on her knees."

Then Cyrus smote his hand upon his thigh, leapt up, and sprang to his horse, galloping to the place of sorrow with a thousand troopers at his back. He told Gadatas and Gobryas to take what jewels they could find to honor the dear friend and brave warrior who had fallen and follow with all speed. He also ordered the herds, cattle, and horses to be driven up wherever he was, so that he might sacrifice on the grave.

When he saw Panthea seated on the ground with the dead man lying there, tears ran down his cheeks, and he cried, "O noble and loyal spirit, have you gone from us?" He took the dead man by the hand, but the hand came away in his own: it had been hacked by an Egyptian blade.

Seeing this, his sorrow grew, and Panthea sobbed aloud, took the hand from Cyrus, kissed it, and laid it in its place as best she could. She said, "It is all like that, Cyrus. But why should you see it?" She continued, "All this, I know, he suffered for my sake, and for yours too, Cyrus, perhaps as much. I was a fool: I urged him to bear himself as a faithful friend of yours, and he never thought once of his own safety, but only of showing his gratitude. Now he has fallen, without a stain on his valor: and I, who urged him, live on to sit beside his grave."

Cyrus wept silently for a while, then said, "Lady, his end was the noblest and fairest that could be: he died in the hour of victory. Take these gifts that I have brought and adorn him." For now Gobryas and Gadatas appeared with store of jewels and rich apparel. "He shall not lack for honor," Cyrus said. "Many hands will raise his monument: it shall be a royal one; and we will offer such sacrifices as befit a hero. And you, lady, you shall not be left desolate. I reverence your chastity and your nobleness, and I will give you a guardian to lead you wherever you choose, if you will but tell me to whom you wish to go."

Panthea answered, "Be at rest, Cyrus, I will not hide from you to whom I long to go."

Cyrus took his leave of her and went, pitying from his heart the woman who had lost so brave a husband, and the dead man in his grave, taken from so sweet a wife, never to see her more. Then Panthea bade her chamberlains stand aside "until," she said, "I have wept over him as I would." But she made her nurse stay with her, saying, "Nurse, when I am dead, cover us with the same cloak." The nurse entreated and besought her, but she could not move her, and when she saw that she did but vex her mistress, she sat down and wept in silence. Panthea then took the scimitar, that had been ready for her so long, drew it across her throat, dropped her head upon her husband's breast, and died. The nurse cried bitterly but covered the two with one cloak as her mistress had bidden her.

When Cyrus heard what Panthea had done, he rushed out in horror to see if he could save her. When the three chamberlains saw what had happened, they drew their own scimitars and killed themselves, there where she had bidden them stand.

When Cyrus came to that place of sorrow, he looked with wonder and reverence on the woman, wept for her, and went his way. He saw that all due honor was paid to those who lay there dead, and a mighty sepulcher was raised above them, mightier, men say, than had been seen in all the world before.

"Cyrus the Great before the bodies of Abradatus and Pantheus" is a significant historical painting by the Spanish artist Vicente López y Portaña, created in the early 19th century. Vicente López (1772–1850)

When Cyrus heard what Panthea had done, he rushed out in horror to see if he could save her. When the three chamberlains saw what had happened, they drew their own scimitars and killed themselves, there where she had bidden them stand.

When Cyrus came to that place of sorrow, he looked with wonder and reverence on the woman, and wept for her. He made sure that all due honor was paid to those who lay there dead, and a mighty sepulcher was raised above them, mightier, men say, than had been seen in all the world before.

VII.4

Adousius's Clever Strategy and the March to Babylon

Summary

The Carians, in constant conflict, asked Cyrus for help. Unable to leave Sardis, Cyrus sent Adousius, a capable Persian leader, who successfully mediated between warring factions in Caria. Adousius's strategy brought peace, leading the Carians to request him as their satrap. Meanwhile, Cyrus sent Hystaspas to Phrygia, where resistance was quelled and garrisons established. Cyrus then left Sardis with Croesus and riches, heading towards Babylon, subduing Phrygians, Cappadocians, and Arabians along the way, significantly boosting his cavalry.

Effective Arbitration Through Building Trust and Unity

Effective leadership involves fostering unity and trust among conflicting parties. Adousius resolved the Carian conflict by presenting himself as a neutral and trustworthy authority. By treating both factions equally and encouraging them to work together for their mutual benefit, he demonstrated that peace and cooperation were achievable. This approach not only resolved their conflicts but also established a lasting peace, showing that fair and transparent leadership can bring harmony to divided groups.

After this, the Carians, who were always fighting with each other because their homes were fortified, asked Cyrus for help. Cyrus didn't want to leave Sardis, where he was having siege engines and battering-rams built to take down the walls of those who wouldn't listen to him. Instead, he sent Adousius, a Persian with good judgment and strong military skills, who also had a pleasant demeanor. He gave him an army, and the Cilicians and Cypriots were eager to serve under him.

Cyrus never sent a Persian governor to rule either Cilicia or Cyprus; he was always content with the native kings, only demanding tribute and troops when needed.

So Adousius took his army and marched into Caria, where both factions were ready to welcome him inside their walls to gain an advantage over their rivals. Adousius treated both sides the same, telling each one privately that he thought their case was just but that they needed to keep his support a secret so he could surprise their enemies.

He insisted they give him pledges of good faith. The Carians had to swear they would let him in without deceit for the benefit of Cyrus and the Persians. He also swore to enter without deceit and for the benefit of those who received him.

He made these agreements with both sides without them knowing about each other. He arranged to enter both strongholds on the same night, taking control of both. At dawn, he positioned himself and his army in the middle and called for the leaders of both sides. Seeing each other, they felt deceived and annoyed.

However, Adousius addressed them, saying, "Gentlemen, I swore to enter your walls without deceit and for the welfare of those who welcomed me. If I destroy either of you, it would harm the Carians. But if I bring peace so you can farm safely, it will be for your benefit. From now on, you must meet as friends, farm your lands without fear, marry your children to each other, and anyone who breaks these rules will have Cyrus and us as enemies."

At this, the city gates were opened wide, people hurried to meet each other, the fields were filled with workers, and there was peace and joy everywhere.

Meanwhile, messengers from Cyrus asked if more troops or siege engines were needed, but Adousius replied that his current force was available for Cyrus to use elsewhere if he wished, and he withdrew his army, leaving a garrison in the strongholds. The Carians begged him to stay, and when he refused, they asked Cyrus to make Adousius their governor.

Meanwhile, Cyrus had sent Hystaspas with an army into Phrygia on the Hellespont. When Adousius returned, he told him to join Hystaspas because the Phrygians would be more likely to obey if they knew another army was coming.

The Greeks on the coast offered many gifts and agreed not to let the Asiatics inside their walls, but only to pay tribute and serve wherever Cyrus commanded. The king of Phrygia, however, prepared to defend his fortresses and sent out orders to that effect. But when his officers deserted him and he was left alone, he surrendered to Hystaspas and left his fate to Cyrus. Hystaspas placed strong Persian garrisons in all the fortresses and departed, taking not only his own troops but many mounted men and infantry from Phrygia.

Cyrus sent word to Adousius to join Hystaspas, take command of those who had submitted, and allow them to keep their arms, while those who resisted were to be disarmed and made to follow the army as slingers.

While his officers were busy, Cyrus left Sardis, leaving a large force to guard the city, and took Croesus with him, along with a long train of wagons filled with riches. Croesus provided a detailed inventory of everything in each wagon and said, as he handed over the lists, "With these, you can check if your officers are delivering everything in full."

Cyrus replied, "Thank you for this, Croesus, but I have arranged for the goods to be managed by those who are entitled to them, so if they steal, they are stealing their own property." He then gave the documents to his friends and officers to help them monitor their stewards.

Aligning Interests Through Vested Incentives

Effective leadership involves aligning interests by giving people a vested stake in the outcomes. This ensures accountability and dedication as individuals have "skin in the game." Cyrus demonstrated this by delegating the management of captured riches to those entitled to them. He explained that if these individuals stole, they would only be stealing from themselves, ensuring responsible and diligent management. This approach made the stewards more invested in the successful management of the resources. In modern days, this is akin to how leaders grant stock options to managers or how venture capital firms compensate partners with shares in portfolio companies, aligning their success with the success of the company or venture. This practice motivates individuals to act in the best interest of the organization, ensuring that their efforts are directed towards common goals.

Cyrus also took Lydians with him, allowing some to carry weapons if they kept them in good condition and tried to please him. Those who didn't lost their horses, which were given to the Persians who had served from the start of the campaign, and their weapons were burned. They were forced to follow the army as slingers.

Cyrus generally made all disarmed subjects practice using the sling, considering it a weapon for slaves. While slingers can be useful with other troops, they can't stand alone against armed soldiers.

Cyrus was marching to Babylon. Along the way, he subdued the Phrygians of Greater Phrygia and the Cappadocians and brought the Arabians under submission. These victories allowed him to increase his Persian cavalry to nearly forty thousand men, with more horses available for his allies.

Finally, he arrived at Babylon with a huge force of cavalry, archers, javelin throwers, and countless slingers.

VII.5

The Siege and Conquest of Babylon

Summary

Cyrus reached Babylon and surrounded it with his forces. To breach the city, he ordered the construction of trenches and towers. These trenches diverted the river that flowed through Babylon, lowering the water level in the riverbed. During a festival, when the Babylonians were distracted, Cyrus's troops entered the city through this now-dry riverbed. They captured the city, secured the palace, and killed the king. Cyrus then established a governance system, ensuring loyalty and emphasizing continuous training and virtue among his soldiers to maintain their empire. He called a council of his Peers and leading men, encouraging them to live by the principles of hard work, self-restraint, and vigilance. He stressed the importance of setting a good example for their children and maintaining their virtues to safeguard their empire and ensure lasting prosperity.

Strategic Planning and Adaptability

A good leader must anticipate potential threats and plan strategically. In this section, Cyrus demonstrates foresight by inspecting the city's fortifications and responding promptly to intelligence about an enemy attack. He reinforces his lines and employs a tactical formation to both protect his troops and bolster their morale. This example highlights the importance of strategic planning and adaptability in leadership.

When Cyrus reached the city, he surrounded it entirely with his forces and then rode around the walls with his friends and the leading officers of the allies. After surveying the fortifications, he prepared to lead his troops away. At that moment, a deserter came to inform him that the Assyrians intended to attack as soon as he began to withdraw because they had inspected his forces from the walls and considered them very weak. This wasn't surprising because the city's circumference was so vast that it was impossible to surround it without thinning his lines significantly.

When Cyrus heard of their intention, he took his position in the center of his troops with his staff around him and sent orders for the infantry wings to double back on either side, marching past the stationary center until they met in the rear directly opposite him. This move boosted the confidence of the men in front by doubling their depth, and those who retired were equally encouraged because they saw that others would face the enemy first. The united wings strengthened the whole force, with those behind protected by those in front and those in front supported by those behind.

With the phalanx folded back on itself, both the front and rear ranks were composed of elite soldiers, encouraging bravery and preventing retreat. The cavalry and light infantry on the flanks moved closer to the commander as the line contracted. When the whole phalanx was in close order, they fell back from the walls slowly, facing the enemy, until they were out of range. Then they turned, marched a few paces, and wheeled around again to face the walls. As they moved further away, they paused less frequently until they felt secure, then quickened their pace and marched uninterruptedly until they reached their quarters.

Once they were encamped, Cyrus called a council of his officers and said, "My friends and allies, we have surveyed the city on every side, and I see no possibility of taking these walls by assault—they are too high and strong. The larger the population, the faster they will succumb to hunger unless they come out to fight. If no one has a better plan, I propose we reduce them by blockade."

Chrysantas then spoke, "Doesn't the river flow through the middle of the city, and isn't it at least a quarter of a mile wide?" Gobryas answered, "Yes, and it is so deep that the water would cover two men, one standing on the other's shoulders. In fact, the city is better protected by its river than by its walls."

Innovation and Creativity

Effective leaders utilize innovation and unconventional creative methods to overcome challenges. Cyrus orders the construction of trenches and towers, intending to divert the Euphrates River and create a path into Babylon through the riverbed, after lowering the level of water. This innovative strategy showcases how creative problem-solving can be crucial in achieving difficult objectives. Leaders must be willing to think outside the box and employ unconventional methods to succeed.

Cyrus said, "Well, Chrysantas, we must forego what is beyond our power. But let's measure off the work for each of us, start digging a trench as wide and deep as we can, so we need as few guards as possible."

Cyrus then took measurements around the city, leaving space on either bank of the river for large towers. He had a gigantic trench dug from end to end of the wall, with his men piling up the earth on their own side. He started building towers by the river, laying foundations of palm trees over a hundred feet long, which could curve upwards under pressure. He built these to give the impression that he intended to besiege the city and prevent the river from carrying off his towers if it flowed into his trench. He also built other towers along the mound to have as many guard posts as possible.

While his army was busy, the men inside the walls laughed at his preparations, knowing they had supplies to last more than twenty years. When Cyrus heard that, he divided his army into twelve parts, each to guard for one month a year. The Babylonians laughed even more, pleased at the idea of being guarded by Phrygians, Lydians, Arabians, and Cappadocians, who they thought would be friendlier to them than to the Persians.

By this time, the trenches were dug. Cyrus learned that it was a time of high festival in Babylon when the citizens drank and made merry all night long. As soon as darkness fell, he set his men to work. They opened the mouths of the trenches, and during the night, the water poured in, turning the riverbed into a highway into the city.

When the river had diverted into its new channel, Cyrus ordered his Persian officers to bring up their thousands, horse and foot alike, each detachment two deep, with the allies following in their old order. They lined up immediately, and Cyrus had his bodyguard descend into the dry channel first to check if the bottom was firm enough for marching. When they confirmed it was, he called a council of all his generals and said, "My friends, the river has stepped aside for us and offers us a passage into Babylon. We must take heart and enter fearlessly, remembering we are marching against men we have conquered before, even when they were awake, alert, sober, armed, and in battle order. Tonight, we go against them when some are asleep, some are drunk, and all are unprepared. When they learn we are within the walls, their astonishment will make them even more helpless.

If any of you worry about volleys from the roofs when we enter the city, set those fears aside. If our enemies climb their roofs, we have a god to help us—the god of Fire. Their porches are easily set aflame because their doors are made of palm wood and varnished with bitumen, the perfect food for fire. We will come with pine torches to kindle it and pitch and tow to feed it. They will be forced to flee or be burned to death. Take your swords in hand; God willing, I will lead you. You," he said, turning to Gadatas and Gobryas, "show us the streets, as you know them; once we are inside, lead us straight to the palace."

Gobryas and his men agreed, saying it wouldn't surprise them to find the palace gates unbarred because the whole city was given over to revelry that night. Still, they expected to find a guard there. Cyrus responded, "There is no time to lose; we must act now and take them by surprise."

They entered the city, striking down some people and causing others to flee into their houses. Some raised the alarm, but Gobryas and his friends drowned out the cries with their shouts, pretending to be revelers. Making their way quickly, they soon reached the king's palace. There, Gobryas and Gadatas's detachment found the gates closed, but they attacked the guards, who were drinking around a fire, and overpowered them.

As the noise grew louder, those inside became aware of the tumult. The king ordered them to investigate, and some opened the gates and ran out. Gadatas and his men saw the open gates and rushed in after the fleeing guards, chasing them with swords into the king's presence.

They found the king on his feet with a drawn scimitar. Overwhelmed by sheer numbers, he and his retinue were cut down. Cyrus sent cavalry squadrons down different roads with orders to kill anyone found in the streets, while those who knew Assyrian warned the inhabitants to stay indoors or face death. While these orders were carried out, Gobryas and Gadatas returned, thanked the gods for vengeance on their unjust king, and expressed their joy and gratitude to Cyrus.

When day broke, those holding the heights saw the city had been taken and the king slain, so they surrendered the citadel. Cyrus took it over, placed a commandant and a garrison there, and allowed the bodies of the fallen to be buried by their families. He proclaimed that all citizens must surrender their weapons, warning that any house found with arms would have all its inhabitants executed. The weapons were surrendered and stored in the citadel.

Freedom, Cultural Sensitivity and Respect for Local Practices

A true leader respects the freedom, religion, and cultures of conquered peoples, fostering loyalty and stability within the empire. Cyrus displayed great respect for the Babylonians after conquering their city. He didn't impose his culture or religion on them but instead allowed them to maintain their practices and traditions. He instructed his officers to treat the captives as subjects, and not slaves, ensuring they were governed fairly and justly. In today's corporate world, successful leaders should respect their global teams diversity and culture and avoid any political, cultural or religious pressure, whether real or perceived, from themselves or from their managers.

Cyrus then summoned the Persian priests, declared the city was now under his control, and ordered the first fruits of the booty to be set aside as offerings to the gods, marking out land for sacred purposes. He distributed the houses and public buildings to those he considered partners in the conquest, giving the best prizes to the bravest men and inviting any who felt unjustly treated to speak to him. He also proclaimed to the Babylonians that they must till the soil, pay dues, and serve those under whom they were placed. He instructed the Persians and allies who stayed with him to treat the captives as subjects.

After this, Cyrus felt it was time to adopt the style and manner of a king, wanting to do so with the goodwill of his friends and in a way that allowed him to appear rarely in public but always with dignity. He devised a plan to achieve this. At daybreak, he took a position in a convenient spot and received those who wished to speak with him, then dismissed them. The people flocked to him in large numbers, struggling and even fighting to gain access. His attendants tried to organize the suitors, but whenever any of his personal friends arrived, Cyrus would bring them to his side, asking them to wait until the crowd was dealt with. However, the crowd kept growing, leaving little time for his friends.

At the end of the day, Cyrus would dismiss them, asking them to return early the next day, expressing his desire to speak with them. His friends were glad to be dismissed, having waited and stood all day without food or drink. The next morning, Cyrus found an even larger crowd waiting for him. He stationed Persian lancers around him and announced that only his friends and generals were allowed access. Once they were admitted, he addressed them.

"My friends, we cannot accuse the gods of failing to grant our prayers. They have given us everything we asked for. But if success means losing our leisure and the company of friends, I would rather forgo such happiness. Yesterday, I listened to petitioners from dawn until evening, and today, there is an even larger crowd with more business for me. If this continues, we will have little time for each other, and I will have no time for myself. Moreover, I find it absurd that strangers should get what they want from me before any of you, my friends. They should be seeking your favor to gain access to me.

I didn't arrange things this way initially because, during war, a commander must be seen and must ensure everything is done properly. But now that the war is over, I feel entitled to some rest. I'm unsure how to balance our needs and the needs of those we must care for, so I seek your advice."

Cyrus paused, and Artabazus the Mede, who claimed kinship with him, stood up and said, "Years ago, when you were a boy, I wanted to be your friend but saw you didn't need me, so I stayed away. Then I had the chance to help you by delivering Cyaxares's orders to the Medes, hoping this would make me your friend. I succeeded and won your praise. But then, new friends like the Hyrcanians joined us, and I felt left out again. After we took the enemy's camp, Gobryas and Gadatas became your friends, making it even harder to reach you. As more allies joined, I hoped that once the war was over, you'd have time for me. But now, with our great victories, it's still hard to see you. Yesterday, I could only reach you by pushing through the crowd. If there's a way for us, your oldest friends, to spend more time with you, that would be great. If not, let me be your messenger again and tell others to step aside for your old friends."

Everyone laughed, including Cyrus. Then Chrysantas the Persian spoke, "Cyrus, it was right for you to be public during the war because we didn't need to be courted, and you had to win over the masses. But now, you should have a private home. It would be shameful for us to enjoy our homes while you endure camp life. You deserve a home, and we should feel guilty if you don't have one."

Many others agreed with Chrysantas, so Cyrus moved into the palace, where the treasures from Sardis were brought and handed over. Cyrus sacrificed to Hestia, Zeus, and other gods named by the Persian priests.

He then organized his affairs, considering how to govern such a vast population and live in the greatest of cities, which was hostile to him. He decided he needed a personal bodyguard. He believed eunuchs, who had no families to love more than their master, would be the most loyal.

Eunuchs, he thought, would value his favor the most because they had no other source of support. Despite common beliefs, he didn't think eunuchs were weak or cowardly. He observed that animals, even when castrated, retained their strength and usefulness. He concluded that eunuchs, cut off from passions, would be gentler but not less brave or skilled. They had proven loyal during their masters' downfalls, and he decided they would make the best personal attendants.

Cyrus also felt he needed more protection from numerous enemies and thought his fellow Persians, who lived hard lives at home, would value life at his court the most. He chose ten thousand lancers to guard his palace day and night and march with him when he traveled. He stationed a significant garrison in Babylon and had the Babylonians provide their pay to keep them humble and submissive. This royal guard and city garrison remained unchanged.

To maintain his empire and possibly expand it, Cyrus knew he couldn't rely solely on his mercenaries' superiority. He needed to keep his brave warriors, who had won the victory, well-trained and valiant. He didn't want to dictate to them but wanted them to see the benefits of staying with him and maintaining their skills. He called a council of the Peers and leading men, saying, "We owe thanks to the gods for granting us this great country and its support. We have our houses and the right to everything in them. But if we become lazy and indulgent, we will lose our honor and wealth. We must continue to watch over our valor and train ourselves. Founding an empire is hard, but keeping it is harder. We must strive for virtue, remembering that the more we have, the more others will envy us. We must share in our subjects' hardships to prove our superiority and keep our weapons ready, for they are tools of freedom and happiness. A man's enjoyment of good things depends on his efforts to achieve them. We must maintain our strength and skills to enjoy our success and avoid losing it. Let us train ourselves and our children to uphold our standards and remain worthy of our past."

Preserve and Leverage Core Values and Differentiators

To sustain long-term success, leaders must consciously preserve and leverage the core values and differentiators that initially made them successful. Maintaining these strengths requires ongoing effort and vigilance. Cyrus recognized that to maintain and possibly expand his empire, he couldn't rely solely on the initial superiority of his mercenaries. He emphasized the importance of keeping his brave warriors well-trained and aware of the values that led to their victory. Instead of dictating to them, he wanted them to understand the benefits of maintaining their skills and staying with him. He called a council of the Peers and leading men, expressing gratitude for their achievements but stressing that becoming lazy and indulgent would lead to a loss of honor and wealth. He urged continuous vigilance and training to maintain their valor and virtue, proving their superiority through shared hardships and readiness. In a corporate setting, sustaining a company's success involves preserving the core values and unique strengths that differentiate it from competitors.

BOOK VIII

The Old Age
and Death of Cyrus

VIII. 1

Cyrus's Governance Strategies
for Sustainable Stability, Authority, and Prosperity

Summary

Cyrus addressed his people about the importance of discipline and obedience for maintaining their success. Chrysantas supported his views, emphasizing the need for willing service and the benefits of a disciplined society. Cyrus then organized his administration by appointing overseers for various functions and personally training those who would guard the commonwealth. He used strategies to ensure attendance and punctuality among his men, rewarding those who complied and penalizing truants. Cyrus also stressed the importance of piety, modesty, and self-control, setting an example for his followers. He believed in training through hunting and maintaining rigorous discipline to ensure his subjects' loyalty. To manage his vast empire, he implemented a hierarchical structure for efficient governance and promoted loyalty among his closest allies by involving them in state affairs.

The Critical Role of Organization, Discipline

Discipline and obedience are crucial for achieving and maintaining success in any organization. This principle is illustrated by Chrysantas, who emphasizes that undisciplined forces cannot capture cities or maintain peace. Just as a household, a city, a ship, or a company requires a hierarchical structure and adherence to authority to function smoothly, so does an army or any organized group. Their triumphs resulted from their willingness to follow orders and maintain discipline, and this must continue to preserve their achievements. In modern terms, it's akin to a well-coordinated corporate team or sports team, where members trust and follow their leader's strategy, ensuring collective success and sustained performance.

Such were the words of Cyrus. Then Chrysantas stood up and said, "Gentlemen, I've often noticed that a good ruler is very much like a good father. Just as a father ensures his children are always blessed, Cyrus has shown us how to maintain our happiness. However, I think he could have explained one point more thoroughly, and I will try to clarify it for those who haven't learned it yet. Ask yourselves, has an undisciplined force ever captured a hostile city?

Has an undisciplined garrison ever saved a friendly town? Without discipline, has an army ever conquered? Is disaster ever closer than when each soldier only thinks about his own safety? In both peace and war, can anything good come if people won't obey their leaders? Could any city be lawful and orderly? Could any household be safe? Could any ship sail home to her haven? We owe our triumph to our obedience. We were ready to follow the call day and night; we marched behind our leader, our ranks unstoppable; we completed every task we were given. If obedience is the path to achieving the highest good, it is also the path to preserving it.

In the past, many of us ruled no one, we were simply ruled. But today, we are all rulers, some over many and some over few. Just as we want our subjects to obey us, we must obey those who are above us. However, unlike slaves, who serve their lords unwillingly, we must, if we are to be free men, willingly do what we see is best. And you will find that even without a single ruler, a city that carefully obeys authority is the last to bow to its enemies. Let us heed Cyrus's words. Let us gather around the public buildings and train ourselves, so we can maintain everything we care for and offer ourselves to Cyrus for his noble purposes. We can be sure of one thing: Cyrus will never ask us to do anything that benefits him but not us. Our needs are the same as his, and our foes are the same."

After Chrysantas spoke, many others, both Persians and allies, supported him. They agreed that men of rank and honor should continually be at the palace gates, ready to serve Cyrus until he dismissed them. This custom still exists today, with the Asiatics under the Great King waiting at their rulers' doors. The measures Cyrus implemented to preserve his empire, as described here, are still the law of the land, maintained by all subsequent kings. However, just as in other matters, the government remains pure under a good ruler and becomes corrupt under a bad one. Thus, Cyrus's nobles and honorable men waited at his gates with their weapons and horses, as agreed by the brave men who helped establish the empire.

Learning and Development: Incentivize Excellence and Hold Accountable

Incentivizing excellence and accountability is crucial for maintaining a motivated and high-performing team. By recognizing and rewarding positive contributions and penalizing absenteeism or lack of effort, a leader can foster a culture of dedication and responsibility.

Cyrus believed in training his partners and colleagues by directly engaging with them and ensuring their presence. He encouraged attendance by assigning easy and profitable tasks to those who were punctual and taking away possessions from those who ignored gentler measures. This way, he lost a useless friend and gained a valuable one. For those who came forward, Cyrus inspired them to noble deeds by embodying the virtues of a man. He showed that the higher his fortunes rose, the more diligent he was in his service to the gods. This approach ensured that his subjects followed his example and adhered to the standards he set.

In a modern organizational context, this approach can be seen in organizing regular training sessions, leadership training sessions, sales kickoffs, and Presidents' clubs. Recognizing success through awards and incentives while addressing failures by taking corrective actions can help maintain a motivated and accountable workforce. Providing opportunities for continuous learning and growth while ensuring that everyone is aligned with the organization's goals fosters a high-performance culture.

Then Cyrus focused on other matters and appointed various overseers: revenue collectors, finance controllers, work ministers, property guardians, and household superintendents. He also chose managers for his horses and dogs, trusted to keep them in the best condition and ready for use. However, he didn't leave the care and training of those who would be his fellow guardians of the commonwealth to others. He considered it his personal responsibility. He knew that if he ever had to fight a battle, he would need to choose his comrades and supporters, the men on his right and left, from these individuals. He would also select his officers for both horse and foot from them. If he needed to send out a general alone, it would be one of them. He depended on them for satraps and governors over cities and nations. He would also require them for ambassadors, knowing that an embassy was often the best way to achieve his goals without war. He understood that nothing could go well if his agents in critical matters were not up to the task. Therefore, he took on the responsibility of training them and believed that the training he required of others should also be undertaken by himself. No man could inspire noble deeds in others if he did not live up to the standards himself.

The more he thought about it, the more he realized he needed leisure to deal with the most important matters. He knew that neglecting revenues was not an option due to the enormous funds needed for such a vast empire. But he also knew that if he was always occupied with his possessions, he would never have time to ensure the safety of the whole. As he pondered how to achieve both financial prosperity and the necessary leisure, he remembered the old military organization. Captains of ten supervised squads of ten, company-captains supervised them, and captains of a thousand supervised the company-captains, and so on up to the captains of ten thousand. This way, not a single man was left without supervision, and one order to the captains of ten thousand was enough to mobilize the entire army. Cyrus applied this principle to his finances, arranging his departments so that he could control the whole system by consulting a few officers. This allowed him more leisure than the manager of a single household or the master of a single ship. Finally, having organized his affairs, he taught those around him to adopt the same system.

With the leisure he needed, he devoted himself to training his partners and colleagues. He first addressed those who, despite being able to live off the labor of others, failed to present themselves at the palace. He sought them out, believing that attendance would be beneficial for them. They would be less likely to do anything wrong in the presence of their king and the noblest men. Those who were absent were usually so due to self-indulgence, wrongdoing, or carelessness. To bring them to attend, he would have one of his close friends claim the property of the offender, asserting it was his own. Naturally, the truants would appear, claiming they had been robbed. For many days, Cyrus would be too busy to hear their complaints, and when he finally did, he would delay judgment even further. This was one way he encouraged attendance. Another was to assign the easiest and most profitable tasks to those who were punctual, and a third was to give nothing to the offenders. The most effective method for those who ignored gentler measures was to take away their possessions and give them to those who showed up when needed. This way, Cyrus lost a useless friend and gained a valuable one. To this day, the king seeks out those who do not present themselves when they should.

For those who came forward, Cyrus believed that as their rightful leader, he could best inspire them to noble deeds by showing that he possessed all the virtues of a man. He believed that written laws could improve men, but a good ruler, being a living law with eyes that see, could guide, detect wrongdoers, and punish them. Thus, he took care to show that the higher his fortunes rose, the more diligent he was in his service to the gods. It was during this time that the Persian priests, the Magians, were first established as an order. Every morning, Cyrus chanted a hymn and sacrificed to the gods they named. The practices he established remain in place at the court of the reigning king. These were the first ways the Persians began to follow their prince, believing their own fortunes would rise by revering the gods, following the man favored by fortune and their monarch. At the same time, they believed they would please Cyrus by doing so. Cyrus viewed his subjects' piety as a blessing for himself, much like preferring to sail with pious men rather than those suspected of wickedness. He believed that if all his partners were god-fearing, they would be less likely to commit crimes against each other or against him, knowing he was their benefactor.

By demonstrating his desire to always be fair to friends, fellow combatants, and allies, he believed he could encourage others to avoid wrongdoing and follow the path of righteousness. He hoped to instill modesty in everyone by showing that he respected everyone and would never say or do anything shameful. He believed that apart from the fear inspired by kings and governors, men would respect the modest and not the shameless, and modesty in women would inspire modesty in men. He believed people would learn to obey if it was clear that he valued prompt and honest obedience even more than grander virtues that were harder to achieve. His beliefs were matched by his actions. His own temperance and the knowledge of it made others more temperate. When people saw moderation and self-control in the man who had the most freedom to be insolent, they were more likely to give up their own insolence. However, he believed there was a difference between modesty and self-control: the modest man would do nothing shameful in public, but the self-controlled man would do nothing wrong even in secret. He believed that self-restraint could be best cultivated if people saw him as someone who couldn't be swayed from virtue by momentary pleasure, someone who worked hard for the deeper joys that come with beauty and nobility. Thus, being who he was, he established a dignified company at his gates, where the lower-ranked showed respect to the higher-ranked, and they, in turn, showed respect to each other with courtesy and harmony. Among them, there was never a shout of anger or an insolent laugh; their demeanor showed they lived for honor and nobility.

Training and Education on Presentation, Etiquette, and Dignity

Maintaining a dignified appearance and practicing proper etiquette are essential for a leader and their team to command respect and prevent contempt. A leader should ensure that their presentation reflects their status and responsibilities, enhancing their credibility and authority.

Cyrus thought it necessary for a ruler to surpass his subjects not only by his own merit but also through charm and artifice. He adopted the Median dress and convinced his companions to do the same because it concealed physical flaws and enhanced the wearer's beauty and stature. He encouraged the use of ointments to make the eyes brighter and pigments to make the skin look fairer. He trained his courtiers never to spit or blow their noses in public or turn aside to stare at anything, maintaining the dignified air of people who could not be surprised. These measures made it impossible for subjects to despise their rulers.

In today's world, leaders can focus on their standards of presentation and appearance to reflect their commitment to their role. This includes dressing appropriately for different occasions, maintaining a clean and professional look, and practicing good manners and etiquette. By doing so, leaders can enhance their credibility and ensure they are respected by their peers and subordinates. This approach underscores the importance of the look being as important as the mind and actions, creating a holistic impression of competence and authority.

This was the life at the palace gates. To train his nobles in martial exercises, he would lead them on hunts whenever he thought it necessary, believing that hunting was the best training for war and the best way to excel in horsemanship. A man learns to keep his seat on any ground while chasing game, learns to throw and strike on horseback in his eagerness to catch the game and earn praise. Hunting was also the best way to toughen his colleagues, making them endure toil, hardship, cold, heat, hunger, and thirst. Thus, to this day, the Persian monarch and his court spend their leisure hunting. From all this, it's clear that Cyrus believed no one had the right to rule unless they were superior to their subjects. He thought that by imposing such exercises on those around him, he would lead them to self-control and perfect their skills and discipline in war. He would personally lead the hunting parties unless he had to stay home. If he was home, he would hunt in his parks among the wild animals he had raised. He wouldn't eat his evening meal until he had worked up a sweat, nor would he feed his horses until they had exercised. He would invite his mace-bearers to join him in the chase. Because of this constant practice, he and those around him excelled in all knightly accomplishments. This was the example he set for his friends. He also kept an eye on others and singled out those who pursued noble deeds, rewarding them with gifts, high commands, seats at festivals, and every kind of honor. This filled their hearts with ambition, and everyone wanted to outdo their peers in Cyrus's eyes.

We also learn that Cyrus thought it necessary for a ruler to surpass his subjects not only by his own merit but also through charm and artifice. He adopted the Median dress and convinced his companions to do the same because he thought it concealed any physical flaws and enhanced the wearer's beauty and stature. For example, the shoe was designed so that an extra sole could be added without being noticed, making the wearer seem taller. Cyrus also encouraged the use of ointments to make the eyes brighter and pigments to make the skin look fairer. He trained his courtiers never to spit or blow their noses in public or turn aside to stare at anything. They were to maintain the dignified air of people who could not be surprised. All these measures aimed to make it impossible for subjects to despise their rulers.

Thus, he shaped the men he considered worthy of command through his own example, training, and the dignity of his leadership. But he treated those he prepared for slavery differently. He didn't encourage them to noble deeds, wouldn't let them carry weapons, and ensured they never lacked food or drink in any manly way. When beaters drove wild animals into the open, he allowed food for the servants but not for the free men. On a march, he led the slaves to water springs like beasts of burden. At breakfast, he waited until the slaves had eaten enough to stave off their hunger. Because of this, they called him their father, just like the nobles did, because he cared for them. But his care aimed to keep them as slaves forever.

[Editor's note: Although he's praising Cyrus, this note by Xenophon on the existence of slaves is very controversial. In the text written on the Cyrus Cylinder discovered in the Babylon region in March 1879 during a British Museum excavation mission, one can read that Cyrus freed the slaves, including Jews and that he was against slavery. This is also confirmed in the Old Testament. Moreover several stone and clay tablets inscriptions found at the Treasury Hall in Persepolis, written in Akkadian and Elamite, mention that no slaves were used to build the construction insisting not only on their monetary compensation but also on other social benefits such as paid vacations and paid maternity leave. One thing is to do so and another thing is to write it. It means they were conscious of the level of progress they had reached certainly because it took them vision and leadership to get there. These matters were detailed in writing like nowadays financial reports or annual reports. Even if slavery was not totally abolished everywhere in the Persian Empire, the fact that we have so many written inscriptions claiming them, shows at a minimum, their vision and their goals. Therefore it's quite strange that Xenophon does not even mention it as a goal. I suspect that the vision of great leaders such as Cyrus the Great and Darius the Great may have not been executed after them as meticulously as under their reins and with time, some of these practices were overlooked.]

This is how he ensured the safety of the Persian Empire. He felt secure from the masses of conquered people, knowing they had no courage, unity, or discipline, and that none could come near him day or night. However, he was aware of true warriors who carried arms, supported each other, and were often in close contact with him. These included commanders of horse and foot, many of whom were confident in their own ability to rule. He rejected the idea of disarming them, considering it unjust and likely to dissolve the empire. Refusing them access or showing distrust would be a declaration of war. Instead, he found an honorable and effective method: to win their friendship and make them more devoted to him than to each other. Now, I will explain the methods he used to gain their loyalty.

VIII.2

Cyrus Builds Loyalty Through Generosity and Kindness

Summary

In this chapter, Cyrus demonstrated kindness and generosity to his friends and soldiers, believing that these actions fostered loyalty and reduced enmity. Initially, he could only show care and support personally, but later, with access to wealth, he shared his resources generously, distributing food and gifts to those who had served him well. His hospitality and open-handedness extended even to his servants and friends, creating a culture of respect and loyalty. This practice of rewarding loyalty and service with gifts made his followers feel valued and secure. Cyrus's philosophy was that true wealth and security came from enriching his friends, who would then become his most faithful supporters. This chapter takes place within the Persian Empire, highlighting Cyrus's strategies for maintaining loyalty and trust among his people and allies.

Fostering Loyalty Through Empathy and Generosity

Leaders can build strong loyalty and trust through consistent empathy and generosity. By genuinely caring for the well-being of their team members and rewarding their efforts with tangible tokens of appreciation, leaders can foster a culture of mutual respect and dedication. This approach is similar to how successful leaders truly connect with their team members and express empathy. It also relates to companies offering bonuses, stock options, benefits, gym membership and public recognition to their employees, enhancing their sense of belonging and commitment. Cyrus's method of spreading wealth and showing personal care for his people ensured their unwavering support and created a united and motivated community.

Cyrus always showed kindness whenever he could, believing that just as it is hard to love those who hate us, it is almost impossible to hate those who love and wish us well. Before he had the wealth to give gifts, he showed his care for his comrades and soldiers by working for them, sharing in their joys and sorrows, and trying to win them over this way.

When he could finally give gifts of wealth, he understood that giving food and drink was the most natural form of kindness. Therefore, he arranged for his table to be set every day for many guests, just like for himself. After he and his guests dined, he would send the leftovers to his absent friends as a token of affection and remembrance.

He would send these to those who had impressed him with their work on guard, in attendance, or any other service, showing them that no effort to please him went unnoticed. He would also honor any servant he wanted to praise by placing all their food at his table, believing this would win their loyalty, just like a dog's.

If he wanted one of his friends to be courted by the people, he would give them such gifts; even today, people respect those who receive dishes from the Great King's table, believing they are in high favor and can get things done. The delicious taste of the royal meats added to the pleasure of these gifts. It's no surprise, as other crafts in large communities reach high levels of perfection, so should royal dishes.

In small cities, one man must do many crafts, but in great cities, a single craft or even a single part of a craft is enough for a livelihood. For example, some shoemakers only make men's sandals, others only women's. Specialization allows them to excel in their tasks. The same applies to household arts. If one servant has to make the bed, set the table, knead the dough, and cook, the master must accept whatever comes. But when there is enough work for one man to boil the pot, another to roast the meat, another to stew the fish, another to fry it, and someone else to bake different kinds of bread, higher standards of excellence are achieved in each task.

This explains how Cyrus could excel in hospitality. He also triumphed in all other services. As he excelled in revenue, he also excelled in the grandeur of his gifts. This tradition of generosity is still seen in Oriental kings today. No one's friends are as wealthy as the friends of the Persian monarch, adorned with splendid attire and well-known gifts like bracelets, necklaces, and horses with golden bridles, which only the king can give.

Only the Great King could win the hearts of men and turn them away from their families with his splendid presents. Only he could exact revenge on enemies far away and be called 'father' by those he conquered—a title signifying a benefactor, not a robber. This suggests that the offices called "the king's eyes" and "the king's ears" originated from his system of gifts and honors. Cyrus's generosity made countless people eager to inform him of anything useful. Thus, there were many "king's eyes" and "king's ears," known to be such. But it's a mistake to think there was only one chosen "eye." A single man can see or hear little, and assigning the role to one person would make others complacent. Instead, the king listens to anyone who claims to have seen or heard something important.

This is why the saying goes that the king has a thousand eyes and a thousand ears. People feared saying anything against Cyrus or doing anything that might harm him, believing he would always know. This universal feeling towards him likely stemmed from his resolve to be a great benefactor. It's not surprising that the wealthiest man could outdo others in the splendor of his gifts. What's remarkable is that a king could surpass his courtiers in courtesy and kindness. Nothing could shame him more than being outdone in courtesy. He once compared a good king to a good shepherd, saying a king must provide for his cities and subjects just as a shepherd provides for his flock.

Cyrus's ambition was to excel in courtesy and care. A noble example of this is his response to Croesus, who criticized him for his lavish gifts, saying they would lead to poverty. Croesus suggested Cyrus should amass wealth instead. Cyrus asked Croesus how much wealth he thought he could have accumulated if he had collected gold since coming to power. Croesus named an enormous sum.

Cyrus then asked his friend Hystaspas to go to his friends and tell them he needed money for an enterprise, requesting each to write down the amount they could give, seal the letter, and hand it to Croesus's messenger. When the messenger returned with the letters, Hystaspas announced that he had become rich thanks to Cyrus's letter, as his friends had loaded him with gifts.

Cyrus told Croesus to count the sums in the letters, which amounted to far more than the treasure Croesus thought Cyrus could have saved. Cyrus explained that instead of hoarding wealth, which would make him envied and hated, he enriched his friends, making them his treasures and better guards than hired watchmen. He believed that while most men bury or hoard their excess wealth, he used it to help his friends, buying their love and goodwill, which brought him security and renown—fruits that never rot and cause no harm.

He argued that the happiest people are not those with the most wealth to guard but those who gain and use wealth righteously and honorably. Cyrus's actions matched his words. He observed that most people only prepare for a healthy life and neglect provisions for sickness. However, he ensured he had the best physicians and all necessary medical supplies stored in the palace. He visited and cared for those who were ill, especially grateful to doctors who used his stores to cure patients. These efforts won him the loyalty of those whose friendship he valued.

He also held contests and offered prizes to inspire ambition and noble deeds, which enhanced his own reputation as a lover of nobleness while fostering rivalry among the participants. He decreed that in any matter needing arbitration, both parties should agree on a judge, often choosing the most powerful and friendly to themselves. This created envy and resentment among the competitors and made them strive for Cyrus's favor.

Through these strategies, Cyrus ensured that the most capable subjects were more loyal to him than to each other.

VIII.3

Cyrus's Grand Procession
A Demonstration of The United Empire

Summary

Cyrus organized a grand public procession to establish reverence for his rule. The day before, he distributed splendid Median robes to the state officials and instructed them on their roles in the procession. On the day of the procession, a detailed and impressive display of sacrificial animals, chariots, and soldiers took place, with Cyrus leading in his chariot, adorned in royal attire. Throughout the event, Cyrus demonstrated his leadership by addressing petitions, managing the procession, and ensuring everything ran smoothly. The ceremony included sacrifices to various gods and a series of races, where Cyrus himself participated and won among the Persians. The event concluded with feasting and the distribution of prizes. Cyrus's actions showcased his ability to organize and lead, while also highlighting his generosity and strategic planning.

Fostering Unity and Belonging Through Public Processions

Cyrus's use of a grand public procession was a strategic move to foster unity and a sense of identity among his people. This approach can be applied in a modern corporate context as well. Cyrus's procession united the diverse groups within his empire, instilling a sense of belonging and shared identity. By participating in a common, grand event, the people felt a part of something greater than themselves, strengthening their loyalty to Cyrus and the empire. Similarly, in a corporate setting, organizing company-wide events, such as annual meetings, celebrations, or team-building activities, can foster a sense of unity and belonging among employees. These events create opportunities for employees to connect, share experiences, and feel valued as part of the organization. By involving everyone and recognizing their contributions, leaders can strengthen the bonds within their team, inspire collective pride, and enhance overall morale and loyalty.

I will now describe Cyrus's first public procession. The solemnity of the ceremony was one way he earned respect for his rule. The day before, he called the state officers, Persians, and others, and gave them splendid Median clothes. This was the first time the Persians wore them. As they received the robes, he said he wished to drive his chariot to the sacred precincts and offer sacrifices with them.

"You will meet at my gates before sunrise, dressed in these robes, and take your places where Pheraulas the Persian directs you on my behalf. As soon as I lead the way, follow in your appointed order. If you think of any changes to improve the beauty and grandeur of our procession, let me know on our return. We should ensure everything is done in the most beautiful and best way possible."

With that, Cyrus gave the most splendid robes to his chief notables. He also brought out other Median garments—purple, scarlet, crimson, and glowing red—and gave a share to each of his generals, saying, "Adorn your friends as I have adorned you."

One of them asked, "And you, Cyrus, when will you adorn yourself?" But he replied, "Isn't it enough for me to have adorned you? If I can do good for my friends, I will look glorious enough in any robe I wear."

His nobles then left and called their friends to put on the splendid garments. Meanwhile, Cyrus summoned Pheraulas, knowing he was quick-witted, loved beauty, and was eager to please his master. Pheraulas had supported Cyrus in giving honor based on merit. Cyrus asked him how he thought the procession could be made most beautiful for friends and most formidable for enemies.

They discussed it and agreed. Cyrus told Pheraulas to ensure everything was done as planned the next day. "I've ordered everyone to obey you in this matter, but to make them more willing, take these tunics yourself and give them to the captains of the guard, these cloaks for the cavalry officers, and these tunics for those commanding the chariots."

Pheraulas took the clothing and left. When the generals saw him, they called out, "A fine fellow you are, Pheraulas! You are to give us our orders, it seems!"

"Oh yes," said Pheraulas, "and carry your baggage too. Here I come with two cloaks, one for you and one for someone else. You must choose which you like best."

The officer put out his hand for the cloak, forgetting his jealousy, and asked Pheraulas which he should choose. Pheraulas gave his advice, adding, "But if you inform against me and let out that I gave you the choice, next time I serve you, I will be a very different sort of servant."

Pheraulas distributed the gifts and then arranged the procession.

The next day, everything was ready before dawn. Ranks lined the road on either side, as they still do when the king is expected to ride out—no one may pass within the lines unless he is someone of note—and constables were posted with whips to maintain order.

In front of the palace, the imperial guard of lancers, four thousand strong, stood four deep on either side of the gates. All the cavalry were there, standing beside their horses with their hands wrapped in their cloaks, as is customary when the king's eye is on them. The Persians stood on the right, and the allies on the left, with the chariots similarly posted.

Presently, the palace gates opened, and the bulls for sacrifice were led out in front of the procession, beautiful creatures, four by four. They were to be offered to Zeus and other gods named by the Persian priests. The Persians think it's more important to follow the guidance of the learned in matters of the gods than anything else.

After the oxen came horses, an offering to the Sun, then a white chariot with a golden yoke, hung with garlands and dedicated to Zeus, followed by the white car of the Sun, also wreathed, and a third chariot with horses in scarlet trappings. Behind them walked men carrying fire on a large hearth.

Then Cyrus himself appeared, coming out of the gates in his chariot, wearing a tiara on his head, a purple tunic shot with white (which only the king may wear), scarlet trousers, and a purple cloak. Around his tiara, he wore a diadem, as did his kinsmen, a custom still observed today. The king's hands were free outside his cloak. Beside him stood a charioteer, a tall man, but Cyrus seemed taller, whether by design or reality.

At the sight of the king, the entire company fell on their faces. Perhaps some had been instructed to do this to set the trend, or maybe they were genuinely awed by the splendor of the pageant and Cyrus himself, stately, tall, and fair. Until then, none of the Persians had bowed to Cyrus.

As the chariot moved, four thousand lancers led the way, two thousand on each side, followed closely by three hundred mace-bearers on horseback with javelins. Then came the royal steeds with golden bridles and striped housings, over two hundred of them, followed by two thousand spearmen and the first squadron of cavalry, ten thousand men, a hundred deep and a hundred wide, led by Chrysantas. Behind them were the second Persian horse unit, ten thousand strong, under Hystaspas, then another ten thousand under Datamas, and more behind them under Gadatas.

Following them were the Median cavalry, then the Armenians, the Hyrcanians, the Cadousians, and the Sakians, each in their order. After the cavalry came the war chariots, four deep, commanded by Artabatas the Persian.

Along the route, thousands of men outside the barriers had petitions for Cyrus. He sent his mace-bearers, who rode beside his chariot, to tell the crowd that if they needed anything, they should tell one of the cavalry officers, who would speak for them. The petitioners then approached the cavalry to find someone to address.

Cyrus sent messages to friends he wished to be approached, telling them, "If someone appeals to you and you think nothing of their request, ignore it. But if it seems just, report it to me, and we'll discuss and arrange it." Usually, the summoned officers would hurry up, eager to enhance Cyrus's authority and show their allegiance. But Daïpharnes, who fancied himself more independent, didn't rush.

Cyrus noticed this and, before Daïpharnes reached him, sent another messenger to say he had no further need for him. Daïpharnes was never summoned again. When the next officer, summoned later, arrived first, Cyrus gave him a horse from his train and instructed a mace-bearer to lead it wherever he wished. This was seen as a high honor, and even more people paid court to the favored man.

When the procession reached the sacred precincts, sacrifices were offered to Zeus, burning bulls as a whole offering, and to the Sun, burning horses. They also sacrificed to the Earth and to the heroes of the Syrian land, as prescribed by the Persian priests.

After the rites, Cyrus saw the ground was suitable for racing. He marked out a goal and a half-mile course and had the cavalry and chariots race, tribe by tribe. He himself raced among the Persians and won easily, as he was the best horseman there. Artabazus won the Mede race on a horse gifted by Cyrus. The Syrian race was won by their chieftain, the Armenian by Tigranes, the Hyrcanian by the general's son, and the Sakian by a private soldier who left his rivals far behind.

Cyrus asked the young man if he would trade his horse for a kingdom. "No kingdom for me," the soldier replied, "but I'd take the thanks of a gallant fellow."

Cyrus said, "I'd like to show you where you could hardly miss hitting one, even with your eyes shut."

"Show me now," said the Sakian, "and I'll take aim with this clod," picking up one from the ground.

Cyrus pointed to a group of his best friends, and the Sakian shut his eyes and threw the clod, hitting Pheraulas as he galloped by on an errand. But Pheraulas didn't turn, flashing past on his mission.

The Sakian asked who he hit. "Nobody here," said Cyrus. "And nobody not here?" asked the young man. "Oh yes," answered Cyrus, "you hit that officer riding swiftly past the chariot lines."

"How is it he doesn't turn his head?" asked the other. "Half-witted, probably," said Cyrus. The young man rode off to see and found Pheraulas, with his chin and beard bloody from the clod's hit. "Did I hit you?" asked the Sakian. "As you see," answered Pheraulas. "Let me give you my horse," said the Sakian. "But why?" asked Pheraulas.

The Sakian explained the situation, adding, "And you see, I didn't miss a gallant fellow."

"Ah," said Pheraulas, "if you were wise, you'd choose a richer one. But I take your gift with thanks. May the gods help me now and see you never regret your gift. For now, mount my horse and ride back; I'll be with you shortly."

They exchanged horses and parted. Rathines won the Cadousian race.

Next came chariot races, tribe by tribe as before. To all the winners, Cyrus gave valuable goblets and oxen for sacrifice and feasting. He took an ox for himself but gave all the goblets to Pheraulas to show approval of the arrangements.

The manner of this procession, established by Cyrus, continues today, the same in all things, except there are no victims when there's no sacrifice. When it was over, the soldiers returned to the city, spending the night in houses or with their regiments.

Pheraulas had invited the Sakian who gave him the horse and entertained him with the best he had, setting a full table. After dining, Pheraulas filled the goblets Cyrus had given him, drank to his guest, and offered them all to him. The Sakian looked at the rich rugs, beautiful furniture, and many servants and asked, "Pheraulas, are your folks wealthy at home?"

"Wealthy? Hardly!" laughed Pheraulas. "My father worked hard to raise me and get me schooling. When I grew older, he couldn't afford to keep me idle, so he took me to a farm to work. I supported him while he lived, working a small plot of land. The land was good and honest, always giving back what I sowed. Life was simple then. Everything you see here, I owe to Cyrus."

The Sakian exclaimed, "You're lucky! Lucky in everything, but especially in coming from poverty to wealth! Your riches must taste sweeter because you knew hunger first."

Pheraulas replied, "Do you really think my joy in life has grown with my wealth? I neither eat, drink, nor sleep more zestfully than when I was poor. With these goods, I have more to watch over, more to give away, and more trouble managing everything. I have many servants now, each with their needs. It seems to me I suffer more today from having much than I did before from having nothing."

"Heaven help us!" cried the Sakian. "Surely, seeing so much of your own makes you happier than me?"

"The possession of riches is nothing compared to the pain of losing them," said Pheraulas. "No rich man lies awake from joy at his wealth, but have you ever known someone who could sleep while losing it?"

"No," said the Sakian, "nor someone who could sleep while winning."

"True," answered Pheraulas. "If having were as sweet as getting, the rich would be much happier than the poor. And remember, a wealthy man must spend much on the gods, friends, and guests. If he loves his riches, spending will annoy him intensely."

"For myself," said the Sakian, "having and spending much is my idea of perfect happiness."

"Heavens!" cried Pheraulas. "What a chance for us both! You can win perfect happiness now and make me happy too! Take all these things for yourself. Use them as you please, and keep me as your guest. I'll be happy with whatever you have."

"You're joking," said the Sakian.

Pheraulas swore he was serious. "I'll arrange for you to be free from military service and court attendance. Just stay home and grow rich. I'll handle everything for us both. If I earn any treasure, I'll bring it to you. You'll be lord of more, but free me from managing it. If you give me leisure from these cares, you'll be of great help to Cyrus and me."

They struck a deal and kept it. The Sakian thought he had found happiness in wealth, while Pheraulas felt blissful being free from its worries. Pheraulas believed man was the noblest and most grateful creature, returning kindness and cherishing parents. He was happy to be free from wealth's anxiety, devoting himself to friends, while the Sakian loved adding to the store and managing it.

Thus, the two lived their lives.

The Grand Festival
A Celebration of Victory

Summary

Cyrus held a grand festival for his victories, inviting close friends and allies such as Artabazus the Mede, Tigranes the Armenian, the Hyrcanian cavalry commander, and Gobryas. Gadatas, the chief of the mace-bearers, managed the event. Cyrus seated his most honored guests on his left and right to visibly recognize their merit. Gobryas noted Cyrus's generosity, as Cyrus shared delicacies and sent dishes to absent friends. Hystaspas questioned why Chrysantas had a higher honor, and Cyrus explained it was due to Chrysantas's proactive service. Cyrus distributed gifts to his guests and wealth from Sardis to his soldiers, ensuring fairness and promoting generosity.

The Power of Visible Recognition and Generosity

Effective leaders visibly recognize and reward contributions to encourage ambition and foster generosity. Cyrus's seating arrangement at the feast visibly recognized merit, motivating excellence. His generosity, openly distributing wealth and resources, built loyalty and encouraged a competitive spirit for self-improvement among his team.

Cyrus offered sacrifices and threw a huge party to celebrate his victories, inviting his closest friends who had shown him the most affection and support. Among the guests were Artabazus the Mede, Tigranes the Armenian, the commander of the Hyrcanian cavalry, and Gobryas. Gadatas, the chief of the mace-bearers, organized the household as he suggested. When guests were present for dinner, Gadatas didn't sit down but made sure everything was taken care of. When they were alone, he dined with Cyrus, who enjoyed his company. Cyrus honored Gadatas greatly for his services, which led to more honors for others.

As guests entered, Gadatas showed each person to their seat, carefully chosen. Cyrus placed his most honored friend on his left, the side most open to attack, the second on his right, the third next to the left-hand guest, and the fourth next to the right, and so on. Cyrus thought it was important for everyone to see how much each person was honored because visible recognition encouraged ambition. He made it a rule that by good deeds, someone could move to a higher seat, or through laziness, to a lower one. He wanted it known that the most honored guest at his table received the most favors. These customs, started during Cyrus's reign, continue to this day.

At the feast, Gobryas noticed that even though it wasn't surprising to see such abundance and variety at the table of someone ruling a vast empire, it was strange that Cyrus, despite his great deeds, never kept any delicacy for himself but always shared it with the company. He also saw Cyrus send dishes that pleased him to absent friends. By the end of the meal, Cyrus had given away all the food, leaving the table bare. Gobryas then said, "Cyrus, until today, I thought you outshone other men most in generalship, but now I believe it's in generosity."

"Maybe," said Cyrus, "I take more pride in this than in generalship."

"How can that be?" asked Gobryas.

"Because one helps people, and the other causes harm," said Cyrus.

As the wine flowed, Hystaspas turned to Cyrus and said, "Would you be angry if I asked something I've been longing to know?"

"Not at all," answered Cyrus, "I'd be upset if you stayed silent when you wanted to ask."

"Tell me then," said Hystaspas, "have you ever called me, and I refused to come?"

"Of course not," said Cyrus.

"Have I ever been slow to come?"

"No, never."

"Or failed to do anything you ordered?"

"No, I have no complaints."

"Whatever I had to do, I always did eagerly and wholeheartedly, right?"

"Absolutely," answered Cyrus.

"Then why, Cyrus, have you given Chrysantas a more honorable seat than me?"

"Shall I really tell you?" asked Cyrus.

"Yes, please," said Hystaspas.

"And you won't be annoyed if I tell you the plain truth?"

"No, it will comfort me to know I haven't been wronged."

"Well, Chrysantas never waited to be called; he came on his own and did not just what he was ordered but whatever he thought would help us. When something needed to be said to the allies, he would suggest what I should say and guess what I wanted to say but couldn't, and he'd say it as if it were his own opinion. He was like a second, better self. Now he always insists he has enough and tries to find more for me. He takes more pride and joy in my triumphs than I do."

"By Hera," said Hystaspas, "I'm glad I asked. One thing puzzles me: how should I show my joy at your success? Should I clap my hands and laugh, or what?"

"Dance the Persian dance," said Artabazus, and everyone laughed.

As the drinking continued, Cyrus asked Gobryas, "Would you be happier to give your daughter to one of us today than when you first met us?"

"Should I tell the truth?" asked Gobryas.

"Of course," said Cyrus.

"Then yes, I'd far rather give her in marriage today."

"Why?" asked Cyrus.

"Back then, I saw your men's bravery in enduring toil and danger, but today I see their modesty in success. I believe it's harder to handle good fortune well than to endure adversity; success often breeds arrogance, while suffering teaches sobriety and fortitude."

Cyrus said, "Hystaspas, did you hear Gobryas's words?"

"I did," answered Hystaspas, "and if he has more wisdom like this, I'll be an even more eager suitor for his daughter than if he had shown me all his goblets."

"Well," said Gobryas, "I have many such sayings written down at home, and you can have them all if you marry my daughter. As for goblets, if you don't care for them, maybe I'll give them to Chrysantas to punish him for taking your seat."

"Listen," said Cyrus, "if any of you tell me when you plan to marry, you'll see what a clever advocate you have in me."

Gobryas asked, "If one of us wants to give his daughter in marriage, who should he apply to?"

"To me as well," answered Cyrus; "I'm good at this."

"What art is that?" asked Chrysantas.

"The art of finding the right wife for each man."

"Then tell me," said Chrysantas, "what sort of wife would suit me?"

"First," he said, "she must be short because you are not tall, and if you married a tall woman and wanted to kiss her, you'd have to jump to reach her."

"Your advice is clear," said Chrysantas, "and I'm not a good jumper."

"Next," Cyrus continued, "a flat nose would suit you well."

"A flat nose? Why?" asked Chrysantas.

"Because your nose is high, and flatness goes best with height."

"You might as well say," retorted Chrysantas, "that one who has dined well, like me, is best matched with someone who hasn't."

"Quite so," answered Cyrus, "a full stomach is high, and an empty one is flat."

"And now," said Chrysantas, "tell us the bride for a flat king."

At this, Cyrus laughed, and everyone joined in. The laughter continued when Hystaspas said, "Cyrus, there's one thing I envy in your royal state more than anything else."

"And what's that?" asked Cyrus.

"That even though you are flat, you can make people laugh."

"Ah," said Cyrus, "what would you give to have it said of you that you are a man of wit?"

They bantered and exchanged jokes. Cyrus then brought out a woman's attire and valuable ornaments and gave them to Tigranes as a present for his wife because she had bravely followed her husband to war. He gave a golden goblet to Artabazus, a horse to the Hyrcanian leader, and many other splendid gifts to the company. "And to you, Gobryas," he said, "I will give a husband for your daughter."

"Let me be the gift," said Hystaspas, "and then I'll get those writings."

"But do you have a fortune," asked Cyrus, "to match the bride's?"

"Yes, I do," answered Hystaspas, "twenty times as great."

"And where are those treasures?" asked Cyrus.

"At the foot of your throne," answered Hystaspas, "my gracious lord."

"I ask no more," said Gobryas, holding out his right hand. "Give him to me, Cyrus; I accept him."

Cyrus took Hystaspas's right hand and laid it in Gobryas's hand, and the pledge was given and received. Cyrus then gave beautiful gifts to Hystaspas for his bride but drew Chrysantas to his breast and kissed him. Artabazus cried, "Cyrus! The goblet you gave me isn't as fine as the gold you've given Chrysantas now!"

"You'll have the same one day," said Cyrus.

"When?" asked Artabazus.

"In thirty years," said Cyrus.

"I'll wait," said Artabazus, "I won't die; be ready for me."

The banquet ended, the guests rose, and Cyrus stood up with them and walked them to the door.

The next day, Cyrus arranged for all allies and volunteers to return home, except those who wanted to stay with him. He gave land and houses to those who stayed, mainly Medes and Hyrcanians, and sent the others away with gifts, both officers and men. He distributed the wealth from Sardis among his soldiers, with special gifts for the captains of ten thousand and his own staff based on their merits. The rest was divided equally, with each captain receiving a share to distribute among their subordinates. Each officer then gave to the officers directly under him, judging their worth, until it reached the captains of six, who considered the privates in their squads and gave each man what he deserved. Thus, every soldier in the army received a fair share. Some remarked, "How rich Cyrus must be to give us all so much!" Others replied, "Rich? What do you mean? Cyrus isn't a money-maker; he prefers giving to receiving."

When Cyrus heard this talk, he gathered his friends and the chief men of the state and said, "I've known men who wanted people to think they had more than they did, thinking this would make them seem free and noble. But it made them appear the opposite. If people think a man has great riches and doesn't help his friends proportionately, he seems stingy. Others hide their wealth, which I see as a betrayal. A friend in need might hesitate to ask for help because he doesn't know what the other has and is left in the dark and starving. The straightforward way is to make no secret of our resources and use them to win honor. I want to show you all my possessions and give you a list of the rest."

He then pointed out his visible treasures and gave an exact account of those that couldn't be shown. He ended by saying, "All these things, gentlemen, you should consider yours as much as mine. I collected them not to spend on myself but to reward noble deeds and help any of you in need, so you can come to me and get what you need."

These were the words of Cyrus.

VIII.5

Cyrus's March to Persia,
his Coronation and the Pact of Loyalty

Summary

Cyrus prepared to leave Babylon for Persia, organizing his army with precise order and efficiency. While marching, he stopped by Media to visit Cyaxares. During this visit, Cyaxares offered his daughter in marriage to Cyrus. In a significant ceremonial act, Cyaxares's daughter placed a crown on Cyrus's head, symbolizing his acceptance as a ruler. Cyaxares gave his daughter and the entire kingdom of Media as her dowry, effectively endorsing Cyrus's authority and expanding his influence. Upon reaching Persia, Cyrus distributed gifts and offerings, celebrated with his people, and made a covenant with them to mutually support and protect each other. After securing this agreement, he returned to Media and married Cyaxares's daughter.

The Importance of Order and Efficiency in Leadership

A good leader prioritizes order and efficiency in all operations, ensuring that everyone knows their roles and responsibilities to maintain smooth functioning and readiness. Cyrus meticulously arranged his army's camp and marching procedures, ensuring that each unit knew its specific place and duties. This organization allowed the vast army to pack, unpack, and take positions quickly and efficiently, demonstrating the importance of structure and clear instructions in leadership.

Now that everything was stable in Babylon, and Cyrus felt he could leave the region, he began preparing to march to Persia and sent out orders to his men. When everything was ready, the horses were yoked, and he set off.

Let's explain how such a large group could pack and unpack without chaos and quickly take up positions wherever needed. When the king was on the move, his attendants had tents and camped with him, both in winter and summer.

From the beginning, Cyrus made it a practice to have his tent pitched facing east. Later, he set the distance between himself and his lancers. He placed his bakers on the right, his cooks on the left, the cavalry on the right again, and the baggage train on the left. Everything else was arranged so that each person knew their own quarters, including their position and size.

When the army packed up after a stop, each person gathered their own belongings, and others placed them on the animals. This way, all the bearers arrived at the baggage train simultaneously, and everyone loaded their own animals. Thus, all the tents could be struck at the same time.

The same process happened when the baggage needed to be unpacked. To ensure everything was prepared on time, each person knew their task in advance, so all divisions could be provided for as quickly as one. Just as the servants had their assigned places, different regiments had their stations suited to their fighting style, and each unit knew their quarters and went to them without hesitation.

Cyrus understood that orderliness was essential even in a private house, as it allowed everyone to find what they needed. He considered it even more critical for an army, where timing is crucial, and being late can have serious consequences. Therefore, he prioritized order and arrangement above all else.

His position was always at the center of the camp, as this was the safest spot. Surrounding him were his most loyal followers. Beyond them, in a ring, were the cavalry and charioteers. Cyrus believed these troops needed a secure position because their equipment couldn't be kept ready, and they needed time to arm themselves. The targeteers were placed to the left and right of the cavalry, and the bowmen in front and rear.

Finally, the heavy-armed troops and those with large shields surrounded the entire encampment like a wall. This way, if the cavalry needed to mount, the most reliable troops would protect them and allow them to arm safely. Cyrus insisted that the targeteers and archers sleep at their posts like the line soldiers. This way, in case of a night alarm, they could quickly hurl darts and javelins over the heads of the infantry dealing with the assailant at close quarters.

All the generals had standards on their tents, and just as a knowledgeable servant in a city knows most of the important houses, Cyrus's squires knew the layout of the camp, the generals' quarters, and each standard. Thus, if Cyrus needed someone, they could be summoned quickly without searching. This clear arrangement made it easy to identify where discipline was maintained and where it was neglected. With these setups, Cyrus felt that any attack would find not just a camp but a well-prepared ambush.

Cyrus believed that a master tactician should know more than just how to deploy troops. He needed to know how to divide them into smaller groups and place them where they would be most useful. He needed to know how to speed up when necessary and manage a hundred other operations. Cyrus studied all these with equal care. While he varied the marching order to suit the moment's needs, the camp arrangement generally followed the plan described.

Establishing Authority and Building Alliances through Ceremonial Acts

Ceremonial acts and strategic alliances are powerful tools for leaders to establish and reinforce their authority and legitimacy. During his visit to Media, Cyaxares offered his daughter in marriage to Cyrus and had her place a crown on his head in a significant ceremonial act. Cyaxares also gave his daughter the entire kingdom of Media as her dowry, effectively endorsing Cyrus's authority and expanding his influence. This act of alliance and endorsement highlights how ceremonial acts and strategic alliances can strengthen a leader's position and expand their influence.

As they marched into Media, Cyrus turned aside to visit Cyaxares. After they met and embraced, Cyrus told Cyaxares that a palace and estate had been set aside for him in Babylon so that he would have a residence whenever he visited. He also offered other rich and beautiful gifts. Cyaxares was pleased to accept them from his nephew and then sent for his daughter. She came carrying a golden crown, bracelets, a necklace of wrought gold, and a splendid Median robe.

The maiden placed the crown on Cyrus's head, and Cyaxares said, "Cyrus, I give you my daughter to be your wife. Your father married my father's daughter, and you are their son. This is the little girl you carried in your arms when you were young. Whenever she was asked whom she would marry, she always answered 'Cyrus.' For her dowry, I give you the whole of Media since I have no lawful son."

Cyrus replied, "Cyaxares, I thank you for your offer of kinship, the maiden, and the gifts, but I must consult my father and mother before I accept. Then we will thank you together." Nonetheless, Cyrus gave the maiden gifts he thought would please her father. After that, he marched home to Persia.

Fostering Mutual Trust and Commitment

Leadership is an Agreement between a leader and a group of People. A leader should foster mutual trust and commitment with their followers to ensure loyalty and cooperation. Upon reaching Persia, Cyrus made a covenant with the Persian people, promising to protect their land and laws, while they pledged to support him against any rebels or traitors. This mutual agreement and the ceremonial act of making a covenant fostered a strong sense of loyalty and commitment, highlighting how trust and reciprocity are essential components of successful leadership.

When he reached the border of his homeland, he left most of his troops at the frontier and went alone with his friends to the city, bringing enough offerings for all the Persians to sacrifice and hold a grand festival. He brought special gifts for his father, mother, old friends, high officers of state, elders, and all the Persian Peers. He gave every Persian man and woman bounties like those the king confers whenever he visits Persia.

Cambyses then gathered the elders and chief officers and said, "Men of Persia, and Cyrus, my son, you are both dear to me. As the king of my people and the father of my son, I must openly present what I believe to be good for both. In the past, the nation has done great things for Cyrus by giving him an army and making him a leader. With the help of the gods, he has made the Persians famous worldwide and crowned you with glory in Asia. He has made the bravest wealthy and provided for many through his leadership. By founding the cavalry, he has won the plains for Persia. If you continue to support each other, you will all benefit. But if you, my son, try to rule the Persians for your own advantage, or if you, my people, envy his power and try to dethrone him, you will lose many valuable things.

Therefore, to ensure only good comes to you, I advise you to make a covenant and call the gods to witness. You, Cyrus, must vow to defend Persia and its laws with all your strength. You, my people, must promise to support Cyrus against any rebels or traitors. While I live, I am the king of Persia. After my death, Cyrus will be king if he is still alive. Whenever he visits Persia, he should offer sacrifices on your behalf, just as I do now. When he is away, the noblest member of our family should perform the sacred rites."

Cambyses finished, and Cyrus and the Persian officers agreed to all he said. They made the covenant and called the gods to witness, and to this day, the Persians and the Great King keep it. After this, Cyrus returned to Media with his parents' consent and married Cyaxares's daughter, whose beauty is still renowned. After the wedding, he set out for Babylon with his horses yoked.

VIII.6

Appointment of Satraps and Expansion of the Empire

Summary

Back in Babylon, Cyrus decided to appoint satraps to govern the conquered tribes while keeping the commandants in citadels under his direct control to prevent rebellions. He called a council to explain the terms for the satraps and assigned houses and districts to his friends. Cyrus selected satraps for various regions, including Arabia, Cappadocia, Greater Phrygia, Lydia, Susia, Caria, Aeolia, and Phrygia by the Hellespont. He sent no satraps to Cilicia, Cyprus, and Paphlagonia due to their support in the Babylon campaign but still imposed tribute on them. Cyrus established a system of relay stations for rapid communication across the empire and set rules for inspections and maintaining order. A year later, he gathered a massive army in Babylon and expanded his empire to include nations from Syria to the Red Sea and Egypt.

Decentralized Control with Central Oversight

Effective leaders delegate authority to trusted individuals while maintaining direct oversight to ensure loyalty and prevent rebellions. Cyrus appointed satraps to govern various regions but kept the commandants in citadels under his direct control. This strategy ensured that even if a satrap became rebellious, there would be a loyal counterforce within the district, demonstrating the importance of balancing delegation with oversight.

When he was back in Babylon, Cyrus decided to appoint satraps to govern the conquered tribes but kept the commandants in the citadels and garrison captains under his direct authority. This showed his foresight, understanding that if a satrap became rebellious, there would already be a counterforce in the district.

To implement this, Cyrus called a council of leading men to explain the terms for the satraps. He wanted them to know the conditions beforehand, so they wouldn't feel mistrusted or surprised by the restrictions.

He addressed the council: "Gentlemen and friends, you know we have garrisons and commandants in the cities we conquered. They were ordered to guard the fortifications and not interfere otherwise. I don't want to remove them as they've done their duty well, but I plan to send satraps who will govern the inhabitants, collect tribute, pay the garrisons, and handle necessary dues.

Furthermore, some of you who work with these nations should have houses and estates there, so you have places to stay and receive tribute."

Cyrus then assigned houses and districts to many of his friends in the lands he had conquered, and their descendants still possess these estates. He emphasized the importance of choosing satraps who would send valuable resources back to the capital, sharing the wealth of the world with those at home.

After learning which friends were willing to go, Cyrus selected the best candidates: Magabazus to Arabia, Artabatas to Cappadocia, Artacamas to Greater Phrygia, Chrysantas to Lydia and Susia, Adousius to Caria (at the Carians' request), and Pharnouchus to Aeolia and Phrygia by the Hellespont.

Cyrus sent no satraps to Cilicia, Cyprus, and Paphlagonia because they had supported the march against Babylon, but they were still required to pay tribute. According to Cyrus's rules, the citadel garrisons and captains are appointed directly by the king and listed in the royal records.

The Communication Platform: Essential for Support and Supervision

Leaders should establish efficient communication systems and regular inspections to maintain order and quickly address issues. Cyrus set up a network of relay stations for rapid communication across his vast empire and instituted annual inspections by an officer to assist satraps and address any issues. This ensured that the state of affairs was known quickly, and problems could be dealt with promptly, highlighting the significance of communication and preparedness in effective leadership.

Cyrus instructed all satraps to emulate his practices: raising cavalry and chariot forces from the Persians and allies, maintaining readiness, presenting themselves at the palace gates, studying temperance, and hunting to train in warfare. He promised to honor those who excelled in these duties.

Cyrus advised them to give preference to the best men at their courts, as he did, and to host their friends and those who accomplished noble deeds. He encouraged them to breed game, work for their food, and exercise their horses.

Cyrus stressed that he needed good comrades to help preserve the empire's benefits and urged them to train their subordinates similarly.

These principles laid down by Cyrus still guide the royal garrisons and governors. Each province is visited regularly for inspections, and the system of relay stations allows rapid communication across the empire.

A year later, Cyrus gathered his troops in Babylon, reportedly 120,000 horsemen, 2,000 scythe-bearing chariots, and 600,000 foot soldiers. He then embarked on a campaign, subduing nations from Syria's borders to the Red Sea, followed by the conquest of Egypt. His empire extended from the Red Sea in the east to the Euxine in the north, Cyprus and Egypt in the west, and Ethiopia in the south.

Cyrus spent seven winter months in Babylon, three spring months in Susa, and the summer in Ecbatana, enjoying a perpetual springtime. Nations and cities sought to send Cyrus their treasures, plants, animals, or artworks, as doing him a service was seen as a path to wealth. Cyrus accepted their offerings and reciprocated with what they lacked.

Bronze statue of a Persian warrior, inspired by Persepolis bas-reliefs.

The Majestic Farewell of Cyrus the Great
A Beacon for Humanity

Summary

Cyrus, now in old age, journeyed to Persia where his parents had long passed away. One night, he dreamt of a divine figure telling him to prepare for his death. Realizing his end was near, he offered sacrifices to the gods and prayed for blessings on his children, wife, friends, and fatherland. He then called his sons, friends, and chief magistrates to his side, informing them of his impending death. Cyrus reflected on his life, expressing gratitude for his accomplishments and the happiness of his friends and fatherland. He designated his elder son, Cambyses, as his successor, granting his younger son, Tanaoxares, the satrapy of Media, Armenia, and Cadousia. He urged his sons to honor and support each other, emphasizing the importance of loyalty and unity. He asked to be buried quickly without elaborate coffins, to return to the earth. Finally, Cyrus bid farewell to his sons, friends, and allies, covered his face, and died.

Succession Planning and Stability

Clear succession planning is essential to maintain stability and prevent disputes within an organization. In his final days, Cyrus designated his elder son, Cambyses, as his successor and assigned significant roles to his younger son, Tanaoxares. This ensured both sons had important responsibilities, minimizing potential conflicts and maintaining stability after his death.

As the years passed, Cyrus reached a ripe old age and journeyed to Persia for the seventh time in his reign. His father and mother had long since died naturally, and Cyrus offered sacrifice according to the law. He led the sacred dance of his Persians in the manner of his forefathers and gave gifts to everyone according to his custom.

One night, as he lay asleep in the royal palace, he dreamt that someone greater than a man came to him and said, "Set your house in order, Cyrus: the time has come, and you are going to the gods." With that, Cyrus awoke from sleep, and he almost knew that the end of his life was near. He immediately took victims and offered sacrifices to Zeus, the god of his fathers, and to the Sun, and all the other gods, on the high places where the Persians sacrifice. He then prayed:

"Zeus, god of my fathers, and you, O Sun, and all you gods, accept this sacrifice, my offering for many noble enterprises, and allow me to thank you for the grace you have shown me. You have guided me all my life, by victims and by signs from heaven, by birds and by the voices of men, showing me what I should do and what I should avoid. I am deeply grateful that I could recognize your care and never let my heart become too proud, even in my prosperity. I ask you now to bless my children, my wife, my friends, and my fatherland; and for myself, may my death be as my life has been."

Then Cyrus returned home and lay down on his bed, longing to rest. When his attendants came to him at the usual time to take his bath, he said he would rather rest. Others came afterward to set the meal before him, but he couldn't bring himself to eat and only drank water readily. It was the same on the second and third days. Then he called his sons, who had followed him to Persia, and summoned his friends and the chief magistrates of the land. When they were all gathered, he began to speak.

Building Loyalty and Unity

Fostering loyalty and unity within a team is critical for effective leadership. Cyrus emphasized the importance of loyalty and unity to his sons. He advised Cambyses that loyal friends, rather than symbols of power, are the true foundation of a stable kingdom, and urged Tanaoxares to support his brother wholeheartedly.

"My sons and friends, the end of my life is near: I know it by many signs. When I am dead, show by your words and deeds that you think of me as happy. As a child, I had all the joys and triumphs of childhood, and as I grew up, I reaped the treasures of youth and experienced all the glories of manhood. Over the years, my powers grew with them, so that I never felt weaker in old age than in my youth. I cannot think of anything I attempted or desired in which I failed. I have seen my friends made happy through me, and my enemies crushed by my hand. I leave our fatherland, which was once insignificant in Asia, at the height of power. Of all that I won, I believe I have lost nothing. Throughout my life, I have fared as I prayed to fare, and the dread that was ever with me lest in days to come I might see or hear or suffer evil, this dread kept me from becoming too proud or foolishly rejoicing.

If I die now, I leave behind my sons, whom the gods have given me, and my fatherland and friends in happiness. Surely I may hope that people will consider me blessed and cherish my memory. Now, I must leave instructions about my kingdom to prevent disputes after my death. My sons, I love you both equally, but I choose the elder, with more life experience, to be the leader in council and action. I was trained in our fatherland to yield to my elders, whether they were brothers or fellow citizens, in the street, in meetings, or in assemblies. I have trained both of you to honor your elders and be honored by those younger than you. These principles are ingrained in our customs and laws. Cambyses, the sovereignty is yours, given by the gods and confirmed by me. Tanaoxares, I give you the satrapy over the Medes, Armenians, and Cadousians. Though your brother has a larger empire and the title of king, your inheritance will bring you more happiness.

What human joy will be lacking to you? You will have all that gladdens the hearts of men, but the burden of ruling, the constant care, and the ambition to rival my achievements will be his. These responsibilities leave little time for happiness. Cambyses, you know your kingdom is not guarded by a golden scepter but by loyal friends. Loyalty does not grow naturally like grass; it must be earned through kindness. To find loyal friends, start with your brother. Fellow citizens are dearer than foreigners, and brothers are the dearest. Support your brother, Tanaoxares, and you will support yourself. A brother's greatness brings glory and safety.

Tanaoxares, be more eager than anyone to obey and support your brother, as his triumph or danger will be closest to you. From whom else could you expect greater rewards or stronger help? Where is coldness uglier than between brothers? Cambyses, only a brother who holds preeminence in another brother's heart can be safe from jealousy. I implore you both, by the gods of our fathers, to honor each other if you care to please me. Do not assume I will cease to exist when I die. You have never seen my soul, but you know its presence through its actions. Have you not seen the terrors and avenging furies that haunt wrongdoers? The honors of the dead endure because their souls are not powerless.

Humility, Reverence, and Legacy

Humility, respect for traditions, and concern for the future are vital components of responsible leadership. Reflecting on his life and approaching death, Cyrus acknowledged the role of the gods in his success and urged his sons to respect divine and human relationships. He requested a simple burial to return to the earth, demonstrating humility and reverence, and planned for the future well-being of his family and kingdom.

I cannot believe the soul lives only while in the body and dies when it leaves. The soul gives life to the body and does not lose sense upon leaving it. Rather, it reaches its highest wisdom when freed from the body. The body's parts return to their elements, but the soul is unseen. Death and Sleep are twin brothers, and in sleep, the soul glimpses the future, perhaps nearest to its freedom. If the soul is set free, reverence my soul and follow my wishes. If the soul perishes, the everlasting gods, who see all and uphold the universe, remain. Fear them and avoid sin in thought, word, or deed.

Respect humanity, for your deeds will be visible to all. Righteous actions will enhance your power, but if you harm each other, you will lose trust. If my words teach you to love each other, it is well. If not, let history guide you. Most parents and brothers show kindness, but not all. Follow the conduct that brought success, and you will be wise.

When I die, do not lay my body in gold or silver or any coffin but return it to the earth quickly. What could be more blessed than to lie in the earth's embrace, the mother of all things beautiful and good? I have loved people all my life and wish to become part of that which benefits humanity. My life is ebbing away; if you want to hold my hand or look into my eyes, do it now. After I cover my face, let no one see me again. Invite the Persians and our allies to my burial and rejoice with me that I am free from suffering. Show kindness to your friends, and you will have the power to deal with your enemies. Goodbye, my dear sons, bid your mother goodbye for me and farewell to all my friends."

With these words, he gave his hand to them, covered his face, and passed away.

VIII.8

Epilogue

Editor's Introduction to Xenophon's Epilogue and Warning

Before you read the epilogue, I want to provide a warning: the authorship and tone of the epilogue of Xenophon's Cyropaedia have sparked debate among scholars regarding the authenticity of this Epilogue. The critical and negative portrayal of the Persian Empire and its decline, contrasts sharply with the more positive references to the Persians throughout the main text. This epilogue suggests a drastic decline of the Persian Empire following the death of Cyrus the Great. It highlights a remarkable contrast between the disciplined, just, and honorable society that Cyrus cultivated, according to Xenophon and the subsequent degeneration into impiety, corruption, and inefficacy under his successors.

Those who believe that Xenophon is the real author of the epilogue argue that this deterioration is evidence of what Xenophon explained at the beginning of the book about the challenges of ruling over people. They see it as proof of the fragile nature of empires reliant on the virtue and leadership of a single ruler. They explain this is why Xenophon admired Cyrus as the greatest leader. I understand their view, but in my opinion, if he held such a view of Persian society post-Cyrus, he wouldn't refer to the nobility of Persians "today" (in his time), several times in the whole book. On the contrary, Xenophon explains that the way Cyrus built the Empire and educated the foundation of the society, was the reason why Persians, as he was seeing them during his time, were so noble.

Moreover, it should be noted that Xenophon (431 BC – 354 BC) lived after Darius the Great (reigned from 522 to 486 BC) and Xerxes (reigned from 486 to 465 BC). We know that these periods were as glorious as the reign of Cyrus the Great. In fact not only Darius the Great expanded the Empire geographically but also he innovated in many aspects of government such as the creation of a professional, full time employed army and the creation of the postal services. Similarly, Xerxes was known as a fierce conqueror. Xenophon, if we assume he wrote this epilogue, makes no reference to them. Given the achievements and glory of Darius the Great and Xerxes, the epilogue of Cyropaedia, which criticizes the decline of Persia after Cyrus's death, indeed raises questions about its authenticity and Xenophon's perspectives. With that in mind, enjoy this piece called epilogue.

220

Of all the powers in Asia, the kingdom of Cyrus was the greatest and most glorious. To the east, it was bordered by the Red Sea, to the north by the Euxine, to the west by Cyprus and Egypt, and to the south by Ethiopia. This vast empire was ruled by the mind and will of one man, Cyrus. He cared for his subjects as a father cares for his children, and they revered him like a father.

But as soon as he died, his sons started fighting, cities and nations revolted, and everything began to fall apart. I can prove this is true, starting with their impiety. In the early days, the king and his subjects always kept their oaths and fulfilled their promises, even to the worst criminals. If they hadn't been known for this, none of the Greek generals who marched with the younger Cyrus would have trusted a Persian, just as they don't trust them today. Back then, they relied on their old reputation and put themselves in their hands, and many were taken to the king and beheaded. Many Asiatics who served in the same war were also killed, deceived by false promises.

In other ways, the Persians have also degenerated. In the past, noble achievements brought fame: the man who risked his life for the king or conquered a city or nation was honored. Now, if someone like Mithridates betrays his father Ariobarzanes or Reomithres leaves his wife, children, and friend's sons as hostages in Egypt, breaking the most solemn promises, they are the ones who receive the highest honors if they seem to benefit the king. With such examples, all the Asiatics have turned to injustice and impiety. As the leaders are, so are the people. Lawlessness has increased among them. Injustice and thievery have grown. Innocent men are arrested and forced to pay fines for no reason. Being wealthy is more dangerous than being guilty, so the rich avoid the powerful and don't even risk appearing at the royal musters. When anyone makes war on Persia, they can roam the country freely without fighting because the Persians have forgotten the gods and are unjust to their fellow men. In every way, their hearts and minds are lower than before.

They don't care for their bodies as they used to. They once never spat or blew their noses, not out of concern for the body's humors, but to strengthen themselves through toil and sweat. Today, this habit continues, but they no longer harden their bodies through exercise. They used to eat only one meal a day, allowing time for business and exercise. The single meal is still the rule, but it starts early and continues until the latest hour. Chamber pots were once forbidden in banquet halls to avoid excessive drinking, but now, although the rule remains, they drink so much they must be carried out. They once refrained from eating and drinking on the march or being seen attending to nature's calls, but now they march so briefly that abstinence is easy.

In the past, they hunted often, giving enough exercise and training for man and horse. But when Artaxerxes and his court fell to drink, the king-led hunts stopped. If anyone hunts with their followers, jealousy and hatred follow. They still bring boys to the palace gates, but fine horsemanship is gone as there's no place for skill to be applauded. They once learned justice by hearing judges decide cases; now, they see that the verdict goes to the highest bidder. Children once learned about plants for health, but now seem to learn only to harm; poisonings are common. Persians today are more luxurious than in Cyrus's time. They used to embrace Persian education and self-restraint, adopting only Median dress and grace. Now, they ignore Persian hardiness in favor of Median softness. They demand luxury, like carpets under bedposts to prevent jarring and inventing new dishes and condiments. In winter, they need warm sleeves and gloves; in summer, servants hold screens for shade. They take pride in having many cups and goblets, regardless of how they were obtained. In the past, no Persian was seen on foot to ensure they were perfect horsemen. Now, they care more for soft saddles than firm seats.

As soldiers, they have declined. Landowners once provided troopers from their estates, and men served actively while garrison troops received regular pay. Now, Persian grandees have a new type of cavalry who work as butlers, cooks, and servants rather than fighters. They look splendid but are useless in battle. Enemies can move through their country freely. Cyrus stopped long-range fighting, arming men and horses with breastplates and short spears for close combat. Today, they fight neither way. Infantry still carry large shields, battle-axes, and swords but never engage the enemy. Scythe-bearing chariots are misused, with untrained men failing to reach the enemy, causing more harm to friends than foes. Aware of their poor fighting condition, Persians give up easily and won't fight without Greek help. Whether fighting among themselves or against Greeks, they need other Greeks to face them.

I believe I have shown that today's Persians and their allies are less religious, less dutiful to family, less just and righteous, and less valiant in war than before. If anyone doubts this, they can examine their actions and find full confirmation.

Editor's Conclusion on This Epilogue

In addition to my note at the beginning of this epilogue, and considering Darius and Xerxes's significant military and administrative achievements and successes, I would like to remind you that Xenophon, writing from a Greek perspective, might have viewed their reigns through a biased lens. The Greco-Persian Wars, particularly Xerxes' invasion of Greece, could have colored Greek perceptions negatively. Cyrus didn't invade Greece, only Lydia.

Moreover, since Cyropaedia is written in Greek, in Greece, one possible scenario is that other Greek members of the Academia, may have had a less positive view of the Persians than Xenophon; they may have added the epilogue to counter Xenophon on the nobleness of the Persian society.

Some other scholar who believe Xenophon did write the epilogue, argue that Xenophon admired Cyrus for his personal virtues, unique style, and effective governance. Even if the Persian Empire remained powerful under Darius and Xerxes for a longer period, with more development, organization, and a larger empire, in the eyes of Xenophon, any perceived moral or ethical decline even very small, could be seen as a decay of the foundational principles that Cyrus established. These principles were justly perceived as rare, deserving the book and all the lessons of leadership and humanity that we have learned and continue to learn from Cyropaedia. I am extremely grateful to Xenophon, whether he was the real author of the epilogue or not.

CONCLUSION

I hope you liked this book.

Let me remind you this part from Cyrus's first motivational speech at a very young age:

*From boyhood, we've been **trained** in the ways of honor and nobility. Now, let's face our enemies. They may be skilled with javelins and bows and ride well, but they aren't true warriors if they fail when endurance is needed.*

*You, however, are not like them. To you, night is like day. Your **training** has taught you that **hard work** leads to **happiness**. Hunger is a daily companion, and water quenches your thirst like a lion at a stream. You have something rare and valuable: **the love of victory**. You seek **honor** and gladly face **hard work** and danger to **earn it**.*

Training and practice are the keywords.

So next is to put all the above into practice. Like every lesson that we learn in our personal or professional life, only practice allows the lesson to become a habit.

We come across lessons every day, every hour; we either practice them and they become habits, or we forget them. It's your choice!

Check out our leadership courses and programs at:

https://infinite-sales.com

https://meddic.academy/

WILL YOU DO ME A FAVOR?

If you enjoyed the book LEADERSHIP By CYRUS THE GREAT, would you mind taking a minute to write a review on Amazon? Even a short review helps, and it means a lot to me.

If your friends, family, parents, team members, colleagues or any friend you care about may be interested in this book, please send them these links:

https://cyropaedia.us
https://cyrus-the-great.com

Finally, if you'd like to stay in touch with me, connect with me on LinkedIn by using my email: darius@meddic.academy

Thank You!

This was,

LEADERSHIP BY CYRUS THE GREAT

Unlocking Xenophon's Cyropaedia

DARIUS LAHOUTIFARD

Made in the USA
Columbia, SC
06 October 2024

30d1dcde-2645-4da8-9347-2097cb434667R01